Travel as Metaphor

Travel as Metaphor
From Montaigne to Rousseau

Georges Van Den Abbeele

University of Minnesota Press
Minneapolis   Oxford

Library of Congress Cataloging-in-Publication Data

Van Den Abbeele, Georges.
 Travel as metaphor : from Montaigne to Rousseau / Georges Van Den Abbeele.
  p. cm.
 Includes bibliographical references and index.
 1. Philosophy, French—16th century. 2. Philosophy, French—17th century.
3. Philosophy, French—18th century. 4. Travel. 5. Montaigne, Michel de, 1533–1592—Views on travel. 6. Descartes, René, 1596–1650—Views on travel.
7. Rousseau, Jean-Jacques, 1712–1778—Views on travel. I. Title.
 B1809.T72V35 1992
 910′.01—dc20   91-13248
                                                          CIP

A CIP catalog record for this book is available from the British Library

Published by the University of Minnesota Press
2037 University Avenue Southeast, Minneapolis, MN 55414
Printed in the United States of America on acid-free paper

The University of Minnesota is an
equal-opportunity educator and employer.

In memoriam Robert Maes

per la Juliana e la Christina

VOYAGE, *s.m.* (Gram.) *transport de la personne d'un lieu où l'on est, dans un autre assez éloigné. On fait le* voyage *d'Italie. On fait un* voyage *à Paris. Il faut tous faire une fois le grand* voyage. *Allez avant le temps de votre départ déposer dans votre tombeau la provision de votre* voyage.

VOYAGE, (Commerce.) *les allées & les venues d'un mercenaire qui transporte des meubles, du bled & autres choses. On dit qu'il a fait dix* voyages, vingt voyages.

VOYAGE, (Education.) *les grands hommes de l'antiquité ont jugé qu'il n'y avoit de meilleure école de la vie que celle des* voyages; *école où l'on apprend la diversité de tant d'autres vies, où l'on trouve sans cesse quelque nouvelle leçon dans ce grand livre du monde; & où le changement d'air avec l'exercice sont profitables au corps & à l'esprit.*

–Encyclopédie

[VOYAGE, *masculine noun* (Grammar.) *transport of a person from the place where one is to another place that is far enough away. One makes the* voyage *to Italy. One makes a* voyage *to Paris. It is necessary for everyone to make the great* voyage *once. Ahead of your departure time, go deposit into your tomb the provisions for your* voyage.

VOYAGE, (Commerce.) *the comings and goings of a mercenary who transports furnishings, wheat and other things. One says that he has made ten* voyages, *twenty* voyages.

VOYAGE, (Education.) *the great men of antiquity judged that there was no better school for life than that of* voyages; *a school where one learns about the diversity of so many other lives, where one incessantly finds some new lesson in that great book of the world; and where the change of air along with the exercise is of profit to the body and to the mind.*]

Contents

Acknowledgments

A number of persons and institutions have encouraged the realization of this book. Initial research on the topic was begun under a Sage Graduate Fellowship at Cornell University. The Andrew Mellon Foundation at Harvard University later gave me leave time to pursue more intensive work. Faculty research grants from the University of California at Santa Cruz and from Miami University in Ohio were also invaluable. William Ray deserves thanks for first suggesting the topic of travel to me. Philip Lewis, Richard Klein, Piero Pucci, Jonathan Culler, and Louis Marin were crucial to the elaboration of the project from its earliest moments. Further encouragement and helpful criticisms came from Michel de Certeau, Fred Jameson, Jean-François Lyotard, Tom Conley, Dan Brewer, Harry Berger, Tom Vogler, James Creech, and Mitchell Greenberg. I wish most especially to thank Peggy Kamuf and Tim Murray for their scrupulous and supportive readings of the final manuscript. The University of Minnesota Press was extraordinarily helpful in preparing the book for publication, and I particularly wish to thank Biodun Iginla and Terry Cochran for their editorial assistance. Ann Klefstad was an excellent and instructive copyeditor.

An early and much abbreviated version of the second chapter was published in *Biblio 17: Récits et imaginaire (Actes de Montréal)* 11 (1984), 3–14; and a portion of the third chapter initially appeared in *L'Esprit Créateur* 25 (no. 3: Fall 1985), 64–74. I thank these two journals for permission to reprint.

Finally, I wish to thank my grandfather, Robert Maes, for inspiring me to study French literature, Christina Schiesari-Safron for bringing her exuberance and spirit into my life, and Juliana Schiesari for her conceptual clarifications and queries, her exhaustive stylistic suggestions, and her endlessly caring love.

Davis, California

Introduction
The Economy of Travel

When one thinks of travel, one most often thinks of the interest and excitement that comes from seeing exotic places and cultures. Likewise, the application of the metaphor of travel to thought conjures up the image of an innovative mind that explores new ways of looking at things or which opens up new horizons. That mind is a critical one to the extent that its moving beyond a given set of preconceptions or values also undermines those assumptions. Indeed, to call an existing order (whether epistemological, aesthetic, or political) into question by placing oneself "outside" that order, by taking a "critical distance" from it, is implicitly to invoke the metaphor of thought as travel.

The following study aims to investigate the relations between critical thinking and the metaphor of the voyage in the context of French philosophical literature from the late Renaissance through the Enlightenment. Before considering the specificity of that context, I would like, however, to reflect upon the travel motif as such at the more abstract level of its general epistemological presuppositions. Despite its association with the interesting or the innovative, the motif of the voyage counts among the most manifestly banal in Western letters. From Homer and Virgil, through Dante and Cervantes, Defoe and Goethe, Melville and Conrad, Proust and Céline, Nabokov and Butor, and on up through the most "postmodern" writers, one can scarcely mention a piece of literature in which the theme of the voyage does not play some role. The very image of thought as a quest is a commonplace in the history of philosophy and features prominently in such canonical works as *The Republic, The City of God,* the *Essays* of Montaigne, Vico's *New Science,* Hegel's *Phenomenology of Mind,* Freud's *Beyond the Pleasure Principle,* Heidegger's *Being and Time,* Lévi-Strauss's *Tristes Tropiques,* and Lyotard's *The Postmodern Condition.* But if one grants the banality of the genre commonly associated with innovation, the question that needs to be raised is whether the commonplace quality of the metaphor of travel does not at some point constitute a limit to the freedom of critical thought.

This question might be rephrased at a still more abstract level in terms of the relationship between an institutional or ideological framework and that which claims to call it into question. What if the critique of a system were itself encoded as an institutionalized part of the system? It would seem, in fact, that the ways in which we question our world are themselves products of that world. Should one conclude pessimistically, then, that critical thought can never escape its entrapment by that which it supposedly criticizes? It is difficult to answer the question when it is phrased in so absolute a form. The hypothesis this study instead attempts to support is that the critical gesture is always entrapped in some ways and liberated or liberating in others. The assumption, in other words, is that no liberating gesture, no theoretical breakthrough, is absolute. Rather, there is always a concomitant degree of entrapment, which I suspect to be the condition of possibility for the liberation that does take place. Moreover, the element of entrapment may even function in certain writers as a desired safeguard that keeps the critical adventure within certain bounds. Granted this paradoxical status of the critical act, it is incumbent upon the critic to explore the conditions for critical discourse, to locate and describe the specific moments where entrapment or radical innovation takes place.

The metaphor of travel as critical trope is at least as paradoxical in its determinations as the critical act. If we are obliged to speak of the voyage as the most common of commonplaces in the Western tradition, a *topos* of the most fixed, conventional, and uninteresting kind, then such a formulation is paradoxical to the extent that a voyage cannot be restricted to or circumscribed within a place unless it is to cease being a voyage—that is, what necessarily implies a crossing of boundaries or a change of places. A voyage that stays in the same place is not a voyage. Indeed, the very notion of travel presupposes a movement away from some place, a displacement of whatever it is one understands by "place." For literature then to make of the voyage a commonplace is to deprive it of its very movement. But then again, if literature returns with such frequency to this *topos* (if it can still be considered to be one), the theme of the voyage must not be simply one literary theme among others but one that in some way or other raises the question of the status of literary discourse itself.[1]

It would seem, moreover, that the very banality or banalizing of travel to be found in literature both veils and unveils its importance for Western culture. The voyage is undoubtedly one of the most cherished institutions of that civilization, and banal as it may be, travel is persistently perceived as exciting and interesting, as liberating, and as what "opens up new horizons." The dearest notions of the West nearly all appeal to the motif of the voyage: progress, the quest for knowledge, freedom as freedom to move, self-awareness as an Odyssean enterprise, salvation as a destination to be attained by following a prescribed pathway (typically straight and narrow). Yet if there is such a great cultural investment in the voyage, that locus of investment is nonetheless one whose possibility of appropriation also implies the threat of an expropriation. The voyage endangers as much as it is supposed to assure these cultural values: something can always go wrong. The "place" of the voyage cannot be a stable one.

A Classical appreciation of the problem of travel can be found in the *Encyclopédie* article of 1765, "Voyage," written by the Chevalier de Jaucourt and whose opening paragraphs figure as the epigraph to this volume.[2] This attempt to define what one means by a voyage at the high-water mark of the age of discovery, at a time when the likes of Cook and Bougainville were preparing to circumnavigate the globe, analyzes travel according to three categories: grammar, commerce, education. The explication of the concurrence of these three definitions, or rather their mutual conjugation and articulation, should provide an initial set of terms with which to pursue an analysis of travel in early modern French philosophical literature.

A voyage is initially defined in grammatical terms as the "transport of a person from the place where one is to another place that is far enough away." Travel is thus first defined from an anthropological perspective: it refers to the movement of human beings, of "a person," from one place to another. To be sure, the agent of this transportation remains unclear: the person is transported. The following three sentences in this article are governed in French by the impersonal forms *on* and *il faut*, and maintain this depersonalized anthropology even as they present three examples of voyages. The first two designate a persistent axis of the specifically French reflection on travel from before Montaigne to after Butor, namely, the axis between Italy and Paris, one to which I will repeatedly return. The third example brings an abrupt switch from the literal to the figural: "It is necessary for everyone to make the great *voyage* at some point." The metaphorical voyage that is death is not simply something "one does," such as travel to Italy, but what "it is necessary for everyone to do." This ultimate "transport of the person" induces the imperative form of a moral pre-scription by which de Jaucourt closes this initial definition: "Ahead of your departure time, go deposit into your tomb the provisions for your *voyage.*" Beneath the anthropological perspective that guides the grammatical definition of travel lurks a risk and an anxiety, the risk—both necessary and inevitable—that the limit to the motion of the *anthropos* is to be found in the limit to the latter's existence: "le *grand* voyage." The anxiety is an economic one, that of not being prepared on time, of not having set aside the necessary "provisions."

As if to follow up on this economic anxiety, the second definition of the word is stipulated as "commercial": "the comings and goings of a mercenary [*mercenaire*] who transports furnishings [*meubles*], wheat and other things." If death is a voyage with no return, commerce is predicated precisely upon the going *and* coming of movable objects (the etymological sense of *meubles*): furniture for the house, wheat for the body, and so on. In the commercial sense of travel, it is not so much the person that is moved, but things that are moved back *and* forth, the latter being shunted about by a particular type of person, a "mercenary," a word whose primary meaning at this time was still simply that of someone working for monetary remuneration. His "mercenary" activity or *revenue* thus depends upon his return, upon the successful completion of his circular movement, by which the voyage can be counted as such: "One says that he has made ten *voyages,* twenty *voyages.*"

The third definition of "voyage" posits another kind of increment, namely, the educational value of travel: "The great men of antiquity judged that there was no better school for life than that of *voyages.*" Here, and in the ensuing paragraphs of the article, the great masters of learning (in a long catalogue from Homer and Lycurgus to Montaigne) are themselves enlisted to support the value of travel as better than any actual school, not unsurprisingly because it brings one to read the grandest textbook of them all: "that great book of the world" wherein "one incessantly finds some new lesson." As the anthropological agent of the voyage is thus secured by the revenue (in profits, in knowledge) of a return, so does the space of that trajectory become available to be read as the grammar of a topography.

And in a clause that impressively recombines the triple definition of the voyage as it brings this paragraph to a close, travel is stated to benefit the body as well as the mind: "The change of air along with the exercise is of profit to the body and the mind." The profits to be gained from travel are as corporeal as they are intellectual or commercial. If travel posits the risk and anxiety of death, it also signals the way to health, wealth, and wisdom. The triple definition of the voyage thus triangulates its object as a zone of potential loss or profit. But if one wants to economize on travel—that is, to minimize its risks and reappropriate any possible loss as profit—one soon discovers that the notion of economy already presupposes that of travel. For the exchange of objects that defines commercial activity implies by its back-and-forth movement some kind of travel. Historically, the great economic and commercial powers have been those most successful at manipulating the means of travel, and vice versa. If there is a great investment in travel, it is perhaps because travel models the structure of investment itself, the *transfer* of assets that institutes an economy, be it political or libidinal, "restricted" or "general."[3]

Now, if there is an insecurity or anxiety associated with travel, it is that insecurity associated with the menace of irreparable loss. This loss can affect not only one's monetary assets but one's very life or sanity. Or one can simply lose one's way, since the possibility of there being no return is always implied in travel. Every voyage is potentially a voyage into exile, a voyage to the "end of the night." La Fontaine's famous fable "The Two Pigeons" provides an eloquent statement of this negative notion of travel. In this satire of the urge to travel, one of the two pigeons, "crazy enough to undertake / a voyage to some faraway land," suffers one disaster after another in his journey until, "half dead and half limping," he decides to return home.[4] Voltaire's *Candide* (1759) takes a similar point of view: after recounting the horrendous series of brutal misfortunes that befall both major and minor characters in their peregrinations around the globe, the "philosophical tale" ends with the famous didacticism, "it is necessary to cultivate our garden," the epitome of sedentariness.[5]

But just as travel poses the danger of loss so also does it propose the possibility of gain (whether this gain be in the form of greater riches, power, experience, wisdom, or whatever). Otherwise, there would be no incentive to travel. Semiotic research on tourism has demonstrated how, in even this apparently most innocent and innocuous mode of travel, strong economic and ideological motives are at work: tourists accumulate "cultural experiences" that then increase their social value within their home communities.[6] A positive evaluation of travel likewise occurs when the voyage is seen as an escape either in the banal urge to "get away from it all" or in the Baudelairean flight from ennui. Perhaps the most explicit—and brutal— form of travel understood as opportunity for gain is to be found in imperialist or colonialist ventures, of which those described in the narratives of the Spanish conquest of the New World offer a particularly forceful rendition.[7]

Both of these evaluations of travel, however, remain circumscribed within an economic point of view. Whether the voyage be loss or gain, what is at stake is a certain property, something that *can* be lost or gained. To be able to talk about loss or gain, however, also requires that something in the transaction remain unchanged, something in relation to which one can register a loss or a gain. In other words, in order to be able to have an economy of travel, some fixed point of reference must be posited. The economy of travel requires an *oikos* (the Greek for "home" from which is derived "economy") in relation to which any wandering can be *comprehended* (enclosed as well as understood). In other words, a home(land) must be posited from which one leaves on the journey and to which one hopes to return—whether one actually makes it back home changes nothing, from this perspective. The positing of an *oikos*, or *domus* (the Latin translation of *oikos*), is what *dom*esticates the voyage by ascribing certain limits to it. The *oikos* defines or delimits the movement of travel according to that old Aristotelian prescription for a "well-constructed" plot, namely, having a beginning, a middle, and an end.[8] Indeed, travel can only be conceptualized in terms of the points of departure and destination and of the (spatial and temporal) distance between them. A traveler thinks of his or her journey in terms either of the destination or of the point of departure.

While the *oikos* is most easily understood as that point from which the voyage begins and to which it circles back at the end, its function could theoretically be served by any particular point in the itinerary. That point then acts as a transcendental point of reference that organizes and domesticates a given area by defining all other points in relation to itself. Such an act of referral makes of all travel a circular voyage insofar as that privileged point or *oikos* is posited as the absolute origin and absolute end of any movement at all. For instance, a journey organized in terms of its destination makes of that destination the journey's conceptual point of departure, its point of orientation. Thus, a teleological point of view remains comfortably within this economic conception of travel.

The economic conception of travel thus implies the attempt to keep travel enclosed within certain limits, that of the closed circle of the home, the *oikos*. On the other hand, so circumscribed a voyage can no longer be considered a voyage, since it never goes outside the range of the *oikos*. Home, the very antithesis of travel, is the concept through which the voyage is "oikonomized" into a commonplace. Hence, while the voyage can only be thought through this "economy of travel," the economy is precisely that which conceptually stops or puts an end to the voyage by assigning it a beginning and an end in the form of the *oikos*. To economize on something, or as the French say, *faire l'économie de quelque chose,* is to try to reduce or dispense with the object of that economy, to avoid or evade it. The voyage, it would seem, can only be thought at its own risk.

If, however, a voyage can only be conceptualized economically in terms of the fixity of a privileged point (*oikos*), the positing of a point we can call home can only occur retroactively. The concept of a home is needed (and in fact it can only be thought) only *after* the home has already been left behind. In a strict sense, then, one has always already left home, since home can only exist as such at the price of its being lost. The *oikos* is posited *après-coup*. Thus, the voyage has always already begun.

Such a voyage, however, is literally unthinkable if it is pre-positional, that is, anterior to the positing of that originary position which I have been calling the *oikos*. What is commonly called "travel" is but an attempt to contain that other prototravel through a kind of reverse denegation that denies travel precisely by affirming it. When I say I am taking a trip, I feel confident in my ability to define it according to an itinerary between points. This "definition" is a containment of travel which allows it then not only to be thought but to be thought as a narrative, as a story—that is, if we accept the idea that it takes at least two movements to constitute a narrative. These two movements, according to the narratology of Thomas Pavel, include the "transgression" of an initial situation and its "mediation" or attempted resolution.[9] The travel narrative is then one in which the transgression of losing or leaving the home is mediated by a movement that attempts to fill the gap of that loss through a spatialization of time. This articulation of space with time smooths that initial discontinuity into the continuity of a line that can be drawn on the map. Through this instituted continuity, the voyage is found not only to conform to the rules of a narrative but also to be one of its canonical forms. Michel de Certeau has even gone so far as to declare that "every narrative is a travel narrative."[10]

What cannot be shown, however, in the drawing of such a line is the concomitant temporalization of space effected by travel, so the home that one leaves is not the same as that to which one returns. The very condition of orientation, the *oikos,* is paradoxically able to provoke the greatest disorientation. One need only cite here the stereotypical image of the traveler, who, à la Rip van Winkle, returns home only to find that it (or the traveler) has changed beyond all recognition. Such a disorientation at the point of return indicates the radical noncoincidence of point of origin and point of return. For the point of return as repetition of the point of departure cannot take place without a difference in that repetition: the detour constitutive of the voyage itself. Were the point of departure and the point of return to remain exactly the same, that is, were they the same point, there could be no travel. Yet if the *oikos* does not remain selfsame, how can one feel secure in it, especially given the fact that this identity of the *oikos* is what is necessarily presupposed by the economic view of travel, the only way we can think a voyage as such?

Be they real or imaginary, voyages seem as often undertaken to restrain movement as to engage in it, to resist change as to produce it, to keep from getting anywhere as to attain a destination. The theory of an economy of travel is an attempt to explain via recourse to an alternative set of

metaphors the paradoxical and contradictory ways in which travel is understood and practiced in our culture. The establishment of a home or *oikos*
places conceptual limits on travel, supplies it with a terminus *a quo* and
a terminus *ad quem* which allow one to conceive of the potentially dangerous
divagation of travel within assured and comfortable bounds. The economy
of travel thus domesticates the transgressive or critical possibilities implied
in the change of perspective travel provides. Nevertheless, the very activity
of traveling may also displace the home or prevent any return to it, thus
undermining the institution of that economy and allowing for an infinite
or unbounded travel. This complex economics of travel rehearses once more
the paradoxical play of entrapment and liberation evinced in critical
thought.

The problems raised in the analysis of travel also recall those commonly
encountered in recent theories of textual analysis: the blurring of identity
and difference, the undecidable effects of repetition, and a structured inability to isolate the object of discourse (that is, to talk about either texts
or travel without becoming embroiled in another text or without embarking
on a voyage, be it only a discursive one).[11] But if one finds the same
anxieties and the same pleasures in both, it is not, in my opinion, because
of a mere coincidence or accident. On the contrary, it is difficult to escape
the impression that both problems are part of the same problem, one rooted
in the decision of Western metaphysics to privilege presence over absence,
voice over writing, and hence the near over the far. What I have been calling
the economy of travel is but a moment in the history of metaphysics, which
is also distrustful of language and which similarly seeks an economy of
signification such that the persistent mediation of the sign is reduced to a
minimum in the conveyance without residue of "full meaning."[12]

Not only, however, do both text and voyage raise the same set of problems, but one finds with surprising frequency that the problems associated
with one are posited or described in terms of the other. It is as if the
domestication or economy of the one proceeded from the other. On the
one hand, one finds topological theories of language in which utterance
becomes a question of choosing the right "route"; on the other, a tex-
tualization of topography such that travel requires the interpretation of
signs; the ability, for instance, to "read" a map. This interpretation can
also be written down in the form of travelogues or what the French writers
of the Classical period referred to as *relations de voyage*. This latter appel-
lation well denotes the domesticating aim of such writing. A *relation de
voyage* is what relates the events of a voyage; it re-lates the voyage, brings
it back by way of the narrator's discourse.[13] The "relation" (from *refero,*
to bring back) itself acts as a voyage that brings back what was lost in the
voyage. It institutes an economy of the voyage. If it acts as a voyage, it

is because *qua re*lation it repeats the voyage by recounting the itinerary in chronological order at the same time *qua* re*lation* (from *latus,* borne or transported) it displaces the topography into a topic of discourse.[14] The result is a mimetic narrative, which is nonetheless instituted by the very loss of what it claims to bring back, to relate. The *relation de voyage* can only mime and recount (can only mime as it recounts) what is already lost, what has already transpired. Not everything can be included or even should be. The most thoroughly detailed travel narratives can be the most boring and tedious. At the other extreme, some amount to little more than an enumeration of dates and place names.[15]

But if the narrative can be constituted by such a repetition and displacement—that is, if it is as much a *trans*lation as it is a *re*lation—the constitution of that narrative can only take place if the voyage is somehow already a kind of text, that is, if there is already in place a differential structure of relationships that allows the "voyage" to be cognized or recognized as such. This structure can be a map or any similar system containing points of reference ("reference" from *refero,* the same word from which "relation" derives). The idea of a reference point refers back to the *oikos* as the transcendental point of reference to which all others are referred. We can now add, though, the further qualification that this referential economy is of a textual order. In other words, a place can only "take place" within a text, that is, only if it can be marked and re-marked from the area in which it is inscribed.[16] Only in this sense can we speak of a topo*graphy,* for insofar as the very perception and cognition of a landscape requires an effect of demarcation, the latter can only be constituted as a space of writing. This space of writing is both the precondition for the referential mastery of the *oikos* and that which implies the inevitable decentering of this referential economy into an endless chain of reference. Such an eventuality, however, implies the loss of whatever mastery was thought to be gained through the positing of travel as text, even as it bears unwelcome witness to the justice of that thesis.

Conversely, the seemingly irresistible propensity of theories of language to use topological terms[17] suggests again that the relationship drawn between traveling and writing is not necessarily unwarranted, although once again perhaps it is not the relationship one would like. For what does Classical rhetoric with its network of topics and its catalogue of tropes pretend to, except, as Cicero declares in the *Topics,* a "disciplinam invendiendorum argumentorum, ut sine ullo errore ad ea ratione et via perveniremus" [a system for inventing arguments so that we might make our way to them without any wandering about][18]. The rhetorical treatise presents itself as a kind of guidebook to the traversal of linguistic space, a discursive Baedeker. The metaphor is literalized, so to speak, in that division of rhetoric known as memory (*memoria*) wherein a prescribed technique to help one remember the points one wishes to make during one's discourse consists of associating each of those points with a familiar place. One can then reproduce one's argument by imaginatively traversing the designated places.[19] Nevertheless, the history of rhetoric, constituted by the interminable haggling, down to our own day, over the correctness of the divisions and schemata proposed by various rhetoricians, stands as a monument to the failure of its attempt to master language, a failure due not to the particular weaknesses of individual rhetoricians but to the structure of language itself.

Nowhere is this inability to maintain the stability of the rhetorical map more evident than in the problems encountered by theoreticians of figural language. Agreement cannot even be reached on the number of tropes or figures to be classified. Now, what a theory of figural language in principle proposes is a complete enumeration and consequent mastery of the ways in which language can mean something other than what it habitually means, ways in which meaning departs from itself. As Du Marsais writes, "Figures are manners of speaking *distanced* from those that are not figured."[20] The presupposition is that something like the literal or "proper" meaning of a word can be precisely determined, in relation to which all figural meanings can then be understood, contained, and mastered. For such a system to work, however, the "proper" meaning must be a stable one, an unchanging point of reference that dominates the field of figural meanings, which can then be grasped as wanderings, deviations, or departures from that proper meaning. At this point, the rhetorical problem of figural versus literal meaning is congruent in structure to the economic problem of travel, with "proper" meaning in the place of the *oikos*. The very language Classical rhetoric used to talk about figures would itself be borrowed from the vocabulary of travel. A more recent theorist of rhetoric has likewise written: "Every structure of 'figures' is based on the notion that there exist two languages, one proper and one figured, and that consequently Rhetoric, in its elocutionary part, is a table of *deviations* of language. Since Antiquity, the meta-rhetorical expressions which attest to this belief are countless: in *elocutio* (field of figures), words are *'transported,' 'strayed,' 'deviated'* from their normal, familiar habitat."[21]

Given such an understanding of figural language as *divagation,* it is not surprising that there should have arisen early on the possibility of seeing in a particular trope, the metaphor, the general form for all figural language, especially if we accept the Aristotelian definition of metaphor as the "application of an alien name by *transference (epiphora)*."[22] "Metaphor" comes from *metaphorein,* to transfer or transport. What better word to denote the transport of meaning than a word whose modern Greek equivalent, *metafora,* commonly refers to vehicles of public transport, such as buses?

But if the concept of metaphor can be used to effect an economical reduction of tropological difference—that is, if metaphor is to become the *proper* name for every figural impropriety—it can only attain that status meta-phorically, by transporting the concept of transportation to that of the text—such a transportation taking place nonetheless within a text and as a text. Travel then becomes the metaphor of metaphor while the structure of the metaphor becomes the metaphor for the travel of meaning.[23] And if, as we have seen in our analysis of travel, the identity of the home is breached by the very movement that constitutes it, are we not entitled to ask if the *metaphorein* of meaning does not have similar consequences for the notion of proper meaning? In his commentary on Aristotle's definition of metaphor, Jacques Derrida suggests just such an eventuality:

> [*Métaphor*] risks disrupting the semantic plenitude to which it
> should belong. Marking the moment of the turn or of the detour
> [*du tour ou du détour*] during which meaning might seem to
> venture forth [*s'aventurer*] alone, unloosed from the very thing it
> aims at however, from the truth which attunes it to its referent,
> metaphor also opens the wandering [*errance*] of the semantic. The
> sense of a noun, instead of designating the thing which the noun
> habitually must designate, carries itself elsewhere [*se porte ailleurs*].
> If I say that the evening is the old age of the day, or that old age
> is the evening of life, "the evening," although having the same
> sense, will no longer designate the same things. By virtue of its
> power of metaphoric displacement [*déplacement*], signification will
> be in a kind of state of availability, between the nonmeaning
> preceding language (which has a meaning) and the truth of
> language which would say the thing such as it is in itself, in act,
> properly. This truth is not certain.[24]

Both the homeliness of meaning and meaningfulness of the home can only be constituted at the risk of an infinite detour.

In the view of this slippery path leading one back and forth between text and travel, it is my suspicion that what might otherwise be construed as idle statements on travel in a writer's discourse allow on the contrary for the elaboration of a critical discourse of considerable force. And in light of the congruencies between the problems of travel, textuality, and critical thinking, the following study aims to discern the role played by the motif of travel in the economy of critical discourse. It is appropriate that this study should take place on the terrain of early modern French thought, since in that historical period there occurs a remarkable conjunction between the vogue of exoticism and imaginary voyages, on the one hand, and the philosophical trends of skepticism, relativism, and *libertinage,* on the other.

So if ever the motif of travel inhabited the critical spirit or *esprit critique,* it would have been in the Classical age.[25]

In exploring, then, the articulation of the discourse on travel with the critical tradition leading up through the *philosophes,* I find that a writer's sustained recourse to the figure of travel inevitably points to underlying concerns with the status of his position, vis-à-vis his own theories as well as in relation to earlier thinkers. Rather than attempt, however, a full-blown historical study of the relation between exoticism and the rise of French free thought,[26] the following study implements a rhetorical or textual approach in order to test the strength of the relationship between theory and travel in the discourse of particular writers of the Classical era. In order to see how far one could pursue an analysis of their writings by following the route indicated by their use of the voyage motif, I have accordingly chosen philosophical writers who also traveled as well as wrote on travel: Montaigne, Descartes, Montesquieu, and Rousseau. Needless to say, the choice of such a corpus is arbitrary to the extent that the problem under consideration extends well beyond the area circumscribed by these particular writers. On the other hand, the names of these writers have been traditionally associated with the notion of travel (Montaigne has even been christened by one critic the "first tourist"[27]) as well as the related issues of exoticism and philosophical relativism. As such, their names denote particularly strong or emblematic moments in the development of prerevolutionary French thought. I have limited myself, then, to a set of extended readings based upon what each writer says about travel (whether explicitly in the form of travelogues or implicitly in the travel metaphors used in their nominally philosophical writings). And if the theme of travel is commonly accepted to be at work in all these writers, my reading intends to corroborate another kind of filiation that binds them together at the level of what we can call their textual production. In each case, traits linked by the writer to travel trigger an associative chain that inevitably leads to concerns fundamental to the writing of the text itself, to the economy of its discourse, and to its authorial propriety. Hence, the writer's discourse on travel is found in each case to allow for the elaboration of a powerful metadiscourse opening onto the deconstruction of the writer's claims to a certain *property* (of his home, of his body, of his text, of his name). For if the property of the home is put in doubt by the voyage as the properness of meaning is by the figurality of discourse, it should not be too surprising to find that what is at stake in the discourse of our writers is that most fundamental of all properties, the property or properness of the proper name, a name whose properness becomes suspect the moment its signature is stamped with the sign of the voyage.

It might well be argued, at this point, that such an analysis would be in no way historical. The figure of travel is so generally implicated in Western metaphysics that it becomes difficult to grant any kind of historical specificity to the texts or analyses that appropriate that figure. The deconstructive potential of the voyage would be lodged in that figure itself and not in any particular or historical uses of it. Just as the privileging of voice over writing could be said, after Derrida, to define the *epochè* of logocentrism in the West, so the privileging of the *oikos* in the economy of travel not unsurprisingly underpins the ethnocentrism and imperialism that have consistently marked Western thought even in its best efforts to "comprehend" the other.[28] In fact, the very use of the terms "same" and "other," drawn as they are from Hegelian dialectics, with its systematic reduction—"sublation"—of differences in the progressive development of the subject of absolute knowledge, reinforces the problem whenever nonwhites, nonmales, or non-Europeans are designated as "others," a designation that presupposes the point of view of the white, the male, the European. The former are, of course, no more (or less) "other" to themselves than the latter are "self-same."

Another, perhaps less immediately obvious, centrism is also at work in the economy of travel: the phallocentrism whereby the "law of the home" (*oikonomia*) organizes a set of gender determinations. One need go no further than the prototypical travel narrative that is the *Odyssey* to find a modeling of the sexual division of labor: the domestic(ated) woman, Penelope, maintains the property of the home against would-be usurpers while her husband wanders about. Away from home, the latter encounters "other" women, who remain, at least for him, alluring and/or menacing, seductive and/or castrating. The call of the Sirens is a dangerous pleasure only for the sailor not securely lashed to the fixity of his phallic shipmast or whose ears are not made deaf to the cry of women. From the perspective of such a gendered topography, it is not hard to read the unpredictable pleasure/anxiety of travel in terms of a male eros both attracted and repulsed by sexual difference. When travel is not explicitly invested with eros such as in the male fantasy production of exotic/erotic enchanted islands such as those of Circe, Cythera, or Tahiti (populated by eagerly willing but fatally attractive women), desire is displaced onto the land itself ("virgin" territories to be conquered, "dark continents" to be explored) or onto the very means of transportation: the at once womblike and phallic enclosures of boat, plane, train, or carriage that allow the explorer to "penetrate" the landscape. At the same time, such vehicles foster male bonding to the exclusion of women, stereotypically left at home or sought after as objects abroad.[29] And while there is nothing inherently or essentially masculine about travel (women have most certainly traveled as well as written about travel),[30] Western ideas about travel and the concomitant corpus of voyage literature have generally—if not characteristically —transmitted, inculcated, and reinforced patriarchal values and ideology from one male generation to the next, whether by journeying conceived as the rite of passage to manhood or by the pedagogical genderization of children's literature whereby little boys are led to read *Robinson Crusoe,* the novels of Kipling and Verne, or that modern corollary of adventure literature, science fiction. As such, the discourse of travel typically functions, to use Teresa de Lauretis's term, as a "technology of gender," a set of "techniques and discursive strategies" by which gender is constructed.[31]

The workings of such a technology can be found, for example, in Melanie Klein's psychoanalysis of the case of little Fritz, a young child whose attitude toward motion, as exemplified by his daily walk to school, vacillates between pleasure and anxiety. Not unsurprisingly, Klein finds at the core of this affective dilemma the castration anxiety of an unresolved Oedipus complex, wherein the boy's pleasure in motion, sense of orientation, and, more generally, his interest in learning are inhibited or motivated by the degree to which the "sexual-symbolic" determinant of these activities as coitus with the mother are repressed. Situated at the home, as what can be lost or regained by the daily excursion to that institutionalizing locus of paternal law that is the school, stands the mother. And, as if to underscore the phallic dimension of the road to school, the child's anxiety is especially evoked by its being lined with large and menacing trees. Interestingly, the lifting of the repression and the reconversion of anxiety into pleasure are marked by the apparently simultaneous sexualization of the topography as maternal body and of the mother's body as a fantasmatic landscape whose various "entrances and exits" elicit in the child a desire for "exploration."[32] To the extent, then, that little Fritz is caught between a good and a bad economics of travel, Klein's analysis thus provides a psychoanalytic reconfirmation of our own initial insights regarding the economy of travel even as it further elaborates the gender paradigms of the journey in the Western male unconscious. That Oedipal narratives of fathers and sons should accordingly emerge repeatedly through the discourse on travel in the texts of the male philosophers analyzed in this study obviously points less to their escape from than to their entrenchment within phallocentrism, and therefore to another limit on the critical possibilities of their discourse. On the other hand, such a conjunction between travel and phallocentrism also reveals a motif that invites a rereading of these texts from more explicitly political, psychoanalytical, or feminist points of view: the disruptive liminality women are represented as occupying in such texts. The analysis of travel in the writers studied here is intended to prepare the ground for such thoroughgoing critiques of the institutional roles and complicities assumed by these writers.

And here it does seem pertinent to reintroduce a certain historicism into my reading of the problem of travel. There is a particular force to such an analysis when it is carried out in the context of French Classical thought. A deconstructive opportunity is provided by that era's strong and insistent representation of the thinker as traveler, concretized in such literary stereotypes as the *picaro,* the knight errant, and the prudent navigator, or more abstractly in the Baroque theme of the *homo viator.*[33] Such representations, as well as the desacralization of the traditional Christian image of the path to salvation (typified in the notion of pilgrimage), themselves take place within the postmedieval crisis of feudal society, whose institutions, among other things, situate the lord's name as the name of his home. It is in the early modern texts of Montaigne, Descartes, Montesquieu, and Rousseau that we are told the manifold consequences of setting adrift the signifying relations that define where one is, who one is, or what is one's own. The so-called age of discovery (roughly spanning the fourteenth through nineteenth centuries) is also the era during which "economics" itself is discovered by European society and formulated progressively into a discernible object of knowledge and discipline of thought. The "science of wealth" was one that developed by discontinuous reactions to unprecedented and unsettling phenomena such as rapid inflation and sudden devaluation. Only through successive critiques of political economy does there eventually occur (after mercantilist theory, after Colbert, Law, Montesquieu and the Physiocrats, after Smith, Ricardo, and Marx) a theory of the production of value that is abstracted from its simple representamen (money, precious metals) and that is able to explain the unexpectedly disastrous effects of the mere accumulation of precious metals, effects made manifest by Spain's ruinous importation of vast quantities of gold and silver from its American empire.[34]

Concomitant with the initial period of European exploration and expansionism is the development and refinement of the new printing technology, which enabled both vast new liquidities through the invention of printed paper money and the commodification of knowledge itself in the form of the printed book. As has been amply demonstrated elsewhere, this new phase of textual objectification triggered an entirely new set of problems relative to the property (as well as propriety) of the book, notably the issue of author's rights and privileges.[35] In the last two decades and in the wake of even newer technologies of symbolic reproduction, it has been fashionable to speak of the death of the author, but this very notion of writerly authority that links name and text in an author's signature and whose wake we now celebrate is one born and circulated during an age that dislodged the bond between name and land.[36]

Another kind of name aggressively figures in preindustrial Europe, the paternal surname, whose instance points to a distinct inflection within the history of Western patriarchy. If the aristocrat's name is his title (to a piece of land), the prototypical bourgeois surname designates the father as such, whether it be in terms of his trade, physical appearance, or place of origin. The surname linguistically consolidates a family unit headed by a father, the king of this diminutive body politic, just as the king in post-Renaissance political thinking is characteristically designated as the father of that extended family which is the nation.[37] Concomitant with the new, public role played by the father was the increased privatization of women's world, what Sarah Kofman (in a transparent allusion to Foucault's "great confinement [*grand renfermement*]" of madmen in the seventeenth century) calls the "great immurement [*grand enfermement*]" of women carried out in the Classical era.[38] The same age that saw the birth of nation-states and that sent men scouring the four ends of the earth also shut women up within the home, a historical coincidence perhaps but one that legitimated the gendered topography of the male imaginary in the very organization of daily life. The birth of the modern family, marked by the patrilinearity of the surname, and reproduced on the macropolitical level by the consolidation of the "fatherland" under the royal paternalism of absolute monarchy, sustained the economics of the home as an ideological complex at a time when the traditional relation to land, concretized in the feudal institution of the fief, underwent a slow but seismic upheaval. That domestic economy headed by an unyielding paterfamilias and typified by the productive mode of cottage industry casts an important historical bridge between manor and factory, between feudal and capitalist worksites.

Within this context of a fundamental dislocation of property relations, a dislocation affecting almost everything that can be comprehended within the figure of the *oikos* or home, it does not seem sufficient to limit an analysis of the travel motif in early modern French philosophical literature to the mere unveiling of the obvious (mis)representations of cultural others such as Montaigne's cannibals, Lahontan's "good savage," Montesquieu's Persians, or Diderot's Pacific Islanders. While the critical analysis of such (mis)representations is of crucial import to any understanding of the ideological self-justification for European expansion as well as of the often suspect development of the discipline of anthropology,[39] the entire discourse of travel in these writers can be seen to thematize a fundamental economic anxiety in the widest sense of the word "economic," an anxiety whose repression is coincident with modern forms of subjectivity: selfhood, authorship, patriarchy, proprietorship. So not only are their texts particularly

available to a reading of their preoccupation with travel as indicative of
some larger anxiety, but that reading, generally applicable as it may be, is
also precisely what leads us to account for the specificity of these texts. In
each case and in each chapter of this study, the same problems and anxieties
are traced in a way specific to the text under consideration. Each time, a
new point of departure leads to a different point of arrival, although the
steps along the way indicate the existence of a set of associations and
assumptions common to all the writers studied, a set that, at least in the
limited context of this study, sketches a tale of the history of French
philosophical writing as a continual rewriting and retraveling of the text
of Montaigne. The belated discovery, in 1774, of the latter's journal of his
trip to Italy historically closes the period under study here even as the
writing of that travelogue pinpoints its beginning. And, as if to underscore
this Montaignian frame, it is by citing from the *Essays* that de Jaucourt
closes the *Encyclopédie* article, "Voyage," with which I chose to begin these
introductory remarks:

> The main thing, as Montaigne says, is not "to measure how many
> feet there are in the Santa Rotonda, and how much the face of
> Nero on some old ruins is bigger than it is on some medallions;
> but what is important is to rub and polish your brains by contact
> with those of others." It is here above all that you have an
> occasion to compare ancient and modern times, "and to fix your
> mind upon those great changes that have made each age so
> different from every other, and the cities of this beautiful country
> [Italy], once so populated, now deserted and seeming to subsist
> only to mark the places where those powerful cities, of which
> history has said so much, were."[40]

The above passage from the *Encyclopédie* also demarcates a geographical
limit that doubles the historical frame of this book: all four of the writers
studied here traveled to Italy, and their relation to Italian (especially Roman)
culture is particularly charged with intellectual and emotional energy. A
veritable subgenre of European travel narrative, the voyage to Italy enjoys
an exemplary status among travelogues, as it does in de Jaucourt's text.
Not only does it appear as the first example given of a voyage ("One makes
the *voyage* to Italy") but the article's close reinforces Italy's prestige as a
prime locus of historical, aesthetic, and moral reflection as well as the
stereotypical place to finish off a young gentleman's education. The early
modern and secular equivalent of the medieval pilgrimage to Jerusalem,
the voyage to Italy was a cultural institution that accredited transalpine
travelers (typically but not exclusively from England, France, and Germany)
with a knowledge both exotic and familiar. No longer the religious,
economic, or artistic center of Europe, post-Renaissance Italy became the

continent's internal other, a place where Northerners could come to gawk at the evidences of Roman decline, and thus feel smug in the superiority of their nationalities, and could acquire the cultural sensibility to assume positions of power at home. Whence their delight in the spectacle of Italian decadence, a traveler's commonplace passing itself off as a bit of historical wisdom, as in the passage de Jaucourt attributes to Montaigne. Acquiring some bit of the *imperium* Italy had lost, these travelers drew a high revenue from the relatively low-risk excursion to the peninsula, and with rarely any other experience abroad these same travelers returned home to help formulate their countries' political and cultural responses to the discovery of vast new lands, peoples, and cultures beyond the confines of Europe. Montaigne never visited the America he describes, nor Montesquieu Persia, nor Rousseau Oceania, yet their writings are of obvious significance in the history of European colonialism. Critics of the latter typically fail to draw the relations between these texts and their authors' experiences in Italy, as well as their powerful fantasy investments in that country as a privileged exotic locale. Countless more French travelers made the trip to Italy than ever set foot outside Europe. By insisting on the dialectics of the relation between home and abroad in the texts I analyze, I hope to resituate some of the givens in our understanding of European expansionism.

Finally, my reading of theoretical or philosophical texts through the play of a certain figure or motif—that of travel—raises the question of the status of those texts as literature. This is especially the case when the figure in question is one that not only permeates the history of literature but can even be construed as fundamentally characteristic of literary discourse. This book can be read then as an embarkation upon a poetics of philosophical or theoretical writing.

As the very drift of these remarks should demonstrate, it is difficult to stay in one place when meditating on the issue of travel. To talk about travel is inevitably to engage in it, to mime through the movement of one's words that which one is trying to designate with those words. Discourse on travel is thus inexorably contaminated by its object. It is not sufficient, however, to conclude that a rigorous analysis of travel is a fundamental impossibility. Rather, it should be acknowledged that the voyage (even when it appears to be well restrained within the limits of an "economy," or even when it is but an object of contemplation) has a powerful ability to dislodge the framework in which it is placed or understood, to subject it to critical displacement—although that displacement is not always to where one expects, nor is its criticism necessarily what one expects to find. The voyage, in other words, always takes us somewhere. The following study can also be read as an adventure to see what some of those "somewheres" might look like.

Chapter 1
Equestrian Montaigne

We can't afford to take the horse out of Montaigne's
Essays.
> —Ralph Waldo Emerson

Montaigne's *Journal de voyage en Italie* opens with a wound, or perhaps
with a couple of wounds, namely those suffered by an unnamed count in
the liminary episode of the journal and those suffered by the *Journal* itself,
given that the first page or pages of the manuscript have been lost. We are
told in the text that the count's wounds "were not mortal."[1] It remains to
be seen what we are to make of those suffered by the text.

Thanks to them, we find ourselves as readers of Montaigne's *Journal*
already en route, specifically at Beaumont-sur-Oise and not at Montaigne,
the presumed point of departure. But even if we could retrieve the missing
pages, there is no reason to believe that the writing of the journal begins
with the beginning of the journey. We know from other sources that after
leaving his home on June 22, 1580, Montaigne went to Paris to present
Henri III with a copy of the just-published first edition of the *Essays*. He
then took part at the king's request in the siege of Huguenot-held La Fère
before continuing on in the direction of Italy via Basel, Augsburg, and
Innsbruck.[2] Barring the discovery of the missing page(s), there remains,
however, no way to be sure exactly when and where Montaigne began to
have a journal kept. The writing could have begun just as easily at La
Fère, or in Paris, or anywhere in between, as at Montaigne.

Now, if I seem to belabor this accident suffered by the manuscript, it
is because—accident as it is—it nonetheless points to a necessity inherent
in any travel narrative, namely that such narratives are always fragmentary.
A voyage has always already begun; its starting point can only be decided

upon arbitrarily and after the fact. Even were it intact, Montaigne's journal, insofar as it is an account of his trip, could only begin *after* he had set out. Montaigne's voyage begins in a radical discontinuity, one doubly marked by the accidental mutilation of the manuscript. It is the possibility of such a discontinuity (accidental or not) that puts into question the very idea of marking the beginning of a voyage, of inscribing it to contain it. On the other hand, the happy coincidence by which the mutilation of the manuscript makes the text begin precisely with the story of the count's wounds tells us not only that these wounds "were not mortal" but that they are the very condition for the narrative's life. It is only because a cut has been made (here or elsewhere, it matters little) that the story can begin, that there can be a corpus of writing. It is under the sign of such a beneficent wound that Montaigne's discourse on travel will take place—and will take place in a persistent relation with a discourse on the body.

A wound, though, even if construed as salutary, implies a certain loss of property: of the blood of one's body, for instance, or the (at least provisional) loss of one's home, which inaugurates the travel narrative. Another kind of property is also at stake in the *Journal,* that of authorial propriety, for about half of this text attributed to Montaigne is not written by him but by an anonymous scribe ("one of my men" says Montaigne; p. 111). This scribe refers to his master, Montaigne, in the third person, as in the opening words of the manuscript in its current, tattered condition: "M. de Montaigne." In February, 1581, about midway through Montaigne's first of two stays in Rome, the scribe is mysteriously given his leave (p. 111). No explanation is offered as to why this leave was granted, as to whether the scribe left willingly or unwillingly, or whether he had somehow displeased his lord, Montaigne. Noting that the work is "quite advanced," the latter simply states the necessity of his taking over the writing of it himself. To the extent that Montaigne does not simply hire a new scribe the way one would change horses on a long journey such as his, and insists that "whatever trouble it may be to me, I must continue [the writing] myself" (p. 111), one is led to ask whether the sudden, unexplained appropriation of the scriptural task does not point to a desire in Montaigne to appropriate as his own this discourse that speaks of him, and that is "so far advanced" as to constitute a separate work on him, a separate work capable therefore of rivaling his own *Essays.* Such a separate work would be separated from him and therefore would not be "consubstantial with its author."[3] Is it a question of cutting off his servant's words at the moment they threaten to cut his own words off from themselves, that is, off from himself?

A manifest impatience with linguistic mediators is already evidenced in Montaigne's most celebrated essay on exoticism, "Of Cannibals," written no earlier than 1579, a few months before the publication of the *Essays* and the departure for Italy.[4] The essay is framed by its opening critique of contemporary cosmographers, such as André Thevet, whose descriptions of foreign lands are said to contain more fiction than fact; and by the closing anecdote of Montaigne's conversation with the Tupinamba Indians he met in Rouen, the directness of which is marred by the mediation of an incompetent translator: "I had an interpreter who followed my meaning so badly, and who was so hindered by his stupidity in taking my ideas, that I could get hardly any satisfaction from the man" (I, xxxi, 214). The interpreter's poor performance of his oral craft stands in contrast with the idealized orality of the Brazilians, whose designation as "cannibals" foregrounds the issue of what is appropriate for incorporation. Not only does their poetry bespeak an eloquence that is "altogether Anacreontic" but their anthropophagic practices remain strictly limited by a ritualistic framework that underscores personal honor and respect for one's ancestors. Such buccal propriety appears far less barbarous than the butchery or "boucherie" carried out between "civilized" Europeans in their contemporary religious wars: "I think there is more barbarity in eating a man alive than in eating him dead; and in tearing by tortures and the rack a body still full of feeling, in roasting a man bit by bit, in having him bitten and mangled by dogs and swine (as we have not only read but seen within fresh memory, not among ancient enemies, but among neighbors and fellow citizens, and what is worse, on the pretext of piety and religion), than in roasting and eating him after he is dead" (I, xxxi, 209). If ethnocentrism comes down here to a difference of taste ("each man calls barbarism whatever is not his own practice," I, xxxi, 205), European savagery or "our corrupted taste" (I, xxxi, 205) can be defined in terms of an indigestion that stems from overindulgence: "We have eyes bigger than our stomachs and more curiosity than capacity. We embrace everything, but we clasp only wind" (I, xxxi, 203). The Amerindians interviewed by Montaigne at Rouen are shocked to discover in France "that there were among us men full and gorged [*pleins et gorgez*] with all sorts of good things, and that their other halves were beggars at their doors, emaciated with hunger [*décharnez de faim*] and poverty" (I, xxxi, 214). The exploitation of one class by another appears as a cannibalism in disguise that eats not the dead but the living. European injustice as perverse digestion can also be read along the essay's geographical code, where colonialism is allegorized as regurgitation: "In Médoc, along the seashore, my brother, the sieur d'Arsac, can see an estate of his buried under the sands that the sea vomits [*vomit*] before itself. . . . The inhabitants say that for some time the sea has been pushing toward them so hard that they have lost four leagues of land. These sands are its harbingers [*fourriers*]; and we see great dunes [*montjoies*] of moving sand that march half a league ahead of it and keep conquering land [*gaignent païs*]" (I, xxxi, 204). The imperialist advances of the ocean, like the invading conquistadors, represent an appropriation that is not a simple case of ingestion but a truly *disgusting* anthropemy[5] that threatens to overturn the very body of the world in a passage that can be read in terms of either land bodies or bodies politic: "It seems that there are movements, some natural, others feverish, in these great bodies [*ces grands corps*] just as in our own. When I consider the inroads that my river, the Dordogne, is making in my lifetime into the right bank in its descent, and that in twenty years it has gained so much ground and stolen away the foundations [*fondement*] of several buildings, I clearly see that this is an extraordinary disturbance; for if it had always gone at this rate, or was to do so in the future, the face of the world would be turned topsy-turvy [*la figure du monde seroit renversée*]" (I, xxxi, 204). While this last passage first appeared in the 1588 edition of the *Essays,* that is, well after its author's return from Italy, it also continues to make explicit the intersections in Montaigne's writing between travel, the exotic, and corporeal propriety, to underscore the urgency of keeping the body upright, unscathed, and properly delimited.

If we consider now the situation of Montaigne's travelogue within the chronology of his work, we find that the voyage to Italy cuts the writing of the *Essays* into two periods: namely, the first period from 1571 to 1580, during which time Montaigne wrote the primitive version of the first two books of the *Essays* (what Montaigne critics traditionally refer to as the *a* stratum), and the second period, leading up to the publication in 1588 of the third book along with numerous additions to the first two (the *b* stratum). It is in terms of this gap occasioned by Montaigne's voyage that a major current of Montaigne criticism has seen an opportunity to explain the "progress" or "evolution" of the *Essays.* An opposition is thereby posited between the 1580 *Essays* and the 1588 *Essays,* with the latter construed as not only the superior but also the finalized version of Montaigne's project (a view that also diminishes or belittles the importance of the subsequent additions included by Montaigne on the "Bordeaux" copy, or *c* stratum). According to this schema, the earlier essays are seen as "unoriginal" and "impersonal" compared to the "originality" and "personality" of the later ones.[6] The voyage to Italy then becomes responsible at least in part for this striking turn in Montaigne's work, for his "humanization." The voyage can then become the metaphor through which is grasped Montaigne's opus as a whole: his "long meditative journey," as one critic puts it.[7] The cut in the writer's production occasioned by the voyage then becomes the beneficent wound that would define the very essence of his corpus.

The main problem with such an interpretation is not so much that it is wrong but that it does not cut far enough. At the same time, it attributes to the voyage a value of presence. Montaigne's voyage would be what takes him away from his tower and his writing to bring him back enriched with experience in the "real" world. While I certainly do not wish to quarrel with the well-documented fact that the observations made by Montaigne in his journal serve as material for his later writing and rewriting of the *Essays*,[8] one of the points I hope to make in the following pages is that a similar logic is at work in both Montaigne's travels and his retreats to the tower, in both his voyaging and his writing, and in both the early and the late *Essays* (I view the latter, then, less in opposition to the early *Essays* than as what renders explicit the problems already posed in the early work). What Montaigne brings back from his travels may be what led him away in the first place.

Montaigne never published—and probably never intended to publish—his *Journal de voyage*. The *Journal* was not published until its accidental discovery nearly two centuries later, unless one considers it to have been by dint of its influence on the later *Essays*. Indeed, entire passages from the *Journal* are textually reproduced in the *Essays*. The *Journal de voyage* can be said to be both inside and outside the text of the *Essays* to the extent that much of what is said in the *Journal* finds its way into the *Essays* while the *Journal* as a whole is to be distinguished from Montaigne's major work. In the familiar terms of Derridean deconstruction, the *Journal* appears then as a "supplement" to the *Essays,* an excrescence that is both vital and superfluous to it.[9] But this is to assume that the *Essays* itself can be considered to constitute a complete work, a notion impugned by the very structure of the *Essays* built as it is on the practice of a ceaseless commentary only ended by Montaigne's death, and any part of which is indecidably essential and inessential. The *Essays* is built on a mass of excrescences, on the text as excrescence, a growth that can be cut off anywhere and nowhere.[10] Such a situation makes it difficult to know what to consider as in or out of the text, and accordingly demands a rethinking of the category of travel, which normally rests on the assumption that one can decide between what is inside and outside—of the text, of the home, of the body. And if it is the cut of a certain trip that defines the Montaignian corpus, the effects of that cut should be legible in the text whose inaugural scars led us to question the status of writing and travel in Montaigne, the travel journal of his trip to Italy. A preliminary description of that journal in terms of its endpoints, the topography traversed, and the foregrounded modalities of displacement should set our bearings on the symbolic function of travel within the *Essays* itself.

Circulating in Italy: *Travel Journal*

The destination of this voyage is Italy (reached by way of Switzerland and Germany). Italy, however, is no ordinary spot on the map in the context of French literature. Rather it is the destination *par excellence*. Any attempt to construct a list of French travelers to Italy would be tantamount to compiling a who's who of French writing. In the sixteenth century, a considerable number of writers besides Montaigne made their way to the peninsula, among them Erasmus, Rabelais, Marot, Calvin, Joachim du Bellay, Montluc, Brantôme, and Henri Estienne. A few of the most prominent French writers after Montaigne to make the journey were Descartes, Montesquieu, De Brosses, Rousseau, Sade, Chateaubriand, Stendhal, Nerval, Taine, Zola, Gide, Proust, Butor.[11] To study Montaigne's travel in this context would require a study well beyond the scope of this one to discern the significance Italy holds for French culture in general, and for that of Renaissance France in particular.

A few remarks might be ventured, however, for the current purpose. To the extent that French culture is not only the younger of the two but the one that finds its mythical and historical origins in the other, one can detect in the French a desire to appropriate Italy and to make that other culture their own. This desire can just as easily take the positive form of what Roland Barthes has called an "inverted racism"[12] as that of military conquest (repeatedly attempted from medieval times through Napoleon III). The ambiguity of this desire is demonstrated, for instance, in the article "Voyage" of the *Encyclopédie*. There, what begins as a description of a French traveler's first view of Italy evokes and then swiftly gives way to a long development on Caesar's crossing of the Rubicon. After this condensation of tourist and conqueror, the article ends by citing a long passage from none other than Montaigne on the educational value of travel to Italy.[13] And if Montaigne's visit to Italy may be seen, therefore, to be exemplary of such voyages, it is not merely because he obliges so many after him to follow his footsteps. There is also found in Montaigne both a great lover of Italy (a "reverse racist" driven to seek and obtain Roman citizenship) and a writer whose work was judged even by some contemporaries to be on a par with that of the ancient Latin writers. Etienne Pasquier called him "another Seneca."[14] Montaigne's name can be linked then with a victory in the French battle for an autonomous literature of equal stature with that of Italy. Perhaps it is here that we are to find the genesis of the unsubstantiated myth of Montaigne's trip to Italy as a spy mission for the French king, ever intent on conquering Italy.[15] In any case, Montaigne's journey takes place in the context of the Italian wars undertaken by Charles VIII, Louis XII, and François I, wars in which Montaigne's father took part.[16] These wars eventually led to the massive importation of Italian art and artists, the traditionally ascribed cause for the spread of the Renaissance into France.[17] The contemporaneous revival of interest in antiquity brought about by the Humanists could be shown to display the same ambiguous attitude toward that antiquity as does France toward Italy: a mixture of love and rivalry, both of which are expressed in the desire to appropriate the Latin other.[18]

Bearing in mind what we have said about travel to Italy, let us turn now to the way Montaigne proceeds to travel in and describe that already over-determined landscape. The *Journal* is punctuated and divided by the names of places where Montaigne stayed, and which are placed in the order of his itinerary. A typical entry includes, after the place name, the amount of distance traveled since the previous place name and some comment on the locality's situation (what Montaigne calls its *assiette,* or site) in terms of its political allegiance as well as its topography (characteristically described in terms of the vertical difference between plain, valley, and varying levels of mountain height): "CASTELNUOVO, sixteen miles, a little walled village belonging to the house of Colonna, buried away among hills [*montaignetes*] in a site that strongly reminded me of the fertile approaches to our Pyrenees on the Aigues-Caudes road" (p. 135). The travelogue as narrative genre is anchored by what would seem to be the most steadfast referentiality, that of the map. This referential system, however, only functions as a grid to pinpoint another set of references, which includes the historical facts, literary reminiscences, and other bits of trivia by which Montaigne grasps the topography he is traversing.[19] In other words, a complex process of recognition is set in motion such that the landscape he encounters is a significant one, one that signifies. The literal inscriptions and monuments encountered by Montaigne only render explicit the semiosis implied in the topography.

But if the topography turns out to be a sort of text, how then shall one characterize the activity of travel? At a certain moment, Montaigne seems to lean toward the metaphor of reading: "He also said that he seemed to be rather like people who are reading some very pleasing story and therefore begin to be afraid that soon it will come to an end, or any fine book; so he took such pleasure in traveling that he hated to be nearing each place where he was to rest, and toyed with several plans for traveling as he pleased, if he could get away alone" (p. 65). But if to travel is to read the text of a certain topography on the one hand, it is also to make certain inscriptions in that text on the other: the tracks left on the ground, for example, by horse hooves or the "evidences of having been there" (p. 68) that Montaigne leaves behind him, such as the family coat of arms he has painted at the baths he visits. The trail of the traveler obliges us to supersede the opposition between reading and writing and to understand in its stead a complex circulation of signs as much written as read which modifies the traveler as much as he modifies the terrain in an endless differential positioning, at once the infinite detour of the text and the text of an infinite detour. This is a prospect embraced by a Montaigne whose potential for digressive peregrination proves daunting to his own scribe and fellow travelers: "I truly believe that if Monsieur de Montaigne had been alone with his attendants he would rather have gone to Cracow or toward Greece by land than make the turn toward Italy; but the pleasure he took in visiting unknown countries, which he found so sweet as to make him forget the weakness of his age and of his health, he could not impress on any of his party, and everyone asked only to return home" (p. 65).

To contain and master this differential network written by the traveler as it writes him, one needs to appeal to a certain notion of referentiality, one that posits the possibility of an identification—such as the identification of the place in which one finds oneself. To make an identifying reference, one needs to refer one position to another (be it only in the act of consulting a map) according to a hermeneutical schema that brings one term back to the other, positing their sameness through the act of *identification.* This act of reference brings the unknown back to the known, the strange back to the familiar. The Apennines near Castelnuovo, as we saw, are understood in terms of the familiar French Pyrenees. The referential act (that is, a certain interpretative act) aims to institute a signifying economy infinitely capable of appropriating the other or the new. Such an economy implies the positing of an *oikos,* a same, to which everything and anything can be referred back. The voyage can then accumulate a certain capital (money, knowledge, experience, and so on), a process that goes hand in hand with a humanistic, individualistic, or anthropocentric ideology. It should not be surprising, then, if contemporaneous with the unfolding of such an ideology during the Renaissance we find descriptions of landscapes in anthropomorphic terms, for Renaissance man conceived of his position in the world in terms of a specular relation between himself and the universe, that of microcosm and macrocosm.[20] The voyage aims at such a speculation and speculates to that end: "This great world, which some multiply further as being only a species under one genus, is the *mirror* in which we must look at ourselves to recognize ourselves from the proper angle" (I, xxvi, 157; my emphasis).

The end of the speculative voyage is the return to the beginning, to the same. The last stop on Montaigne's trip, as noted in his *Journal,* is Montaigne, that is to say, the place that bears his name, or rather, the place from which he takes his name. The name, Montaigne, is as much Montaigne's proper name as it is the name of his property. "Moy" is difficult to distinguish from "chez moy." For the subject who occupies this place, the mastery of one's geography is implied in the mastery of one's language, and vice versa. In both cases, we are dealing with the circular structure of a return to the same through the process of identification: identity of place, identity of name, identity of the subject. We will have occasion to return to the implications of this identification of place with name in our analysis of the *Essays*.

For the moment, we need to insist upon the fact that an identification does not go without saying. One can be mistaken about a name as well as about a place. The reference can be lacking or be made with difficulty or remain doubtful. One cannot always be certain that the walls that surround Rome are in fact vestiges of the ancient walls (*Journal,* p. 135). Moreover, the referent itself can have changed, as in the case of the ruins encountered by Montaigne all along his route but especially at Rome: "An ancient Roman could not recognize the site of his city even if he saw it" (p. 105). The half-effaced inscriptions and the monuments in ruin resist as much as they encourage the act of reference. The ruin remains as an index of what it once was at the same time that its very state *as* ruin blocks the full recovery and reconstruction of that anterior state. Even if one could reconstruct the monument, it could never be exactly the same as it once was. The inevitability of loss works against the hermeneutic appropriation we have posited as the basis of the economy of travel.

This loss denotes a fundamental alteration that at the limit renders impossible any return to the same and that alters the voyager as he proceeds on his voyage. Such a conception is also to be found in Montaigne's text, especially in such anecdotes as that of the Italian become more Turk than Italian merely by spending too much time among Turks (pp. 163-64) and the story of the young girl transformed into a man after having made a leap (p. 5)[21]—an act we can read as the ellipsis or ultimate abbreviation of the voyage. In these examples, we find an interpretation of travel as loss of that identity which should have been assured by the economy of referential identification.

The precariousness of the economy of travel is especially to be remarked in Montaigne's anxiety about his "colic" at the baths of Lucca. For his condition to improve and for the mineral water to purge his body of kidney stones, the amount of mineral water drunk must be exactly rendered in his urine. Any imbalance between the two prompts a state of anxiety that drives Montaigne to note down his every urination and to check it against his intake of mineral water. Not that Montaigne is unaware of the comical aspect of such an obsessive notation: "It is a stupid habit to recount what you piss" (p. 165). It is nonetheless Montaigne's very health that is at stake in the ingestion and elimination of a certain quantity of a certain kind of liquid, a circulation that aims at domesticating something interior to Montaigne's own body. Thus the need to master the circulation of an exterior element, namely the mineral water, exists only in view of the need to master an internal alteration, the growth and movement of his stone. Such a hydraulics is exceedingly difficult to master. He may be able to drink as much water as he wants but he cannot so easily "make water." Somewhere in the circulation of these liquids, something radically unmasterable intervenes as a kind of blockage that places this movement out of the control of the subject, Montaigne.

These circulatory economies of landmarks and body liquids shed light, moreover, on Montaigne's fascination with the fantastical hydraulic technology he sees in Augsburg, at the Prattolino, in Tivoli, and elsewhere. What could better fulfill the dreams of an ailing Montaigne than the closed structure of a fountain in and out of which circulates water without loss and in a perfect equilibrium; in other words, the figure of an absolute self-sufficiency? We come back to the desire for something proper that would elude the structural necessity of a fundamental alienation. But in the economies we have been analyzing (those of writing, of travel, of the monument, of the hydraulics of the body as well as of the fountain), the very opposition between the apparently contradictory terms of appropriation and disappropriation seems to be put in question. Montaigne travels to improve his health but the mineral waters seem to aggravate his condition as much as they aid it.[22] As for the appropriation implied by the writing of a journal to register and keep a record of events, that appropriation is further subject to question, as we have already seen, by an intermediary, a scribe who seems at times to be writing under Montaigne's dictation and at other times to be writing for himself.[23]

The problem of an appropriation that is simultaneously a disappropriation is perhaps most dramatically brought into relief by Montaigne's decision to write a portion of the *Journal* in Italian as if to mime the progress of the voyage by writing in the same language as that spoken in the area traversed. Hence, he returns to the French language upon crossing the Alps back into France. If by such a mimetic device he seeks to master the traveler's situation, the text nonetheless escapes all the more from his grasp insofar as Montaigne is trying to use a foreign language which, as he himself as well as his commentators have pointed out, he manipulates with considerable difficulty.[24] (This problem is at once effaced and strangely mimed in its totality in all French editions, which replace the Italian text of Montaigne by Meusnier de Querlon's French translation, dating from the *Journal*'s first publication in 1774.)

Finally, another kind of appropriating device can be located in the means of transportation, a particular mode of which may be phantasmically privileged by the individual traveler. Oppositions may be set up between different ways to travel: a modern traveler may consider trains to be good, safe, and pleasant while planes are bad, dangerous, and unpleasant, or vice versa. In other words, a certain vehicle of mastery may define the good or economical voyage, as opposed to the bad or risky one. In a well-known passage near the beginning of "Of Coaches," Montaigne states his preference for horse travel: "Now I cannot long endure (and I could endure them less easily in my youth) either coach, or litter, or boat; and I hate any other transportation than horseback, both in town and in the country" (III, vi, 900). And once again, the discourse on travel comes under the sign of the body. According to Montaigne, coach or boat travel upsets his stomach and aggravates his kidney stones while horseback riding actually gives him relief (*Essays* III, vi, 899-901 and III, xiii, 194; *Journal,* p. 58).[25] The strength of Montaigne's feelings on the matter can be judged by his choice, upon returning from Rome, to go to Milan by the more arduous land route of Pontremoli rather than by way of Genoa because the latter would require a sea journey (p. 227). He does, however, agree to take a barge into Venice, "since the boat is drawn by horses" (p. 73). What is to be feared in the boat is the motion of water (p. 73), for if Montaigne adores the well-ordered and well-mastered flow of fountain water, what he abhors is the unbridled and uncontained water of the sea, the water caught up in a perpetual flux. Such water upsets his stomach, that is, it upsets the hydraulic equilibrium of his body. Such a flux means that travel takes place as much inside the body as outside of it, with the result that the very notions of inside and outside are jeopardized along with that of the body itself as proper to itself.

The horse, on the other hand, is not only what does not leave terra firma but also that mode of transportation whose movement ideally responds to its master's bridle. Indeed, mastery over the horse exemplifies mastery in general. *Chevalier* is a title of nobility, the sign of one's adherence to a ruling class. It is to this class that Montaigne belongs. In the Latin document proclaiming him a Roman citizen, Montaigne is noted down as an *eques,* a member of the equestrian class (III, ix, 999). And if mounting a horse signifies one's ascension to the rank of the high and mighty, it is also what allows a man of small height, such as Montaigne, to attain another kind of stature: "Since my early youth, I have not liked to go except on horseback. On foot I get muddy right up to my buttocks; and in our streets small men are subject to being jostled and elbowed" (III, xiii, 1096). Being in the saddle puts one in a position of both physical and political domination. Small wonder, then, that Montaigne should say that were he allowed to lead the life he desires, "I should choose to spend it with my ass in the saddle" (III, ix, 987). Such is the kind of life he tries to lead in his trip to Italy, a trip made on horseback. Hardly a page of the *Journal* passes without at least some mention of a horse or horses, as if the situation of being on horseback merited in itself repeated attention. In fact, "horses [*chevaus*]" is the very last word written by the scribe before Montaigne takes over the writing of his own journal (p. 110). Given Montaigne's small height and the relatively recent entry of his family into the nobility,[26] his obsession with horseback riding is manifestly overdetermined, and it should not be cavalierly dismissed as of mere biographical interest. For what is at stake in the figure of the horse is nothing less than Montaigne's status as master in terms of the property of his name, of his land, and of his body. The consequences of such an investment in the horse can only be gauged, though, if we turn to the *Essays,* a text in which the motif of the horse is as prolific as the other categories unearthed by our analysis of the *Travel Journal:* the insistence of the body, the referentiality of the name, and the symbolism of Rome.

Unbridled Leisure: "Of Idleness"

Where should we begin our reading of this prolific horse if not in an essay where it metaphorizes a certain perverse prolificacy? The essay in question, "Of Idleness [De l'oisiveté]" (I, viii) invites such primacy in other ways as well. It is probably one of the earliest essays in point of composition as well as one of the first chapters in the ordering of the book, the eighth essay of the first book. More significantly, it is the first essay in which Montaigne tries to define and justify his purpose in writing the *Essays.* The essay corresponds then to a moment of self-reflexivity in Montaigne's discourse wherein he begins to form and define the autobiographical project that is the key to the success of the *Essays* in the history of French writing.[27] Furthermore, this metadiscursive moment coincides with what is, if not the first appearance of the horse in the *Essays,* at least the first sustained recourse to that figure.[28]

The essay on idleness begins with what appears to be a commentary in the moralist tradition on the dangers of that condition.[29] Now if there be any risk in idleness, one would think that this risk would be a function of the immobility implied in such a state of repose and would take the form of boredom, or what a latter tradition would call ennui. Montaigne, however, reverses these polarities, for the danger he sees in idleness is certainly not that of too great a domestication. Rather, idleness, for Montaigne, far from being a state of immobility, is a state of "agitation." The danger of idleness lies in its propensity to produce an unmasterable movement, which can itself lead to madness: "And there is no mad or idle fancy [*rêverie*] that [idle minds] do not bring forth in this agitation" (I, viii, 32).[30] Idleness, despite the connotation of the word, is paradoxically what sets one in motion, but in a bizarre, unsettling kind of motion, a motionless motion or a mad motion that sends the idler on a journey going nowhere.[31]

Such a voyage raises an economic problem, since it is the *oikos* itself that is at stake when the home becomes unstable and the familiar becomes unfamiliar. The need to establish a certain *domus* or domestication is therefore precisely what is put into relief by the metaphors Montaigne uses to describe the dangerous state of idleness: "Just as we see that idle land, if rich and fertile, teems with a hundred thousand kinds of wild and useless weeds, and that to set it to work we must subject it and sow it with certain seeds for our service; and as we see that women, all alone, produce mere shapeless masses and lumps of flesh [*des amas et pieces de chair informes*], but that to create a good and natural offspring, they must be made fertile with another kind of seed; so it is with minds. Unless you keep them busy with some definite subject that will bridle and control them [*qui les bride et contreigne*], they throw themselves in disorder hither and yon into the vague field of the imagination" (I, viii, 32). Although, at first glance, it seems possible to understand these examples in terms of the opposition between nature and culture, a closer reading plays havoc with the distinction, since the state of nature reveals itself to be less a terrestial paradise than a condition characterized by a kind of perverse excess. In the first simile, uncultivated land is not marked by sterility or the absence of vegetation but rather by an overabundance of plants. The second simile repeats the same argument, this time in relation to women. Women, says Montaigne as if it were an incontrovertible fact, require the male seed only for the purposes of assuring a "*good* and *natural* offspring." Without the intervention of the man, they would still produce "shapeless masses and lumps of flesh."[32] One sees in both these examples that nothing is more unnatural from the point of view of culture than nature itself. The state of nature (and of idleness) is dangerous, then, since it implies an unchecked process of useless and vertiginous propagation.

This perverse germination man will try to domesticate and cultivate through agriculture and attention to conjugal duties. Culture can then be defined as the institution of a certain kind of procreative labor, the antithesis of idle perversity, of idleness as perversity. So it is a particular kind of activity or motion which is to bring into bounds the mad motion of idleness. The metaphor used by Montaigne is that of a certain "bridling" of the idle mind, an image that presages a more elaborate horse metaphor at the end of the essay. Here, however, the domestication of the horse is the metaphor for domestication itself, the domestication that consists in the establishment of a proper *domus*. What role then does the domesticating bridle play in the institution of this *domus* if not that of ensuring a certain teleological or proleptic creation, a pro-creation (and it is for this reason that the bridle can be compared to the seed)? In other words, the *domus* is what is pro-created to the extent that the bridle *dom*esticates by keeping the idle mind headed to a particular destination. The movement is mastered by the setting up of a goal: "The soul that has no fixed goal loses itself; for as they say, to be everywhere is to be nowhere" (I, viii, 32).

The danger raised by idleness is that of the loss of one's bearings, that is to say, the loss of the property or properness of the *oikos*. This loss takes place because idleness makes it impossible to establish any kind of property or differentiate between what is proper and what is not. Even the word "idleness" (*oisiveté*) itself seems to have lost any proper meaning it once might have had save to denote impropriety itself. Rather than con-noting such notions as those of repose, ease, leisure, solitude, or immobility, idleness is interpreted in this essay as if by design in terms of agitation, madness, and perverse overabundance. The problem of idleness, as evi-denced by Montaigne's ensuing citation of Martial, is that of property itself, of property as the proper habitat: "Quisquis ubique habitat, Maxime, nusquam habitat [He who dwells everywhere, Maximus, nowhere dwells]" (I, viii, 32).

It is immediately after this quotation from Martial that Montaigne reveals that the state of idleness he has been describing describes, in fact, his own experiences upon taking up his retreat. The preceding negative description of idleness should not lead us, however, to conclude that Montaigne detests idleness as in itself a pernicious or particularly damaging vice. Far from excluding idleness on moral grounds, Montaigne often takes pleasure in describing himself as an idle or even slothful person (see, for example, II, xvii, 642–43; III, ix, 969, 992). Furthermore, the very reason for which he took up his famous retreat, or so he says, was to find the kind of rest and tranquillity one would normally associate with a state of idleness. But, as he continues, this was not what he found: "Lately when I retired to my home [*chez moy*], determined as far as possible to bother about nothing except spending the little life I have left in repose and seclusion, it seemed to me I could do my mind no greater favor than to let it entertain itself in full idleness and stop and settle in itself, which I was hoping it might henceforth do more easily, having become weightier and riper with time. But I find—idleness always makes the mind distracted [*variam semper dant otia mentem*]—that, on the contrary, like a runaway horse [*faisant le cheval eschappé*], it gives itself a hundred times more trouble than it took for others, and gives birth to so many chimeras and fantastic monsters [*et m'enfante tant de chimères et monstres fantasques*], one after another, without order or purpose, that in order to contemplate their ineptitude and strangeness [*l'ineptie et l'estrangeté*] at my pleasure, I have begun to put them in writing [*les mettre en rolle*], hoping in time to make my mind ashamed of itself [*luy en faire honte à luy mesmes*]" (I, viii, 33). Montaigne sought repose in idleness, but what he found was just the opposite: instead of rest, a ceaseless agitation; instead of a mind in peace, the frantic production of tempestuous thoughts which are compared to "chimeras and fantastic monsters." The monstrosity, if there is one, is that idleness turns into its opposites. This monstrosity is engendered by the idle mind itself, which is compared to a "runaway horse."

And here, the horse comes back although precisely in the guise of a horse that refuses to come back. The horse, which had earlier appeared as the metaphor of domination and domestication, now emerges as the dominant metaphor in a piece of writing rife with mixed metaphors. And it is somehow in the positing of the problem of idleness as a runaway horse that Montaigne is able to conceptualize his predicament. The metaphor of the horse defines the dangerous divagation of idleness. The solution, then, if we recall the first part of the essay, should be a certain bridling.

Before discussing how this bridling takes place or why the return of the horse spurs or is spurred by Montaigne's move into self-reflection, we need to concede that the very desire to bridle the horse implies the persistence of Montaigne's desire to be "idle." For if Montaigne's project to write seems a reaction against the idleness he describes, it is because what he seeks is another idleness, the absolute idleness of pure repose. If the act of putting "en rolle" (of recording) the productions of his idle mind is supposed to master mental activity by directing it toward some goal, that goal is nothing other than the repose of the mind. The mind will supposedly stop running like an unbridled horse when it confronts the "rolle" or scroll of its monstrous acts, an event that will "make my mind ashamed of itself." The bridling of the horse or the recording of one's thoughts comes down to a therapeutic project that takes the form of a self-analysis. A dialogue is instituted in which one part of the self, or "moy," strives to domesticate the other ("make it ashamed of itself") through a rhetorical strategy that consists of making that other confront its own babble. This discursive confrontation will, in principle, provoke a heightened self-awareness that will, in turn, bring about peace of mind or the repose of absolute idleness, which Montaigne calls wisdom or "sagesse." Now, this quest for repose is not a mere anecdotal detail from Montaigne's personal life; it is something fundamental to the very basis of his thought and a constant element in it despite the *Essays'* often noted vagaries and vicissitudes. To follow Villey's tripartite division of Montaigne's career,[33] we could argue that in each period Montaigne's thought is teleologically focused upon a concept of repose as the *summum bonum*: the tranquillity of the soul and the calm in the face of death posited as virtue in his Stoic period; the spiritual repose or *ataraxia* to be obtained by the suspension of judgment in the skepticism of his second period; and the praise of ignorance as the greatest value in life in his last or so-called naturalist period.

The descriptive project, then, of "Of Idleness" is the prescription for achieving absolute quietude, or "idleness," in the mind. The Montaigne who writes describes his thoughts in order to silence them. In other words, he describes his thoughts in order to have no thoughts. We are in the paradoxical situation of he who seeks repose through activity. This active quest for repose is paradoxical to the extent that the desire or effort to attain repose functions as the immediate obstacle to the attainment of that repose. Rigorously speaking, to make a movement toward a state of rest is precisely to put oneself in motion, that is, to do the opposite of putting oneself at rest. And if that state of rest, once attained, should turn out once more to be a state of agitation, one runs the risk of being condemned to a perpetual motion and an impossible quest for repose. One needs to move in order to stop, but when one stops one finds oneself all the more in motion.

What has become of our bridle? For if the horse as the dominant metaphor of the essay is what should be the metaphor of domination, it is nevertheless not Montaigne who holds the bridle on idleness but idleness that holds Montaigne by the bridle. It is the horse, in short, who leads the rider, and the latter's hope to tame that horse remains just that, a *hope,* as Montaigne proleptically suggests in the last line of the essay: "I have begun to put [my idle thoughts] in writing, *hoping* in time to make my mind ashamed of itself."

But what Montaigne says he *has* begun to write is also, evidently, the very text we are reading. The first part of the essay is thus given a retroactive significance. The "rolle" is the text of the *Essays,* the writing Montaigne produces in his strenuous efforts to attain a state of repose. But again, this "mise en rolle" itself perpetuates the motion it is supposed to restrain. The putting into writing of the idle thoughts can only master them to the extent that it repeats them, but this repetition is simultaneously what makes them repeatable. Once the "mise en rolle" has begun, one is "rolling" in a writing there is no way to stop. It is neither an accident nor a mere quirk of Montaigne's personality that he should keep writing and rewriting the text of his "idle thoughts" until his death. The economy of this textual journey is thus opened onto an infinite divagation.

If the writing is also a "rolling," it is because the function of that writing is to retrace the steps of the horse's itinerary. The effort is to describe or note down the thoughts described or traced out by the movement of the horse. But if the *Essays* then describe the same trajectory as the horse, there are at least two differences to be remarked. First, the writing *follows* after the horse, thereby instituting the regimen of repetition already alluded to. Secondly, the "mise en rolle" follows exactly the same path as the horse only to the extent that it is motivated by the hope of bridling the horse. If it accepts following the horse, it is only because it counts on eventually being ahead of it, on being at the endpoint to which the horse will ideally move. The endpoint of the voyage is the hoped-for (but only hoped-for) moment when the horse stops after having come back to itself, seen what it has produced, and felt shame thereupon. The discursive voyage of the *Essays* is teleologically closed by the *hope* of teleological closure, of the bridle, of a proleptic creation or "pro-creation" of the self as *domus*.

The jest here in connecting these terms is nonetheless in earnest. We have already seen the connection at work in the first part of the essay. More to the point, what underlies the passage in question is precisely the issue of a certain *progeny,* namely the "chimeras and fantastic monsters" to which the "runaway horse . . . gives birth." These offspring are, according to Montaigne, characterized by "ineptitude and strangeness" and invite comparison with the "shapeless masses and lumps of flesh" Montaigne says women produce when they are without the bridle of the male seed. It is these offspring of which the idle mind should be ashamed. The problem, necessarily stated in terms of hope since one cannot easily predict the nature of one's offspring, would be that of engendering a body that is "good and natural." Such a body would presumably be not inappropriate or foreign [*inepte ou étrange*] but proper and one's own.

What kind of body are we talking about? Or more exactly, *whose* body is it? Following what we know from "Of Idleness," we can already deduce that that body is a "body of thought" proper to its thinker. Such a notion is, in fact, not at all uncommon to Montaigne if we remember, for instance, the long development at the end of "Of the Affection of Fathers for their Children" (II, viii, 399–442) in which Montaigne compares the relation between writers and their books to that between fathers and their children. Moreover, Montaigne privileges the former of these relations because, so he says, literary offspring are "more our own" (II, viii, 400). To support that contention, he adds that "we are father and mother both in this generation." Elsewhere, Montaigne makes claims for his own book that would seem to make it even more proper to him than one's own child: "a book consubstantial with its author" (II, xviii, 665); "I am myself the matter of my book" ("To the Reader," p. 3). Leaving aside for the moment the question of the validity of Montaigne's claims, we can conclude that the body we are dealing with is a corpus of writing, which is understood to be a body proper to its author. Whether that body is the writer's own or that of his "progeny" is an issue of lesser importance—once the claim to property has been made. That body is always *called* one's own no matter what shape it takes.

If we return once more to "Of Idleness," we must conclude that if there is a proper body produced there, it must be related to that "mise en rolle" of the "chimeras and fantastic monsters." The implication, though, is that the proper body is made out of improper ones. The paradox can be resolved, at least momentarily, if we remember the example of the "idle" women. The "shapeless masses and lumps of flesh" they produced became proper human bodies if they were "worked over" [*embesoigner*] by "another kind of seed [*une autre semence*]." The male seed would give form to feminine matter. In the case of the shapeless bodies produced by idle thoughts, that other seed must be the writing itself, which forms those ideas into a body of writing. In phallocentric terms, the pen(is) would *define* the properness of the body.[34]

If the productions of the mind, as they are retraced in writing, constitute the body of writing as Montaigne's own, what "property" is described or circumscribed by that idle wandering if not the territory proper to Montaigne, namely his domain of Montaigne? Thus, the text of the *Essays* constituted as a pro-creative journey aims to institute an *oikos* as the habitat proper to Montaigne. This "property" is that topographical body carved out by the text, a mountain or Monta(i)gne in writing.[35] "Montaigne" is the name affixed to that property, whether it be a text, a place, or a body. These three terms can then function and do function in "Montaigne" as metaphoric equivalents. So if Montaigne describes his text as a body, he can also describe his body as a space, even as a room or building (when it is not the very particular space of the third-story room in his tower where he writes surrounded by his library).[36] Perhaps no single expression better captures the flexibility of Montaignian space than the prepositional clause, *chez moy,* which appears for the first time in "Of Idleness" ("Lately when I retired to my home [*chez moy*] ... ") and which designates an interiority as vast as the entire surrounding region of Gascony or as restricted as the innermost core of Montaigne's private being, his "back shop [*arrierebou-tique*]." Indeed, the metaphorics of interiority that construct the space of the self [*moy*] as a place [*chez moy*] reaches its height in such expressions as "As for me, I hold that I exist only in myself [*Moy, je tiens que je ne suis que chez moy*]" (II, xvi, 626), or "If I am not at home, I am always very near it [*Si je ne suis chez moy, j'en suis toujours bien pres*]" (III, ii, 811).

What the *Essays* of Montaigne seeks to do then is to delimit an anthropomorphic or corporeal topography in and through a text whose economy is proleptically assured by the signature of the proper name, Montaigne, or the *moy* whose name appears right from the title page. The signature would thus appear to be the stroke of the pen(is) or bridle which pro-creates the proper body of Montaigne by defining the bounds of that property.

The bounds of the signature, however, only offer the teleological closure for what we can already see to be an autobiographical project. The signature is the *hope* of property, its *pro*creation, which nonetheless still leaves a body to be defined or produced through the writing that delimits or demar-cates that textual corpus. But if Montaigne's discourse describes the limits of his body or his property, the limits of that proper body are the limits of his discourse. The body or the property of Montaigne about which we are speaking is of a textual order. In other words, "Montaigne" is what he *states* himself to be: "It is not my deeds that I write down; it is myself, it is my essence [*c'est moy, c'est mon essence*]" (II, vi, 379). Hence, he can add elsewhere that all arguments "are equally good to me" since "every movement reveals us" (I, 1, 302). Montaigne's discourse is the *discursus*, or running through, of his discourse. Anything can be said, then, since anything Montaigne says describes him and can be attributed to him as part of his proper body, the corpus of writing of the *Essays*.

Yet it is at this very point that Montaigne's claims to property begin to break down, for what could be less his own than the discourse that delimits Montaigne's property? Carried to the limit, Montaigne's project, despite what he writes in "Of Repentance" (III, ii, 804–5) would not so much trace the limits of "a particular man," or even those of "man in general," so much as the limits of discourse itself. The discourse that claims an irreducible personality tends toward an absolute impersonality. The cita-tional mania of Montaigne then only exemplifies this problem inherent to his project, namely, the appropriation of a discourse which to the extent that it comes from elsewhere (a sociolect) can never be fully called one's own. Or should we say that it can be called one's own in name only, only by *calling* it proper in the assignation of the proper name to it?[37]

An Accidental Body; or, The Paternal Limit: "Of Practice"

It should be remembered that if a "proper body" has been procreated, it was in order to seek a certain stability or repose in accordance with a project of self-analysis as self-therapy. This self-reflexivity in itself points, however, to a break in the subject. Such doubling, in itself a loss of property since it separates the self from itself, is nonetheless the condition for the engenderment of a proper body, since the split allows the subject to be *at once* "father and mother" (or, as Mitchell Greenberg has more accurately put it, at once father, mother, and child).[38] Strangely enough, the authorial corpus or proper body is self-engendered by two very improper parents—

namely, improper, idle thoughts and writing as "*another* kind of seed." We may know whose body this is, but *what* it is still remains unclear.

The rudiments of an answer are laid out by Montaigne in the essay "Of Practice" (II, vi), near the end of which he undertakes to defend his work against the charge of another kind of impropriety—that of the self-indulgence implicit in one's talking only of oneself. One passage in this discussion particularly merits attention because it reformulates Montaigne's project in terms pertinent to this analysis: "I principally portray my cogitations, a shapeless subject [*subject informe*] that cannot be brought into artisanal production. It is all I can do to couch my thoughts in this airy body of speech [*ce corps aërée de la voix*]. I expose myself entire: it is a SKELETOS wherein the veins, muscles, and tendons are seen with a single glance [*d'une veuë*], each part lodged in its place [*chaque piece en son siege*]. . . . It is not my deeds that I write down, it is myself, it is my essence" (II, vi, 379). We again have the intercourse of two improprieties, unformed thoughts and linguistic matter, which together produce a proper body: "It is myself, it is my essence." A crucial qualification is supplied, though, by the fact of that body being a "skeletos." We have indeed arrived at a state of repose, the ultimate repose of death. Death defines the body as absolutely proper; it puts everything "in place" ("each part lodged in its place"). But this absolute property is, at the same time, absolutely improper to the extent that the body is a dead one. In other words, it is cut off, separated from the subject to whom it is supposedly proper. For if the proper body is one that can be contemplated "with a single glance," the distance implied in the possibility of such a vision itself implies a subject disconnected from its own body,[39] a proprietor without his property. The proper body is only proper because it is absolutely improper. One can only have a truly proper body, it would seem, if it is a dead one, or one to which one is dead.

If my somewhat heavy-handed use of the Derridean problematics of the proper is allowed, the apparent absurdity of a "proper" that is only proper because it is improper follows coherently from the Montaignian notion of idleness as what is persistently turning into its opposite. This inalterable excitation can only be contained by the delimitation of that matter within the formal bounds of the self-definition authorized by the signature of the *moy,* the inscription of whose unformed, idle thoughts is said to be the matter of his book: "It is myself, it is my essence." If the proper is what is defined as proper, then death is the limit case of that definition, the definitive form of a rigor mortis: an improper delimitation that takes away the properness of the definition itself. Montaigne's "skeleton" is of a very particular kind; not only is it not to be construed as a mere bone structure, but it is described as a full-fledged cadaver ("wherein the veins, muscles, and tendons are seen with a single glance") missing only one significant part of its anatomy, the skin. The proper body of the writer is an *écorché,* literally de-limited, shorn of its limit, stripped of its skin.

At the same time, the morbid metaphorization of the textual body as pro-created *écorché* circumscribes a site of corporeal and rhetorical excess. Curiously, if the textual body has no skin, it is also, insofar as it is but the *tracings* of the unbridled mind, nothing but the line of the limit it describes in its meanderings. If the limit of Montaigne's self-portraiture is the *écorché,* the *volume* it generates is the effect of an accumulated layering whose depth remains crucially at the surface: namely, the limit of words. This layering, like the incongruous sedimentation Montaigne sees in the ruins of Rome,[40] is textually rehearsed as the strata of the *Essays* philologically designated *a, b,* and *c*. This effect of volume gives the proper name its weight even as that proper name is what gives the layered sediment of words its profundity. Concomitantly, Montaigne's rhetoric of sincerity is thematized as a peeling off of layers to reveal the self's intimate and true interior, the naked core of its being.[41] That the sense of the latter is itself but an effect of the metaphorics of undressing is emblematized by the limit case of a self-representation as textual skinning. As Montaigne says elsewhere, "We cannot distinguish the skin from the shirt" (III, x, 1011).

"Of Practice [De l'exercitation]," the essay that closes with the image of the *écorché* in the course of an apology for the autobiographical content of the *Essays,* opens with a meditation on the experience of death, followed by the autobiographical narrative of a near-fatal horse accident that leaves Montaigne "dead" *and* "skinned [*escorché*]" (II, vi, 373). The sixth essay of the second book thus further explores the terrain charted in "Of Idleness," even as its title seems to denote the very opposite of idleness: in French, *exercitation* can mean exercise or activity as well as practice. The unpredictable convertibility of idleness into its opposite, however, was already thematized in the earlier essay. Likewise, the runaway horse of I, viii returns in II, vi not as one who refuses to return but as one whose uncanny return is nothing short of catastrophic: the danger of idleness, an unbridled horse, scarcely differs from the danger of excitation, still a wild and untamed horse. And while "Of Idleness" is probably earlier with respect to date of composition and is certainly prior in the order of presentation, being near the beginning of the first book, "Of Practice" recounts an event prior to the composition—or perhaps even to the conception—of the *Essays.*

Turning now to the first section in "Of Practice," we again encounter the problem of constructing an anthropological space, a body, whose identity and properness is to be assured by the precise demarcation of the limit between its interior and exterior. What seems to be the best way to assure this limit and thereby the integrity of the space it defines is to "test" it, a verb that might translate what Montaigne variously calls *éprouver, expér-imenter, exercer,* and of course *essayer.* By such an experience, we determine our own limits and thus "*form* our soul" (II, vi, 370; my emphasis):

> That is why, among the philosophers, those who have wanted to attain some greater excellence have not been content to await the rigors of fortune in shelter and repose, for fear she might surprise them inexperienced and new to the combat; rather they have gone forth to meet her and have flung themselves deliberately into the test of difficulties. Some of them have abandoned riches to practice [*pour s'exercer*] a voluntary poverty; others have sought labor and a painful austerity of life to harden themselves [*pour se durcir*] against hardship and toil; others have deprived themselves of the most precious parts of the body, such as sight and the members proper to generation, for fear that these services, too pleasant and soft [*mol*] might relax and soften the firmness [*fermeté*] of their soul. (II, vi, 370-71)

These experiences "form," "fortify," "harden" and "make firm" one's "soul" through the contact they provide with some fearful exteriority, the threat of which is somehow preempted by a strategy of direct confrontation. This willed ex-perience defines the interior of the soul ("[we] *form* our soul through experience") and appropriates that exterior as part of the very process by which that interior is defined or delimited. One can no longer fear a danger one has already inflicted on oneself. At the same time, this willed experience is that through which the philosopher engenders or pro-creates himself, since it is what defines and forms his body as something proper to him. In other words, the movement outwards of *expérience,* of *exercitation,* of *épreuve* (from *ex-probare,* to appraise), of the *essai* (from *exagium* or *exagere,* to weigh) makes proper an improper interiority by a movement of disappropriation that is construed as an appropriation.[42] That one of these words, *essai,* is also the title of the book suggests that what we are reading is also to be understood as such an attempt, or *coup d'essay,* to define Montaigne's proper body through its expropriation or expression into writing.

If the expropriation makes proper, it is because that threat to the integrity of the interior comes not from without, but from within the inside itself. If the experience forms and defines an inner self, it is because the latter left to its own devices alters and destabilizes itself: "Here is what I exper-ience [*espreuve*] every day: if I am warmly sheltered in a nice room during a stormy and tempestuous night, I am appalled and distressed for those who are then in the open country; if I am myself outside, I do not even wish to be anywhere else. The mere idea of being always shut up in a room seemed to me to be unbearable. Suddenly, full of agitation, changes and weakness, I had to get used to being there for a week, or for a month. And I have found that in time of health I used to pity the sick much more than I now think I deserve to be pitied when I am sick myself; and that the power of my apprehension made its object appear almost half again as fearful as it was in its truth and essence" (II, vi, 372). If imagining the danger is worse than experiencing it, then imagination is the improper expropriation that takes place when one remains "inside," "shut up in a room." On the other hand, experience is the proper expropriation that puts the self back in its home, so to speak, by taking it out of it. Montaigne thus radicalizes the Stoic contemplation of death or the *tekne alypias* of the Greek *sophos,* which rely on a strategy of mastery through the imaginary representation of the event to be feared.[43] To be sure, Montaigne's critique takes a contradictory formulation. On the one hand, as he says in the very first sentence of the essay, he bases his discussion on an unquestioned opposition between an "impotent" discourse and the "reality" implied by experience: "Discourse and education, though we are willing to put our trust in them, cannot be powerful enough to lead us to action, unless besides we exercise [*exerçons*] and form [*formons*] our soul through experience to the way we want it to go; otherwise, when it comes to the time for action, it will undoubtedly find itself inhibited" (II, vi, 370). On the other hand, we are certainly invited to read the *Essays* themselves as a radical experience of the self, by which is formed Montaigne's corpus in the guise of the skinned cadaver found at the other end of this same essay.

If experience can be said then to define the body, it is because it does not leave the latter intact. We should not be surprised then if self-mutilation becomes exemplary of the experiential appropriation: "Others have deprived themselves of the most precious parts of the body, such as sight and the members proper to generation, for fear that these services, too pleasant and soft, might relax and soften the firmness of their soul." Castration emerges as what defines the body most properly by protecting it against the danger of castration itself by assuring a certain "firmness" or "hardness." Castration is thus paradoxically what erects the body, what (im)properly renders it proper. Experience is a self-procreation predicated upon the loss of one's procreative faculties, a castration that is not to be denied, but rather affirmed as the only hope of denying castration. In Lacanian terms, the loss of the penis would be the prerequisite for gaining the phallus by means of an asceticism that scarcely disguises the displaced eroticism of its sublimation.[44]

There is a limit, though, to this structure of expropriation as phallic appropriation, namely, the limit to be found in the definitive definition of death. One cannot "test" or experience death because death forever remains a radical exteriority. Death, as we are told by the name of the third of the three Fates, A-tropos (the one who cuts the thread of life), is that which cannot be "troped," or brought into a relation, figural or literal, with life. The radical discontinuity of death makes its appropriation impossible. On the other hand, this very inaccessibility of death and the limit it places on the project of experiential appropriation make death a privileged topic of discourse for Montaigne: "Through habit and experience, one can fortify oneself against pain, shame, indigence, and other such accidents; but as for death, we can try [*essayer*] it only once: we are all apprentices when we come to it" (II, vi, 371). The ultimate task of philosophy is somehow to be able to preempt death without being able to experience it. The title of the twentieth essay of the first book says "that to philosophize is to learn to die." And if, as has been often noted, Montaigne should change his mind and contradict himself by first advocating the value of always keeping one's mind on death and then insisting, on the contrary, that one never think at all about death, this change simply represents a change in tactics regarding the best way to domesticate death (which remains as always essentially impossible to domesticate).[45]

There is, nonetheless, at least one way in which an attempt is made to think the unthinkable, one trope continually called upon to trope the a-tropic: "It seems to me, however, that there is a certain way of taming ourselves to death and trying it out [*essayer*] to some extent. We can have an experience of it that is, if not entire and perfect, at least not useless, and that makes us more fortified and assured. If we cannot reach it, we can approach it, we can reconnoiter it; and if we do not penetrate as far as its fort, at least we shall see and becomes acquainted with the approaches to it" (II, vi, 372). In this passage, the radical discontinuity of death is made continuous through the introduction of a topography that places death on its farther side. To die, then, is to undertake a journey, what the *Encyclopédie* euphemistically refers to as "the great voyage." As Montaigne says at another point in the essay, death is like a "passage" out of which those who enter "have not come back to tell us news of it" (II, vi, 371).[46] Death is the voyage of no return, a radical and irrevocable "dislodging [*deslogement*] of the soul" (II, vi, 371). The image of death as travel is a conventional one in expressions such as "to pass away," "to depart," "trépasser," or "untergehen," and in mythological images such as the crossing of rivers (Styx or Jordan). If all this is true, though, then the image of death as a voyage must inevitably coincide with an understanding of travel as containing within itself the possibility of death. According to Freud, "'departing' on a journey is one of the commonest and best authenticated symbols of death."[47] Travel is deadly, and to be feared to the extent that it raises the possibility of there being no return, but without the possibility of no return (of death), there could be no such thing as travel.

When in "That to Philosophize Is to Learn to Die" Montaigne represents a series of events in which to contemplate one's own death, the first on the list is the "stumbling of a horse" (I, xx, 86). But if we are to see death in the figure of the horse, Montaigne's equestrianism is what will allow him, in the ensuing narrative of II, vi, to travel right up to the brink of death and to return alive, though not entirely unscathed.

The story of Montaigne's scrape with death begins in a state of considerable uncertainty that leaves a good deal to be defined: "During our third civil war, or the second (it doesn't quite come back to me which it was), I went riding one day about a league from my home [*chez moy*], who am situated at the very hub [*qui suis assis dans le moiau*] of all the turmoil of the civil wars of France" (II, vi, 373). Considering the importance Montaigne attaches to the ensuing incident, it is rather striking that he is not able to be more specific about the time it occurred. That he cannot even remember during which of the religious wars it took place is surprising in someone who, in the very same sentence, situates his dwelling place at the very hub (*moiau*) of these conflicts. It is as if he were not even involved in these events, or as if he were talking about someone other than himself, a hypothesis given credence by the impersonal construction of "*il* ne me souvient pas bien de cela [*it* doesn't quite come back to me which it was]." If the *moy* is defined at all, it is in terms of the *place* where it is, namely, "a league from my home [*une lieue de chez moy*]." But if the *moy* first appears as not being *chez moy,* the grammatical construction of the succeeding relative clause identifies *moy* with *chez moy:* "my home, which *am* situated in the very hub [*chez moy, qui suis assis dans le moiau*]." In other words, the place where I am *is* me. "I" am situated in a particular part of France. To depart from *chez moy,* which is situated in the "*moi*au," is to depart from oneself. Montaigne leaves Montaigne.[48]

Such a departure is not without consequences. To leave oneself does not mean one can return easily. For Montaigne, it is precisely in returning that he encounters some difficulties:

> On my return, when a sudden occasion came up for me to use this horse for a service to which it was not accustomed, one of my men, big and strong, mounted up on a powerful workhorse [*un puissant roussin*] who had a desperate kind of mouth and was moreover fresh and vigorous [*vigoureux*]—this man, in order to show his daring [*pour faire le hardy*] and get ahead of his companions, spurred his horse at full speed [*à toute bride*] straight into my path, and came down like a colossus on the little man and the little horse, and hit him like a thunderbolt with all his stiffness and weight [*fondre comme un colosse sur le petit homme et petit cheval, et le foudroier de sa roideur et de sa pesanteur*], sending us

both head over heels: so that there lay the horse bowled over and stunned, and I, ten or twelve paces beyond, dead [*moy dix ou douze pas au delà, mort*], spread out on my back, my face all bruised and skinned [*tout meurtry et tout escorché*], my sword [*espée*], which I had had in my hand, more than ten paces away, my belt in pieces [*ma ceinture en pieces*], having no more motion or feeling than a stump [*souche*]. (II, vi, 373)

As the highlighted words show, the accident is recounted quite explicitly in terms of a castration scenario (continued in later passages, such as that in which Montaigne mistakenly believes that he is the victim of "a harquebus shot in the head" [II, vi, 374] or when he describes himself as "disarmed" [II, vi, 375]). But if Montaigne's fall at the hands of this rather phallic horse is described in terms of castration, that fall is similarly to be understood as the death of Montaigne. Montaigne does not say that his state is *like* death; he says that he *is* dead: " I, ten or twelve paces beyond, dead."

What follows then as Montaigne "comes back to himself," is a kind of resurrection: "I came back to life [*je vins à revivre*] and regained my powers" (II, vi, 377). That we are in fact dealing with a tale of resurrection is strangely confirmed when Montaigne later fears that he will "die again [*remourir*]" from the aftereffects of the fall (II, vi, 377). Montaigne's equestrian calvary, however, ends with an arduous journey to a mountain, for it is in coming back up the hill to Montaigne ("chez moy") after having fallen down that Montaigne "comes back" to himself ("moy"). Not until he has returned home, though, is he fully himself. In describing this interim, Montaigne nonetheless evinces great delight in recounting all the movements of his body (and even of his mind) that transpired without his knowing it. These actions "cannot be called ours" given that "they did not come from within me [*chez moy*]" (II, vi, 376). Since "moy" was not "chez moy" when "moy" did these things, they cannot be attributed to "moy." The pleasure in all this lies in being able to appropriate or at least "come close to [*avoisiner*]" (II, vi, 377) death even at the cost of one's own utter disappropriation. As in the case of the proverbial piece of cake, Montaigne can thus both have his death and know it too, a situation replicated by the *skeletos* of the text as dead body, a body claimed nevertheless by Montaigne as his own.

The resurrection of the body in the text, though—is that not too the result of an accident, the risk incurred by a certain horsing around? In a passage just a few lines before the *skeletos* appears, Montaigne describes writing as a metaphorical riding of horses: "to fling oneself well out into the pavement [*se jetter bien avant sur le trottoir*]" (II, vi, 378; *trottoir* in sixteenth-century French means a place to trot horses). We can no longer look at such horseplay without seeing in it the threat of castration and death. But if the horse not only castrates but writes, it now seems to be in a position opposite to that of the horse in "Of Idleness," which was linked to the idle thinking that needed to be formed or cut into shape through writing. We still do not know, after having seen these wild and improper horses and the consequences they entail, why Montaigne should love nothing better than to ride horses. There must be still something else at work in Montaigne's equestrian obsession.

An answer might be found in that other castrating accident that lets Montaigne hold death by the hand—or in his lap. I refer to Montaigne's kidney stone condition, of which, in the final essay of the original 1580 edition, he writes as being "of all the accidents of old age, the one I feared the most" (II, xxxvii, 759). In the same passage and continuing along this line, Montaigne describes his encounter with the stone precisely in terms of an accident suffered during the course of a voyage, the voyage of his life: "I had thought to myself many times that I was going forward too far, and that in making such a long journey, I would not fail to get embroiled in some unpleasant encounter" (II, xxxvii, 759). The "accident" of the stone is nothing short of deadly, so deadly in fact that elsewhere Montaigne approvingly cites a passage from Pliny that mentions the stone as one of only three illnesses the evasion of which justifies suicide (II, iii, 355). Yet it is precisely because the *pierre* is in many ways worse than death that Montaigne takes comfort in the *experience* it offers: "I am at grips with the worst of all maladies, the most sudden, the most painful, the most mortal, and the most irremediable. . . . I have at least this profit from the stone, that it will complete what I have still not been able to accomplish in myself and reconcile and familiarize me [*m'accointer*] completely with death: for the more my illness bears down on me [*me pressera*] and bothers me, the less will death be something for me to fear" (II, xxxvii, 760). The "profit" derived from the stone is in the ceaseless ordeal or *épreuve* of death it provides, in the proximity it brings one to the limit case of experience itself.

Furthermore, if Montaigne can once again claim to appropriate death in this experience of the stone, that experience of death is, like that in "Of Practice," described in terms of castration. Since the stone by its very formation blocks the urethral passage, it effectively puts an end to any cares one may have about procreation. Moreover, one of the few cures for kidney stones in Montaigne's time involved an almost invariably fatal operation that required that one "have oneself cut [*se faire tailler*]" (II, xxxvii, 773). At its best, the expulsion of a stone is a source of erotic pleasure ("that dreamer in Cicero who, dreaming he was embracing a wench, found that he had discharged his stone in the sheets" [II, xxxvii, 762]). More typically, Montaigne complains that "the sharp points press into me [*les aigres pointures me pressent*]" and his stones "diswench me strangely [*me desgarsent estrangement*]" (II, xxxvii, 762). Finally, the stone's phallic significance is made explicit when in the course of his trip to Italy, Montaigne claims to have rendered a stone that had "exactly the shape of a prick" (*Journal,* pp. 207-8).

The stone points back, then, in the direction of Montaigne's voyage to Italy, where we found Montaigne desperately trying to master the movement of that phallic stone through his regimen of mineral water. In a passage of the *Essays,* he comments in typically skeptical fashion on the advantages and disadvantages of this use of mineral water:

> Aperients are useful for a man with the stone because by opening and dilating the passages [*passages*], they move along [*acheminent*] that sticky matter of which the gravel and the stone are built and convey [*conduisent*] downward what is beginning to harden and accumulate in the kidneys. Aperients are dangerous for a man with a stone because by opening and dilating the passages, they move the matter of which the gravel is built along toward the kidneys, which, being apt to seize it by a natural propensity [*propension*], will hardly fail to stop much of what has been carried [*charrié*] to them. Moreover, if by chance there comes along some body a little too large to go through all those narrow passages that remain to be traversed in order to discharge it outside [*passer tous ces destroicts qui restent à franchir pour l'expeller au dehors*], this body, being set in motion [*esbranlé*] by these aperients and cast into these narrow channels [*jetté dans ces canaus estroits*], will stop them and expedite [*acheminera*] a certain and very painful death." (II, xxxvii, 775)

What is implied in the *pierre* is a kind of inner travel that, if not mastered, threatens to disrupt the equilibrium of the body. Exterior travel, a trip to Italy for instance, might be seen as an attempt to master this improper inner divagation.[49] The only way to be rid of that impropriety is to *expel* it. Once again, the movement outwards defines and preserves the inside. Self-castration, as we have already seen, insures that one will not be castrated; witness the deadly operation of the *taille*.

The movement of the stone as phallus castrates by delimiting or tearing the skin off of the *inner* parts of the body. In other words, that castration is worse than the death by skinning we saw in the case of the *écorché* because the stone does not define the body as a proper interior set off against an improper exterior. Rather the stone suggests something exterior that is at the same time inherent to the body's interior. From where does the stone come?

Not for nothing does Montaigne make these extended remarks on his illness in an essay entitled "Of the Resemblance of Children to Fathers" (II, xxxvii): "It is probable that I owe this stony propensity [*cette qualité pierreuse*] to my father, for he died extraordinarily afflicted by a large stone in his bladder" (II, xxxvii, 763). Montaigne resembles his father through their common affliction, the *pierre*. This resemblance between father and son becomes all the more interesting, however, if we take note of the phonic similarity in French between the words *pierre* and *père,* "stone" and "father." It is even more interesting when we recall the name of Montaigne's father: Pierre.[50]

I come then to the question of Montaigne's resemblance to his father in their common bearing of the *pierre*. This resemblance, however, allows for the transmission of something other, namely the name of the father, Pierre, which through the *pierre* takes on substance in the very body of the son. The earlier interpretation of the *pierre,* as something radically exterior that is at the same time somehow inherent to the very interiority of the body, is then borne out. The traveling *pierre* leaves in its wake a certain patronymic inscription that defines properly or improperly the body of the son. That *pierre* is, then, what is both exterior and interior to the son, what is in fact the origin of the son, what makes him what he is. The *pierre* contained in the father's "seed" ("that drop of water [that] lodge[s] this infinite number of forms" [II, xxxvii, 763]) defines the son as a certain property belonging to the father, Montaigne.

Procreation as the transmission of the seed-stone maintains the father's property (his name, his body, his land). For this property to remain intact, however, it must be transmitted by the son to his son and so forth. But if the son has no progeny the father will die: if the progenitor is regenerated through his being incorporated by the son, then the son engenders the father as much as the father does the son.[51] No simple betrayal of his father, Montaigne's lack of male offspring needs to be reappraised in view of the fact that the very thing the father transmits to his son to transmit is itself what makes that further transmission impossible.[52] Montaigne's *pierre* is not only what proves his filial attachment to his father but also what, in its painfulness, is equated by Montaigne with death and castration. But if the *pierre* defines (the son as son) as it delimits or castrates the body, then it would seem that to procreate is to castrate. What is castrating, then, if not precisely the way in which the son resembles the father? It is reproduction as resemblance then which castrates, for it leaves the son able only to repeat the father and to stand for him as a kind of tombstone or *pierre tombale*. The metaphor is not uncalled for since the castration of the son, in the Montaignian imaginary, implies the death of the father. The father can live only as long as his seed is transmitted. If it is the seed itself, however, which cuts off the transmission, as in the *pierre* Montaigne's father gives his son, then the continuity of the resemblance between father and son which is supposed to assure patriarchal continuity only takes place through a radical discontinuity, the castration of the son, the death of the father. To procreate is to risk death even as that death allows for a certain reincarnation or resurrection. In fact, for there to be the possibility of a resurrection, there must be a prior death. One can only live on in *another* body, as other, as son. If the seed cuts, it cuts both ways; the cut that engenders cannot leave the body intact.

We can now return to that other petrifying scene of castration and resurrection: Montaigne's horse accident. The collision, we should note, is between *two* horses, each with its rider. Montaigne's horse is a "little horse" described as "very easy but not very firm"; its counterpart is "a powerful workhorse" that is "fresh and vigorous." While Montaigne describes himself as "little," the other horseman is "big and strong." The only differences noted by Montaigne are those of size and strength, with the advantage in both these areas granted to his opponent. In the accident that leaves Montaigne in the described state of castration, the overpowering size and force that hits him is compared to "a colossus" in its "rigidity" and "weight." This colossus of a horse hits Montaigne with the force of a pillar of stone.

Where does this horse come from? Would we have reason to suspect a certain Pierre? If we consult the language that the father forcibly imposed on the son and in which that son was raised, namely Latin,[53] we find that the word for horse is *equos* and the word for horseman, *eques*. At this juncture, I do not feel it would be unwarranted to place the signifiers of these words (and even more pertinently that of the accusative of *eques, equem*) next to the family name of Montaigne's father: Eyquem.

To be sure, I am not for a moment arguing that the man whose horse hit Montaigne was in empirical or referential terms Montaigne's father. Rather, what our analysis seems to be unraveling is the logic behind a phantasm—and if Montaigne's accident is not in itself phantasmic, the description of it, with its memory lapses and wordplay, certainly is. Some assurance of the validity of this deciphering of the father's name can be had if the play of the patronymic will, in turn, give coherence to our reading of Montaigne.

If we reflect on the insistence with which words particularly cherished by Montaigne begin in *e* or *ex*—*exercer, experimenter, expérience, épreuve,* and of course *essai* and *essayer* (as well as *exercitation*)—and on his *eques*-trian obsessions, we can draw some interesting conclusions. The patronym points to a movement outwards, as in the riding of a horse. The *ek* or *ex* of this movement outwards includes in its very movement the threat of castration and death. Insofar, however, as the *ex* of that movement outwards is what defines or delimits an interior, it is the *ex* itself, the ex-cursion, which castrates, as in the ex-pulsion of the stone. The movement of the *pierre* defines the son as son but only at the cost of internal damage. The body defined by castration is never intact since this defining wound is also a mutilation. Not only is what defines the proper self improper (insofar as it is excentric) but its very movement ensures that that proper is never fully proper. As we saw earlier, the inside (of the body, of the home) can only be assured through the movement outwards which leaves that inside behind, a movement the absolute limit of which is death or the complete loss of that inside. The appropriation that renders the proper proper (or defines the interiority of the inside) is at the same time a disappropriation. Yet that appropriation as disappropriation is the only hope of ever having something that is proper, a property. To stay inside ("shut up in a room"), to guard the stone inside the body, is to jeopardize the very property and properness of that inside. For Montaigne to stay at home is to invite the chaos of an utter dispossession, beginning with the dispossession of what one would think to be most one's own. Only through a radical movement of expulsion can any claim to property be made: the evacuation of the stone, the experience of travel, or for that matter, the externalization of thoughts into writing as excrement.[54] The pro-creation of his proper body can only take place if he assumes his castration, that is, if the seed cuts. The home can only be *dom*esticated, "bridled," if he rides off on a horse. Pushed to the limit, this logic suggests that absolute domesticity is to be found in an infinite excursion, to Italy and beyond. To repeat what the scribe of the voyage to Italy writes, if Montaigne "had been alone with his attendants he would rather have gone to Cracow or toward Greece by land than make the turn toward Italy; but the pleasure he took in visiting unknown countries, which he found so sweet as to make him forget the weakness of his age and of his health, he could not impress on any of his party, and everyone asked only to return home" (*Journal,* p. 65). We remember that this equestrian excursion is also accompanied by the "expulsion" of the stone. In fact, Montaigne repeatedly states that it is on horseback that he finds the greatest relief from the stone (*Journal,* p. 58; *Essays* III, ix, 974, and III, xiii, 1094). And if the twin phallicity, at once internal (kidney stone) and external (horse travel) to the body, is at work in defining the proper limits to that body through the violent exceeding (excision) of those limits, the saddle turns out also to be a privileged locus of erotic fantasy, where Montaigne experiences his "most profound and maddest fancies and those I like the best" (III, v, 876). If our analysis has moved back and forth between the horse and the stone (even in our first glances at the *Travel Journal*), it is because the stone and horse (*pierre* and *equem*) play into the same phantasmic expulsion that in its very enactment would obsessively inscribe the father's name into the son's body-text.

All Roads Lead Back to Rome: "Of Vanity"

Now, this ex-centricity through which the son castrates himself in the name of the father cannot be without consequences for the father, the death of whom is implied in the son's castration. For the son to assume his own castration, then, is paradoxically to celebrate the father's death. Such an Oedipal dilemma can be found at work in the essay "Of Vanity [De la vanité]" (III, ix), where Montaigne, in an essay written entirely *after* his trip to Italy, also makes his most extended observations concerning his interest in travel. The voyage as ex-cursus remains massively Oedipalized.

"Traveling hurts me only by its expense," says Montaigne near the beginning of the essay (III, ix, 949). The only pain in travel is the *expense*. Such a loss is to be discounted, though, continues Montaigne, since he has no male heirs for whose inheritance he would need to provide (III, ix, 949). Already castrated, Montaigne can set out on his travels with no fear of castration. Someone else, though, does stand to lose from both of Montaigne's losses:

> My father loved to build Montaigne, where he was born; and in all this administration of domestic affairs, I love to follow his example and his rules, and shall bind my successors to them as much as I can [*autant que je pourray*]. If I could do better for him [*Si je pouvois mieux pour luy*], I would. I glory in the fact that his will still operates and acts through me. God forbid that I should allow to fail in my hands any semblance of life that I could [*que je puisse*] restore to so good a father. Whenever I have taken a hand in completing some old bit of wall and repairing some badly constructed building, it has certainly been out of regard more to his intentions than to my own satisfaction. And I blame my indolence that I have not gone further toward completing the things he began so handsomely in his house; all the more because I have a good chance of being the last of my race to possess it, and the last to put a hand to it. For as regards my own personal inclination, neither the pleasure of building [*ce plaisir de bastir*], which is said to be so alluring, nor hunting, nor gardening, nor the other pleasures of a retired life, can amuse me very much [*ne me peuvent beaucoup amuser*]. (III, ix, 951)

Antoine Compagnon makes much of this passage, in which he justifiably sees that Montaigne "through a subtle play of denegation . . . marks himself off from his father while protesting his loyalty."[55] Montaigne's ambiguous attitude toward his father is nonetheless not simply a product of his guilt for having no progeny, as Compagnon would have it. Montaigne says he likes to follow his father's example and presents himself as a faithful image of his beloved father in all respects save one, namely his *inability* to "build" Montaigne. This inability is underscored by the use of the verb *pouvoir,* which appears three times in the passage. Montaigne says he would encourage his inheritors ("as much as I *can*") to follow his father's example, an ironic statement considering Montaigne's precise lack of successors. He then adds that he would do more for his father *if* he *could* ("*si* je *pouvois*"), implying that he is incapable of doing more. Finally, he insists that "the pleasure of building" and associated domestic pleasures "can[not] amuse me very much." What is at stake in this inability to "build" the family chateau? As Compagnon demonstrates, the word *bastir* is also used by Montaigne to denote the act of procreation.[56] Montaigne is like his father in every respect except in his inability to produce offspring, to maintain the family property. Once again, though, if Montaigne is a castrated, impotent clone of his father, his father nonetheless stands to lose on the same count. With Montaigne's death, the Eyquem family will come to an end, and its property will pass into other hands. Montaigne himself knows this very well.

If Montaigne is thus forced to view his own inadequacy vis-à-vis his father, he can nevertheless assume that castration and celebrate his father's demise not only by leaving the home unfinished but also simply by leaving the home. The long passage above is preceded by a long development on the joys of travel, of being elsewhere, of the eroticism of the exotic: "And I seem to enjoy more gaily the pleasures of someone else's house [*une maison estrangiere*]" (III, ix, 951). In fact, what is continually asserted throughout this essay is that the home is less of a home than is its negation, travel. Only by leaving the home can Montaigne get "inside" himself. Montaigne systematically denies all the possible dangers and inconveniences of travel and reinterprets them as advantages. Travel itself is what is proper insofar as it removes one from an improper, undomesticated home. And since it is proper in itself, or autotelic, the voyage needs no other goal than itself and can thus take the form of an infinite wandering.

Before concluding, though, that Montaigne situates himself as a nomadic son rebelling against a homebody of a father,[57] we should note that Montaigne's willful cutting off of himself from the home still follows the trace of his father's footsteps. For that Eyquem whose name points to the outward movement of the horse was himself a great traveler, one who in so doing went so far as to jeopardize his health as well as "his life, which he nearly lost in this, engaged . . . in long and painful journeys" (III, x, 1006). Elsewhere, we are told not only that he went to Italy but also that, like his son, he kept a journal of his trip there: "[My father] had taken a very long part in the Italian wars, of which he has left us a journal, in his own hand, following what happened point by point" (II, ii, 344). It is also worth remembering that Montaigne only decides to return home from Italy when, during his second stay in Rome, he receives word of his election to the mayoralty of Bordeaux (*Journal,* p. 221), a position which his father too had once held (III, x, 1005-6).

Now, if there be any direction to the wandering of the essay "Of Vanity," it is precisely from the bad home of Montaigne to its antithesis, the "only common and universal city" (III, ix, 997), Rome. Rome for Montaigne is more of a home than home itself: "I was familiar with the affairs of Rome long before I was with those of my own house: I knew the Capitol and its location before I knew the Louvre, and the Tiber before the Seine" (III, ix, 996). At the same time, though, Rome is a city of the dead, a veritable necropolis with its monuments and historical sites, "the tomb of that city" (III, ix, 996). Amazingly, it is among these dead that we find Montaigne's father: "I have had the abilities and fortunes of Lucullus, Metellus, and Scipio more in my head than those of any of our men. They are dead. So indeed is my father, as completely as they; and he has moved as far from me and from life in eighteen years as they have in sixteen hundred" (III, ix, 996). In retracing his steps, the voyage to Rome ends by celebrating the death of the father. Rome, death, the father: "Its very ruin is glorious" (III, ix, 997). For Montaigne, then, all roads lead to Rome, whether topographical, symbolic, psychological, historical, or literary. If Montaigne is exemplary of French tourists to Italy, as we suggested earlier, then the ambiguous French attitude toward that land is implicitly Oedipal. It is at this moment too, however, that Montaigne chooses to affirm his castration as a virtue: "I have never thought that to be without children was a lack that should make life less complete and less contented. The sterile profession [*vacation sterile*] has its advantages too. Children count among the things that are not particularly to be desired" (III, ix, 998). Finally, Montaigne defends his administration of the home against his father's accusations: "He who left me in charge of my house predicted that I would ruin it, considering that I was of so unhomely a humour [*mon humeur si peu casanière*]. He was mistaken; here, I am as when I first came into it, if not a little better" (III, ix, 998–99). Marking within Montaigne's imaginary the realm of symbolic fatherhood, the ruins of Rome are also described in a passage of the *Journal* (written down by the scribe but said by him to be the very words of Montaigne) as the locus of a corporeal (and implicitly patricidal) violence, not without striking parallel in the scene of Montaigne's horse accident in "Of Practice": "Those who said that one at least saw the ruins of Rome said too much, for the ruins of so awesome a machine would bring more honor and reverence to its memory: this was nothing but its sepulcher. The world, hostile to its long domination, had first broken and shattered all the parts of this wonderful body; and because, even though quite dead, thrown on its back, and disfigured [*mort,ranversé et défiguré*], it still terrified the world, the world had buried its very ruin" (*Journal*, 103–4). If "Of Vanity" imaginatively retraces the itinerary of Montaigne's trip to Italy, itself a retracing of Pierre Eyquem's journey there, the traces of the father have been buried under the monumentality of the son. Which is not to say that the old, dismembered, departed Rome does not remain an object of nostalgia, the recovery of whose ancient values is what motivates Montaigne's praise of Amerindian cultures in his essays "Of Cannibals" (I, xxxi) and "Of Coaches" (III, vi).

"Of Vanity" ends with Montaigne's citation in toto of a document officially declaring him a citizen of Rome. Interestingly, Montaigne's name appears on the document without his family name. Indeed, as Pierre Villey has noted, "Michel would be the first to abandon definitively the family name of Eyquem to bear only the name of his land."[58] Cutting off part of his proper name, Montaigne denies his father's paternity to set himself up instead as self-engendered. But the document also adds that Montaigne is an "Eques sancti Michaelis [a knight of the Order of Saint Michael]" (III, ix, 999), an award he coveted as a youth (II, xii, 577). Montaigne has ceased to be an Eyquem in order to become an *equem,* unless we should want to read this switch as an attempt to dislodge the patronymic from its position of domination and to press it into the service of the son, Michael. Having left home to cure himself of his "pierre," Montaigne returns home to Montaigne *as* Montaigne.[59] Rome is also the place where Montaigne takes over the writing of his journal after dismissing his secretary.

What is inevitably affirmed in all this traveling is the value of inner retreat and the finding of a home (be it the final home of death: "a death all my own" [III, ix, 979]), which for Montaigne must be sought in travel, away from the home. Interiority is attained through the excursion itself in all its castrating definitude. It is only because of this Oedipal determination of travel, which makes of it the very condition for property, that Montaigne can underwrite so willingly the "expense" of the voyage as an incomparable gain. The name of the father thus serves as the reference point, or *point de repère,* that guaranteees an economy in which the more one loses, the more one gains, and the farther off one wanders, the closer one gets to home. Such a perversity (in the etymological sense of a turning over) makes Montaigne's equestrianism as much a comfort for him as it is a bane for a rationalist like Descartes, for whom, as we will see, the horse needs to be kept within strict bounds.

To the extent, though, that this rather carefree assumption of castration is the precondition for an always phallic definition of self, the often debated "liberalism" or cultural relativism of Montaigne finds its axiomatic parameters.[60] The skeptical discourse of the *Essays* deploys a wondrously recuperative machine, one able to posit maximal diversity to the precise extent that diversity is reducible to the same, to the extent that the thesis of proliferating differences results in indifference (even as the *Essays* remain one of the West's greatest critiques of such reductionism). Montaigne's criticism, for instance, in "Of Cannibals" of the "barbarity" of considering all those different from oneself to be "barbarous" finds its limit in his simultaneous praise of Tupinamba culture for its replication of ancient values, for its moral proximity to Roman greatness as the unsullied youth of the Old World. Favorably citing a line from Juvenal, he even finds a precedent for—and hence defense of—cannibalism in the archaic Gascon culture from which he himself descends (I, xxxi, 210). While "Of Cannibals" and "Of Coaches" represent important early moments in the defense of autochthonous American cultures, their hermeneutics of analogical recuperation (whereby the other's threatening otherness is domesticated by the systematic recoding of cultural differences as veiled similarities) also helped crystallize the alternative myth of the *bon sauvage,* a myth whose perniciousness remains masked by its veil of benevolent idealism.[61]

Likewise, if Montaigne can seem to take an apparently "progressive" position toward women's rights in "On Some Verses of Virgil" (III, v), that too can be shown to be in function of a denial of gender difference that veils a fundamental misogyny. Unsurprising in this regard, given Montaigne's Oedipal scenarios, is the telling absence throughout the *Essays* of what one would think to be the significant women in Montaigne's life: his mother, his wife, and his one surviving daughter. No doubt they remain the occluded force of stability, maintaining house and hearth (the ménage whose upkeep Montaigne finds wearisome in III, ix), while the lord of the "mountain" pursues his travels abroad or remains ensconced in the phallic tower of his library, writing the text of his immortal *écorché.*[62] Curiously, it is in a moment of absence, upon his return from the famous horse accident, at a time when his thoughts "did not come from within me" (II, vi, 376), that his wife makes one of her few appearances in the text: Montaigne asks, oddly enough considering the context, that she be given a horse because he sees her "stumbling and having trouble on the path, which is steep [*montueux*] and rugged."[63] Woman appears, then, only as she who cannot walk for herself up the hilly path to Montaigne's height and is in need of his equestrian assistance.

But then horsemanship was already invoked when it was a question of giving "form" to those shapeless masses [*amas et pieces de chair informes*] produced by women in "Of Idleness." Unbridled as Montaigne's thought may be, the *form* it takes is not without its share of (at least, implicit) exclusions even in that apparently most inclusive and democratic of humanist truisms: "Each man [*homme*] bears the entire form of the human condition" (III, ii, 805). If the late Renaissance marks the historical moment when the privatized inner space of individualism is first demarcated, that moment also witnesses the codemarcation of exteriorized zones of otherness (femininity, savagery, madness) that reciprocally implicate the new interiority as exclusivist and limited to those empowered by European masculinity. If the assumption of castration allows for the demarcation of a privileged psychic interiority, Montaigne's "ruling form [*forme maistresse*]" (III, ii, 811) as a secure space of selfhood or *chez moy* (or, at its limit, a phallic fortress),[64] the drawing of those boundaries both requires at least a glance beyond those walls and enables the gazer's self-confidence in confronting the exterior beyond. Aristocratic largesse could occur because of the privileged political and economic status it also signified in its practice. Does not the condition of possibility for the radical skeptical critique lie in the Oedipalized heights of Montaigne, in the security of the tower walls that dominate the landscape below?[65]

It is with a similar confidence or lack of intimidation before the symbolic, then, that Montaigne can conceptualize writing itself in terms of travel: "Who does not see that I have taken a road along which I shall go, without stopping and without effort, as long as there is ink and paper in the world?" (III, ix, 945). To the infinite wandering corresponds an infinite discourse, one whose bounds are nonetheless proleptically secured or preset by the reinscription of the text as book of the self. And if Montaigne can not only describe writing and travel in terms of each other but also switch back and forth between those two experiences, going as he does in and out of his tower, would we not be justified in assuming that they are similarly Oedipalized? What do we find in the *Essays* if not the experience, or *ex-père-ience* (to rewrite the title of Montaigne's last essay), of writing as that movement outwards that celebrates the father's death in the son's castration? Montaigne's first writing experience, his translation of Raymond Sebond's *Theologia naturalis,* came in the form of something imposed on him by the father, be that father described in the same breath as the "the best father there ever was": "It was a very strange and a novel occupation for me [to translate Sebond]; but being by chance at leisure at that time, and being unable to disobey any commandment of the best father there ever was [*du meilleur pere qui fut onques*], I got through it as best I could; at which he was singularly pleased, and ordered it to be printed; and this was executed after his death [*ce qui fut executé après sa mort*]" (II, xii, 440). The "execution" of the writing commanded by the father follows upon the father's demise, an execution in print that also enshrines the son's shift—in the very act of translating—from paternal Latin to French.[66]

But if the son's affirmation of castration consecrates the father's death in the very movement of experience that reenacts the father's name, something else is nonetheless procreated in that castration. What is produced, and in this the son pushes to the limit his resemblance to his father, is a castrated son, namely that definitively defined proper body of the text as *écorché,* a proper body that as we remember, can only "live" (if that word can have any meaning in this context) by its progenitor's death. This body of writing bears a name, though—that of Montaigne, its author. Such a name, which defines Montaigne, can only be assigned *après-coup.* An author's name can only be assigned or affixed if there is *already* a body of writing, a text. The author's name can only take place if the "author" has *already* succumbed to the castration and death of writing. Montaigne's *Essays* finds its *oikos* in this "name of the author," only if it is conceded that this ultimate point of reference is found along the Oedipalized paths of writing as the ex-cursion that repeats (as it entombs or encrypts) the father's name. What the *Essays* performs as a death of the body is also, then, the birth of the author, the properness of whose proper name bespeaks the inauguration of a new historical order, a new set of property relations wherein the feudal proper name as the name of the land the lord owns gives way to a precapitalist name, functioning as a designatum of individuality, to be found in the self as *locus* of its own production. The play of Montaigne's name straddles these two orders by its metaphorization of body, text, and land within a set of equivalences that reinstitute patriarchal law as a new kind of autarky: having no male offspring, Montaigne ends his familial line even as he, as author, situates himself as the father of French philosophy.

The last entry in Montaigne's travel journal is headed "Montaigne," where he arrives on November 30, 1581 (p. 239), but the last line of the preface to the *Essays* had already reinscribed this name, indecidably signature and place name, not too long *before* his initial departure: "So farewell, from Montaigne, this first day of March, fifteen hundred and eighty [*A Dieu donq, de Montaigne, ce premier de Mars mille cinq cens quatre vingts*]."

Chapter 2
Cartesian Coordinates

In the history of thought, Descartes will always be that French cavalier who set off at so fine a pace.
—Charles Péguy

Contemporaneous with the great era of voyages of discovery is the impressive and persistent alignment of the motif of travel with the critical moment in French philosophical literature. In its most positive aspect, the advent of European contact with other cultures engaged a generalized questioning of Western values as embedded in sanctified Greco-Christian paradigms. The masters of medieval synthesis, Augustine and Thomas Aquinas, had succeeded in grafting (respectively) Plato and Aristotle onto the Christian narrative of redemption. This redoubling of the pilgrim's path to salvation by the Socratic quest for the absolute generated the great allegorical journeys found in Dante and the various legends of the Arthurian cycle. Far from seeking new horizons, though, these narratives were organized by the fear of losing one's way, of straying away from the right road, off into error and transgression.

When travel runs the risk of transgression (etymologically speaking, a crossing or stepping over), then voyages to exotic places can quickly open onto the transgression or calling into question of received ideas in the traveler's homeland. As Geoffroy Atkinson has shown, criticisms of traditional theological and philosophical positions abound in the texts of Renaissance explorers and geographers well before such criticisms surface (most dramatically with Montaigne) in more philosophical prose.[1] In Montaigne's *Apology for Raymond Sebond* and other essays, ethnographic information, gleaned from travel literature, about the diversity of human behavior plays a leading role in the debunking of the Western pretension to know. With the Baroque, there even appears a certain pleasure in the discovery of human frailty, self-delusion, and instability. One's drifting in error becomes less a moral (or mortal) danger to be evaded than one's own (necessarily idiosyncratic) experience, to be lived and enjoyed. Instead of Dante's spiritual odyssey we have the mordant irony of Cervantes's deluded knight errant. But if, in the wake of Montaignian skepticism and relativism, the voyage of discovery is what allows philosophy, in the guise of *libertinage* or free thought,[2] to travel out of its accustomed ways of thinking, it can be asked to what extent the risk of that philosophical journey issuing in a nihilistic drift is forestalled by the very way in which the travel project is formulated. When the desire to call a system of thought into question by going outside it becomes a recognizable *topos* or commonplace, is not that movement outwards then what defines the very inside one is supposedly trying to leave? Is this not, after all, the lesson of Montaigne's equestrianism?

These questions also confront us with an interesting imbrication of the philosophical (skepticism, relativism) with the literary (spatial metaphors, travel narratives). For philosophy to think its way out of its own scholasticism, it would seem to have recourse to certain figures or *mythoi* of travel, of the *technai* of "moving outwards," among which is the writing of imaginary worlds or utopias, which proliferated in the aftermath of More's eponymic work. Yet it can be asked to what extent the utopic text can offer a critique that exceeds the analogical reductionism that describes its generic limit: Can Cyrano de Bergerac's lunar fantasy of the "other world," for instance, ever be radically other so long as that other world is said to be "like this one"?[3] Such affirmations of otherness are simultaneously denials of it, to the extent that differences are marked only to be neutralized by an overarching sameness.[4] In order, however, to posit this otherness outside itself, philosophy as pure conceptual cogitation must have recourse to another other, to an outside that is already inside itself, to what we could call here the literary: the figures and uses of language it appropriates to plot its mental itinerary.

While the texts of imaginary voyages or utopias are manifestly informed by such literary concerns, the formal and linguistic framing of philosophical content could also be demonstrated in philosophical systems, such as the empiricism so triumphant in Great Britain, that would deny their literariness by claiming a transparency of signification and an immediacy to reality that would enable them to step out of scholastic obscurantism and formalist preciosity.[5] In France, the best-known advocate of such a "common-sense" rationalism is, of course, René Descartes, a thinker who claimed to have opened "windows" and shed light into the dark "cellar" into which philosophy had obscurely descended with Aristotelian scholasticism (*Discourse,*

VI, 105). Descartes was as opposed to the writers of utopias, whom he considered seditious ("I could in no way approve of these turbulent humors" [VI, 43]), as to skepticism, crystallized in the figure—never named—of Montaigne, the refutation of whose work constitutes the principal driving force behind the Cartesian opus.[6] Yet metaphors and other figures of speech abound in the writings of this exponent of "clear and distinct" ideas, in particular a prolific use of travel metaphors. The latter have been the object of a magisterial study by Nathan Edelman, for whom Descartes's obsession with finding the right road to truth is to be understood as a reflection of his "native uncertainty" and concomitant desire for "utmost certitude."[7] In the following pages, I would like to demonstrate, by looking first at two passages in the Second Meditation, and then more generally through the *Discourse on Method* as well as the *Meditations,* how Descartes's recourse to travel and topographical metaphors not only betrays, as Edelman argues, a fundamental anxiety in Descartes but also, through the presuppositions contained in the use of those metaphors, actively functions to allay that insecurity.

Finding One's Footing: Second Meditation

A key passage in which the play of spatial metaphors seems to inform Descartes's metaphysical speculations occurs at the very beginning of the Second Meditation, just a little before the truth of the *cogito* is presented. In this passage, Descartes describes, in an autobiographical vein, his reaction to the first day's meditation and comments upon his meditative method:

> Yesterday's meditation has filled my mind with so many doubts that it is no longer in my power to forget them. And nevertheless, I do not see in what way I can resolve them; and as if I had fallen all of a sudden into a very deep water [*une eau très profonde*], I am so astonished that I am able neither to find footing on the bottom nor swim to hold myself up above [*ni assurer mes pieds dans le fond, ni nager pour me soutenir au-dessus*]. I shall nevertheless make an effort [*Je m'efforcerai*], and I shall once more follow the same path as the one upon which I entered yesterday by distancing myself from all that in which I can imagine the slightest doubt, just as if I knew it to be absolutely false; and I shall continue always along this path until I have encountered something certain, or at least, if I cannot do anything else, until I have learned with certainty that nothing is certain in this world.[8]

Following the dominant metaphor here, the state in which the subject is placed after the First Meditation is understood as a loss of footing, the sudden disappearance of the terra firma on which he felt secure in standing:

he feels as if he had suddenly fallen into a deep pool of water and can neither touch its bottom nor swim back up to the top.

The Latin text is even more explicit in linking the concept of doubt to a metaphorics of disorientation, which is itself oriented according to a certain topography. The previous day's meditation has "thrown" (*conjectus sum*) the meditating subject "into" so many doubts (*In tantas dubitationes*) that he can neither forget about them nor see a way to resolve them (**VII, 23-24**). This implied figural dislocation effected by doubt is made explicit in the second half of the first sentence, which merits being cited in the original Latin: "sed, tanquam in profundum gurgitem ex improviso delapsus, ita turbatus sum, ut nec possim in imo pedem figere, nec enatare ad summum [but, just as if I had unexpectedly fallen into a deep abyss, so am I thrown into such confusion that I am able neither to place my foot on the bottom nor swim out to the top]." But even as this abyss is opened up in all its threatening vertigo for the doubting subject, it begins to be filled in or out by the very act of its representation. A bottom is placed under this abyss (*gurges:* a bottomless abyss), a bottom that cannot be touched with the foot, but a bottom nonetheless. The void itself acquires a certain consistency, that of water, in which one can swim even if one cannot swim all the way out to the top, but again there is (now) a top and a way to get there even if one cannot actually get there. And if one cannot get there, it is not even because of any objective limitations but solely because the doubting subject himself is simply unable to do it, as the first person subjunctive, *possim* (the verb that governs the last two clauses of the sentence in question), indicates.

The changing of a single letter is now all it takes to complete this filling of the abyss and to turn the abyss itself into the very bedrock of certainty. I refer to Descartes's reprise of the verb "enatare" (to swim out) as "en*i*tar" [the future indicative of *enitor,* literally "to mount up" or "to climb" and figuratively "to exert oneself" or "to make a great effort"—*s'efforcer,* as Descartes's translator, the Duc de Luynes, chose to write in the French edition). The change of verb figuratively puts Descartes's feet on the ground, on terra firma. To climb out of something implies that one already has at least a place on which to stand. Descartes can thus assert in the future indicative that he will *climb out* of what, a moment ago, using a verb governed by the present subjunctive he said he could not *swim* out of: "I will climb out, nonetheless, and I will again try out the same path as the one I had entered upon yesterday [Enitar tamen et tentabo rursus eandem viam quam heri fueram ingressus]."

What Descartes will attempt to do in his efforts to climb out of the abyss is to try out or test out (*tento, tentare,* closer to the verb *essayer* as used by Montaigne in the *Essays* than modern French *tenter* or English *attempt*) the same road as that upon which he had entered the previous day. Descartes's logic seems to have taken a strange if not illogical twist: the road that is to take one out of the abyss is paradoxically the same as the one that led into it during the previous day's meditation. In other words, the way out is the same as the way in. Nevertheless, a certain *progress,* or advance toward a destination, has already been made insofar as we are now dealing with a defined pathway, one that can be recognized as *the same.* A voyage can now be undertaken "into and out of" doubt where previously the very state of doubt involved the loss of any kind of firm footing. A topography of doubt is now affirmed where previously doubt had been linked on the metaphorical level with the loss of all possible topological bearings. The abyss of doubt is now something that can be traversed in the search for truth and certainty, for the certainty of the truth. This certain truth then becomes the *telos* of a philosophical journey wherein doubt and uncertainty are seen as mere detours or obstacles on the path to truth and certainty. And so it is that in following the road of doubt to its very end, one arrives at absolute certainty; again, by following the road that leads into the abyss one comes out of it: "I will again try out the same path that I had entered upon yesterday; removing, that is, all that which allows even a minimum of doubt no less than if I had ascertained that it was wholly false; and I will proceed onwards until I know either something certain or, if nothing else, at least this itself for certain, that nothing is certain" **(VII, 24)**.

Such a teleological closure allows the doubt to be methodical, and allows belief in the fiction of a "point that is certain and unshakable [*punctum certum et inconcussum*]" before it has been discovered. In other words, the very act of positing certainty as a destination already puts the philosopher on firm ground and keeps him from slipping into the drift of aimless nomadism. To say where one is going is to orient one's position in relation to that destination, to define one's position *as* a position in relation to the destination, toward which one can then proceed teleologically. Once such a preliminary positioning or pre-positioning has taken place, the philosopher can then proceed with great assurance ("pergamque porro donec aliquid certi"). The subject of the meditation "will proceed onwards" to certainty. He will proceed onwards to certainty, one might add, *with* certainty.

The Latin phrase *pergamque porro* reveals something else, however, about this progression or journey to certainty, something effaced by the French translation ("et je continuerai toujours dans ce chemin," IX-1, 19). The adverb *porro,* which I have translated as "onwards," could, in fact, if we follow Lewis and Short's *Latin Dictionary,* be translated here in three different ways. The first meaning of *porro,* that of "forwards" or "farther on," refers to movement in space and thus corroborates once more the metaphorics of the voyage so far unearthed in this passage. The second meaning of *porro,* "hereafter" or "in the future," refers to movement in time. In the passage under analysis, this second meaning is nonetheless readily reconcilable with the first meaning since a voyage, such as that undertaken by our philosopher, moves forward in time as much as it does in space. But *porro* has another meaning, a meaning found in logic and rhetoric, that of a conjunctive adverb that can be translated as "furthermore," "moreover," or "besides," in order to indicate a discursive progression. That the meaning of *porro* is left indeterminate in this passage from the *Meditations* indicates that the journey through hyperbolic doubt is as much a discursive movement as it is a movement in space and time.

If it is granted that Descartes's philosophical project is tantamount to a quest for stability and fixity in a post-Montaignian world of "perennial movement" (*Essays* III, ii, 804), it should be remarked that this quest takes place via the discursive voyage of the metaphysical meditation, via the itinerary, or *methodus* (a Greek word for a pathway), of methodical doubt. Implied, however, in this metaphor of the road is a certain security, the security by which the subject (of doubt, of travel) can map out where the text (of his doubt) is taking him, can domesticate the text (of his doubt) through a representation of it in spatial or topographical terms. But then the metaphor of the voyage applies to the text of the meditation as well as to the process of doubt. The text like the abyss of doubt (if it is not the abyss of doubt itself) becomes a space to be traversed on the way to "what is certain and unshakable [*quod certum sit & inconcussum*]" (**VII, 24**). This search for what is certain and stable is compared by Descartes to Archimedes' request for a "firm and immobile" point (*punctum firmum & immobile*), from which place he could move the entire world (*integram terram loco dimoverit* [**24**]). What is "certain and unshakable" will be a point (*punctum*), from which can be mastered the (discursive) space of doubt. As the course of the meditation will show, the conditions for such a "point of certainty" will be found in the enunciation of the *cogito:* "Ego sum, ego existo; certum est [I am, I exist, that is certain]" (**27**). The positing of the *cogito* provides the Cartesian coordinates for the discursive meanderings of the doubting subject, that is, it provides a transcendental reference point (*oikos*) in relation to which he can always locate himself.[9]

Once posited, the *cogito* should allow for the mind to find repose after its peregrinations through doubt, which were "upsetting" it so: "conjectus sum," "turbatus sum." The expected repose is not to be had, however, as we can see if we turn to a passage a few pages later, after the *cogito* has been discovered. Although the proof of the *cogito* has been arrived at, there remains some difficulty in believing its truth: "But I cannot help believing that corporeal things, whose images are formed by my thought and which occur to the senses, are known more distinctly than this unknown part of myself that does not fall under the imagination: even though it is in effect a very strange thing that those things I find doubtful and far away are more clearly and easily known to me than those things which are true and certain, and which belong to my own nature" (IX-1, 23). The problem here is less that of the mind's doubting the transcendental reality of the subject as evidenced in the *cogito* than it is that of the persistence of its desire to believe in empirical reality as being the more certain and truthful of the two: "But I see what it is: my mind enjoys wandering off [*s'égarer; aberrare*], and it cannot yet contain itself within the limits of the truth. Loosen its bridle one more time [*Relâchons-lui donc encore une fois la bride; laxissimas habenas ei permittamus*], so that, after awhile, when it is led back, it will let itself be ruled more easily" (IX-1, 23, **VII, 29-30**). The mind will not hold steadfastly to the truth of the *cogito* because it "enjoys" straying among the suspect objects encountered in empirical reality. Even though it recognizes the truth, it persists in its error. It knows one thing, but wants to believe something else.[10]

In an image fraught with the shades of Montaigne, such a perverse persistence is metaphorized as a runaway horse that refuses to stay within its assigned limits, those of the truth. The wanderings (*s'égarer, aberrare*) of this horse are its errors. Error, in other words, is a wandering (*aberrare*) from the truth. This metaphor is all the more striking given that the Latin text often cannot distinguish between the two senses of the verb *erro:* to wander or to err. (The French text obfuscates this ambiguity in Descartes's language by translating *erro* by *s'égarer* when its meaning is deemed to be that of wandering.) What is at stake in this passage on the horse's "error" is the return of the mind to the repose of the *cogito;* that is, its willingness to let itself be restrained within the "limits of the truth." The tactic involved is basically that of letting the mind indulge in its "extravagance," that is, to let the horse run its course so that after the reins have been brought back in, the horse-mind will allow itself to be ruled or led more easily. What is projected is a circular journey, a wandering that is not at all aimless but in fact always already circumscribed such that it must inevitably return to the point of departure. As the Latin text specifies, the reins are only to be loosened to their laxest (*laxissimas habenas*), not let go of entirely. The horse can be allowed to wander as far afield as it likes, to persist in its "error," because there is no danger of its actually wandering away; the bridle can always be suitably drawn back at the appropriate moment ("after awhile").

All that will happen in the wake of this wandering is that the *cogito* will be proven true once again, but this time not by hyperbolic doubt but, as it were, by a hyperbolic credulity. Instead of examining what can or cannot be doubted, we are to see what—if anything—can be believed. The mind will be provisionally allowed to believe whatever it pleases; that is, to believe the evidence of the senses or, if one prefers, to believe in the primacy of "external" reality over the "reality" of the subject. Our passage thus prefaces Descartes's ensuing and famous argument about the piece of wax, whose purpose is to demonstrate that the clarity and distinctness of objects does not so much prove their reality as the reality of the mind that perceives them. Extracted from the honeycomb, the wax has a certain color, shape, size, and texture, all of which are altered when the same piece of wax is melted by fire. One believes that the piece of wax remains the same despite contrary evidence from the senses. The philosopher concludes that it is not the piece of wax that is "clear and distinct" but the activity of the mind perceiving that wax, not through the senses but through the understanding (*intellectus, entendement*). Having completed this meditative trajectory, Descartes can then conclude, "here am I imperceptibly brought back to where I wanted" (IX-1, 26). The logic of the argument, in following the grapplings of the mind in the latter's effort to understand what it takes to be reality, comes back around "imperceptibly [*insensiblement*]" to the truth of the *cogito*.

Clearly, this argument presupposes the prior demonstration of the *cogito*.[11] Indeed, it is only because the *cogito* has already been ensconced that Descartes can feel safe in saying "loosen the bridle." It can be deduced that the wanderings of the horse must lead back to the point of origin, given that the proof of the *cogito* rests not on objective criteria but on the very fact of the subject's thinking. For the *cogito* to be true requires only that the subject think (cogitate), whether rightly or wrongly, whether in truth or in error. So whatever errors the mind indulges in, the truth of the *cogito* remains unchallenged—so long, that is, as the mind engages in error, as the horse continues to wander.[12] In other words, it is the very wandering or erring that constitutes the subject: *J'erre donc je suis.*[13] But if it is the wandering that defines the truth of the *cogito* as the certain and unshakable point—the place from which all the instability and loss of grounding occasioned by radical doubt can be stabilized and resolved—then one is led to wonder if this wandering of the mind is still a wandering. What the *cogito* does, in fact, is to neutralize this wandering, to turn it into nonwandering, to ensure in short that this wandering will not wander anywhere, that this error not be decisively in error but rather accompanied by the truth. What the *cogito* provides is an economy of error such that there is never any possibility of loss to the subject, whose mental expenditures can only provide it with surplus value in the shape of an ever increasing belief in his own autonomous existence. In other words, the more he thinks, or the more he errs, the more he knows he is. There is thus no danger in relaxing or letting off on the mind's bridle, and the gesture that would seem to allow for the *cogito* to be put in question only paves the way for the continued affirmation of its truth.

Even the very metaphor of the errors and delusions of the mind as the wanderings of an unbridled horse points to the containment (in both senses of the word) of the error within "the limits of truth." For the very understanding of that error as "wandering" implies a topography or space of wandering, which, be it ever so vague, already sets limits to the wandering: *veritatis limites,* the limits of the truth. The horse's very field of movement already in itself substitutes a comforting horizontality for the vertiginous verticality of the initial plunge into the bottomless waters of doubt. The very metaphor of wandering precludes wandering; that is to say, it excludes certain radical "wanderings" of the mind that, for example, by not respecting the spatialization of the temporal continuum the metaphor of wandering implies, would begin to call into question the assumptions and presuppositions upon which the *cogito* and its attendant topographical metaphors rest. In other words, only certain types of error can be admitted: those that allow themselves to be understood by or within the metaphor of wandering. In this sense, an "error" is merely a deviation from an assured truth and not what, for instance, aggressively calls into question the status of the truth itself.

It must be said, however, that the metaphor of wandering as deviation from the truth is the only way to put the security of the *cogito* to the test once we have accepted the truth of the *cogito* as a topographical point. The calling back into question of the *cogito* that Descartes claims to be undertaking at this juncture of the *Meditations* further supposes that metaphor, insofar as we are dealing with a certain transgression of what has previously been established in the *Meditations*. Instead of examining what can or cannot in fact be put in doubt, we are to see what, if anything, can be believed in. But this deviation from the rhetorical strategy of Descartes, as in the case of any such transgression, is always already framed, comprehended by some more encompassing bounds that take the very transgression of the bounds into consideration. No notion, in sum, is more circumscribed than the notion of transgression—and yet how else can the notion of transgression be understood? Like the error of Descartes, a transgression can only be affirmed or posited *as such* if it has somehow already been neutralized, contained, or codified within a certain preestablished structure, and this is the case even when such boundary-crossing is positively valued for its own sake and affirmed in all sincerity. Such is not, to be sure, the case in Descartes, where the unbridling of mental "error" remains heuristically and manifestly in the service of a strategy to contain or restrain such error, wandering, or transgression.

Are we not also invited to read in Descartes's preoccupation with the unbridled horse of error the scene of his confrontation with Montaigne, his predecessor or spiritual father, the thinker most linked with the skepticism he is trying to refute? In the light of such an Oedipalization, Descartes's situation seems less happy than Montaigne's. *Error* is what is proper to Montaigne, improper as that may be. If Montaigne cheerfully assumes the castration of ex-perience, Descartes seeks instead to deny that castration, and with it the parental example set by Montaigne, by resorting to the category of intuition, construed as what is most inner and proper to the thinking subject: his "own" thoughts as they present themselves to him. But if Montaigne rides off on his horse while Descartes stays at home cogitating in his celebrated *poêle,* or stove-heated room, it is because each in his own way makes the same claim to their own property or properness.[14]

Wanderings in Error: *Discourse on Method, Meditations*

Descartes's economy of error (wherein no wandering or illusion would lead to loss because the very fact of its occurrence would prove the *cogito* right) is in sharp contrast to the useless wanderings and errors he describes in the autobiographical first part of the *Discourse on Method.* In fact, it is because of these errors that Descartes shuts himself up in his *poêle* in order to choose "which paths I ought to follow" (VI, 10). Implicit in the full title of the work (*Discours de la méthode pour bien conduire sa raison et chercher la vérité dans les sciences:* Discourse on the Method for well conducting one's Reason and for seeking Truth in the Sciences), the metaphor of thought as travel appears almost from the beginning. Right after his celebrated opening remark about the equitable distribution of "good sense" in men, Descartes reverts to the travel metaphor in order to be able to explain differences in intelligence: "The diversity of our opinions does not arise because some men are more rational than others, but only because we lead [*conduisons*] our thoughts along different ways [*voies*] and do not consider the same things" (VI, 2). While everyone has the same quantity of "good sense," we all use it in different ways, giving rise to the diversity of our opinions. But these different ways are also different "ways" or paths (*voies*), as Descartes implicitly proposes a topography of thought in which each person follows a different itinerary.

But not all itineraries are good ones, as Descartes is quick to point out; his description of the various uses to which the mind may be put takes on ethical overtones: "The greatest souls are capable of the greatest vices, as well as the greatest virtues; and those who walk only very slowly may advance much farther, if they always follow the straight path, than those who run and go astray from it" (VI, 2). A certain moral imperative surfaces in Descartes's resuscitation of the Christian dead metaphor of *le droit chemin,* the "straight and narrow" path. Those that wander off the path are in error, they err in their wandering, like the Second Meditation's unbridled horse. At this point in the *Discourse,* however, error is still something to be avoided as opposed to something in which one can indulge freely and safely, knowing that that error will always lead back to the truth. In the *Discourse,* the problem for Descartes is how to get on the right path and stay on it, or even how to recognize it when one stumbles upon it. Only by finding a sure solution to this traveler's dilemma can this error or aimless (and by implication both stupid and sinful) wandering be avoided.[15]

And it is Descartes's story of how he found a "method" (*methodus:* an itinerary) to arrive at this solution which we are told in the *Discourse on Method:* "I shall not be afraid to say that I think I have had a lot of luck [*heur*], for since my youth I have found myself on certain *paths,* which have *led* me to considerations and maxims, out of which I have found a *method*; through which it seems to me that I have the means to increase my knowledge *step by step*" (VI, 3; emphasis added). Something has happened, however, to the organization of Descartes's topography. Here, the philosopher's position is not merely the result of a moral and intellectual choice, but it is also an effect of one's good fortune (*heur*). Descartes has merely had the good luck, or *bonheur,* to find himself on certain paths and not others, in certain ways of thinking and not others. Now, too, differences between people are said to be "accidental": "Only between *accidents* is there 'more' or 'less' and not between the *forms,* or natures, of *individuals* of the same *species*" (VI, 2-3; Descartes's emphasis). Given this revision of the topographical schema, one is always already in error to the extent that one finds oneself on certain paths, good or bad, out of which one must find one's way to the "right" one. Later, in the third part of the *Discourse,* while Descartes is developing his "provisionary" morals by which to guide his actions in the world until such time as he can undertake a global and systematic reappraisal of his opinions, the finding of the right or straight path (*droit chemin*) merely becomes a question of following straight on or *tout droit* the path on which one is: "In this, I would imitate travelers lost [*égarés*] in a wood; they must not wander about [*errer*] turning now to this side, now to that, and still less must they stop in one place; but they must keep walking as straight as they can in one direction [*marcher toujours le plus droit qu'ils peuvent vers un même côté*] and not change course for slight reasons, even if at the beginning their choice was determined perhaps by mere chance; for in this way, even if they do not arrive just where they wish, they will at least finally get somewhere where they will probably be better off than in the middle of a wood" (VI, 24-25).[16] While the meditations leading up to the discovery of the *cogito* require the rejection of the probable as well as the improbable, the moral of this extended analogy is that, in the conduct of one's day-to-day affairs, one should stick merely to what is most probable, at least until the time when a true and definitive morals will have been found to replace its provisional counterpart. More generally, what the sought-for method should do is propose a definitive way out of this labyrinthine and stereotypical forest of error. Part One of the *Discourse* accordingly presents the narrative of an exemplary education, of the "progress I think I have already made in the search for truth" (VI, 3). To the extent, though, that everyone finds himself elsewhere in the topography of thought and must follow a different itinerary, Descartes can only tell of those paths he himself has taken. The exemplary narrative is also or only an autobiography, the tale of Descartes's personal odyssey in search of truth, "à la recherche de la vérité," an exemplum that, as he is at pains to remind his readers, is not generalizable.[17] The journey is a solitary one.

To find his own way out of the labyrinth of error, Descartes tries three solutions or paths. The first involves the pursuit of scholarly erudition, a task itself compared to a journey: "For it is almost the same thing to converse with men of other centuries as to travel. It is well to know something about the manners of different peoples in order to judge our own manners more sanely, and not think everything contrary to our own fashions absurd or irrational, as do customarily those who have never seen anything. But when one spends too much time traveling, one finally becomes a foreigner in one's own country; and when one is overly curious about the kinds of things pursued in centuries past, one typically remains very ignorant about those things that are pursued in this one" (VI, 6). Reading the scholarly masterpieces of antiquity is the temporal equivalent of traveling through space. But while Descartes does not want to deny a certain utility to both literal voyages and the figural travel of scholarship, there is a certain economy in the use of one's time that must always be taken into account. At the time he is writing the *Discourse,* Descartes believes he has already "given enough time to languages, and likewise to reading".[18] Then, there is the danger of spending too much time on either kind of travel: that of becoming a foreigner in one's own land in the case of literal travel, that of becoming a stranger to one's own time in the case of scholarly travel. The threat would be that of an *error* so sweeping as to prevent the very possibility of return. In the case of the overly diligent reader, there is the danger of a Quixotic folly: "Those who govern their conduct by examples drawn from ancient histories and fables are liable to fall into the extravagances of the paladins of our romances and to conceive designs beyond their powers" (VI, 7).

Confronted with the danger of such error, Descartes tells how he abandoned the course of his studies and began to wander literally: "Resolving not to seek any knowledge but what might be found within myself or in the great book of the world, I spent the rest of my youth in travel, in visiting courts and armies, in frequenting people of various dispositions and ranks, in *collecting a variety of experiences,* in testing myself in the circumstances fortune dealt me, and in reflecting everywhere upon the things that presented themselves in a way that might enable me to derive some *profit* from them" (VI, 9; my emphasis). Suddenly, the topography of thought has become the map of Europe, and the latter in turn a book, "the great book of the world." But if literal travel is a figural reading, that reading is understood to be more literal than its literal equivalent: "It seemed to me that I could encounter much more truth [*plus de vérité*] in the reasonings that every man makes about the affairs that concern him and whose issue will very quickly punish him, if he has judged badly, than in the reasonings of a man of letters in his study, about speculations that produce no effect" (VI, 9-10). There is an implicit economics that qualifies the "profit" that Descartes derives from his "variety of experiences." The reasonings he encounters in the book of the world have "much *more* truth," thus confirming the latter book's economic superiority over literal books. For once in Descartes, it is the error of the mind which is undone by the error, or wandering, of the body. But while the profit derived from literal travel is said to deliver him "little by little from a lot of errors" (VI, 10), it cannot itself arrive at the assurance of certainty. Consequently, a third solution is attempted: "After I had spent some years studying thus in the book of the world, and in trying to acquire some experience, I resolved one day to study also in myself and to use all the powers of my mind to choose which paths [*choisir les chemins*] I ought to follow. This succeeded much better, it seems to me, than it would have, had I never distanced myself [*si je ne me fusse jamais éloigné*] from my country or from my books" (VI, 10-11).

Following the narrative put forth in the *Discourse,* Descartes decides to put an end to both kinds of error in his life (mental and corporeal), first by enclosing himself in the *poêle,* and then by embarking upon an introspective meditation that will decide once and for all "which paths I ought to follow." This moment of retreat, out of which we are invited to believe the entire Cartesian system, including the rules of the method and the provisionary morals, suddenly sprung forth,[19] has all the trappings of an event, datable to the winter of 1619, at which time the young Descartes was serving as a volunteer for the Duke of Bavaria in the early stages of the Thirty Years' War. Some of his earliest extant writings date from this period, as well as the occurrence of his famous dream (November 10), for if his daytime cogitations successfully attain the security of a method to follow, the opening section of his dream vividly represents the anxiety of dislocation in pointedly theological terms:[20] blown about by a powerful wind and enfeebled on his right side, Descartes "turns over onto his left" and hobbles along, fearful he may fall "at every step," until he manages to attain the shelter of a college chapel. As he turns back around to greet a passerby, the wind "violently" pushes him back against the church. He is told that someone has a gift for him, which he believes to be "a melon brought from a foreign country." He also notices that everyone else is standing "straight and firm on their feet" while he is still "bent over and tottering on the same terrain" (X, 181). The wind dies down, and he wakes up with the uneasy feeling that some "evil genius" has wanted to "seduce" him. Interpreting his own dream, Descartes decides that this wind was nothing other than "the evil genius who was forcefully trying to throw him into a place where his design was to go of his own will" (X, 185). Instead of leading him astray (se-ducere), presumably by allowing movement only along Descartes's left or "sinister" side, this diabolical agent forces him toward a saintly destination, a church inside a school. Despite the symbolism of the *via sinistra,* Descartes does end up on the "right" road. What does it mean, though, to be forced to go where one wants to go? Descartes's own interpretation suggests an oneirical refiguration of the rhetorical moves we have already noted in Descartes's meditations: the way out of the abyss is the way back into it, the hyperbolic doubt is the vehicle to certainty, the pursuit of error leads to truth. And is it not by letting himself be "blown away" by the radical skepticism enabled by the *malin génie* at the end of the first meditation that he is brought, via the indubitability of his necessarily being something, no matter how fooled he is by this almighty trickster, to the "rational" proof for the existence of God, itself based on the intuition of a being more perfect than he? The question of which way to go is repeated later in the dream when Descartes finds himself before a book, an anthology of Latin poetry entitled the *Corpus poetarum,* which he just happens to open up to a verse from Ausonius: "Quod vitae sectabor iter? [What path of life shall I follow?]." Oddly, this question of where to go is esteemed by Descartes to be "the good advice of a wise person, or even Moral Theology" (X, 182–84). The "wise" prescription is the question itself, the relentless pursuit of which, in turn, provides the answer. The dreamwork with its symbolism of left and right thus presages the lesson of the meditation, that wandering in error does not fail to lead back to the truth. In the rendition given some eighteen years later in the *Discourse* (1637), no mention at all is made of this dream, and whatever insights may have been gleaned nocturnally are credited to the diurnal intensity of

Descartes's rationalist contemplation within the *poêle,* a locus curiously unmentioned in the same *Cogitationes privatae* that contains the dream.

But if the positing of the *cogito* is what will eventually allow Descartes conceptually to contain or comprehend error and in fact to derive further proof of the *cogito* from the latter, the entire practice of meditation leading up to the *cogito* was called for precisely because the problem of error had inserted itself so pervasively not only in Descartes's writing and thinking but also in the text of his life. As if to recapitulate Part One of the *Discourse* in an utterly elliptical way, the very first paragraph of the *Meditations,* published four years later, once again states the necessity of a retreat into oneself in order to undo all the "false opinions" acquired in the course of one's life (IX-I, 13; **VII, 17–18**). The time for this meditative exercise is given as "today" (*hodie,* **VII,** 17), not the "one day" or "all day" (VI, 10, 11) of a November long past. Nonetheless inscribed within the same trajectory of a self-extrication from error via a conscious deliberation over the right path to follow, the metaphysical meditation is thus paradoxically at once a voyage of discovery, a refusal to voyage, and a quest for the proper way to voyage. It is a journey undertaken to find one's bearings so that the voyage can be undertaken with assurance, so that the movement of error can be definitively mastered. As in the unbridling of Descartes's horse, the travel metaphor seems to be invoked not as the occasion for a critical appraisal, but as precisely the move that reaffirms what has previously been supposed. Strangely, it is by indulging in error that one hopes to do away with it, by pursuing a kind of travel that one hopes not to travel.

The labyrinthine topography of error in its threat of an infinite wandering figures Descartes's predicament as one that is inextricably textual. Confronting this predicament, Descartes has recourse to the supremely logocentric gesture of the *cogito,* of a scientific method grounded in innate ideas and intuition; in the declaration, that is, of the subject's unmediated and pure presence to itself as thought, an insight made secure by what he poetically calls "natural light." That the problems of travel, or error, and of the text are construed by Descartes as facets of the same problem is evidenced by the metaphors noted earlier in Part One of the *Discourse:* the danger incurred by working too much with texts is that of a certain estrangement that is "almost the same" as the estrangement that comes from too much travel. And in the case of travel, errors are corrected through one's wandering in the book of the world. But these errors are only corrected "little by little" through the slow, painful work of interpretation. Although Descartes does not say it in the *Discourse,* the danger, which he will reckon with in the *Meditations,* is that the interpretation will be infinite, that is, an infinite wandering to undo an infinite number of errors. Such a prospect is suggested by the imperfect tense of the verbs Descartes uses: "I was learning [*j'apprenais*] not to believe anything too firmly"; "thus I was delivering myself [*je me délivrais*] little by little from a lot of errors" (VI, 10). Descartes does not want to get involved in the kind of ceaseless balancing and weighing of issues marking, for example, Montaigne's thinking in the *Essays*. Such an infinite wandering would also be an infinite squandering, a squandering, that is, of Descartes's mental and physical resources for a doubtful "profit."

The metaphysical meditation must, therefore, also answer an economic imperative, and in fact the purpose of his "methodical" doubt is to avoid the "infinite labor" entailed in examining every issue case by case to determine its truth or falsehood: "I shall apply myself, seriously and freely, to the task of destroying all of my former opinions. Now, in order to arrive at this end, it will not be necessary to prove that they are all false, a task I would probably never bring to an end . . . there is no need for me to examine each one in particular, which would be an infinite labor but, because the ruin of the foundation necessarily brings down with it the whole remainder of the edifice, I will first attack the principles upon which all my former opinions were set" (First Meditation, IX-I, 13–14; **VII, 18**). Here as in the second part of the *Discourse* (11–14), Descartes uses an architectural metaphor, representing the economic value of leveling the entire edifice of one's thought at once rather than trying to rebuild it piecemeal. And it is by such a claim to economy that Descartes continues to ward off or plug up the infinities that repeatedly threaten to intrude on his discourse, to lead it astray, to lead him into an infinite *error.* In the following passages alone, taken from the Second Meditation, Descartes upholds his resistance to being snared by a search that would be infinite and thus inconclusive:

> But what is a man? Shall I say "a rational animal"? Certainly not: for then I should have to go on to ask what an animal is, and what "rational" is, and so from a single question, we would fall imperceptibly into an infinity of other questions that would be more difficult and cumbersome, and I would not want to waste that small amount of time and leisure that remains to me, by using it to unravel subtleties of this kind. (IX-1, 20)

> Can I assure myself of having the least of all the things I have here above attributed to the nature of a body? I stop to think about it attentively, I review and review again all these things in my mind, and I encounter none that I can say is in me. There is no need for me to stop and enumerate them. (IX-1, 21)

> Is it not that I imagine the wax being capable of passing from a round to a square shape, and from a square to a triangular one? Certainly not, since I conceive it capable of receiving an infinity of

such changes, and I cannot run through this infinity in my imagination. (IX-1, 24)

And so many other things are encountered in the mind itself, which may contribute to clarifying its nature, that those which are derived from the body scarcely merit counting [*ne méritent quasi pas d'être nombrées*]. (IX-1, 26)

We can conclude, then, that error appears in its most threatening form as infinity, whether as infinite wandering or infinite text, and that it is the broad purpose of the Cartesian project (including not only the *cogito* itself but also the provisional morals, the rules of the method, and even the invention of coordinate geometry), to comprehend and contain that infinity.[21]

It is interesting that the infinite error that Descartes seeks so vigorously to avoid resembles closely what Kant calls in the *Critique of Judgment* the "mathematical sublime"[22]—with the qualification that such a mathematical infinity appears to Descartes as anything but sublime. The sublime does appear in Descartes, however, and in conjunction with a recurrence of the notion of infinity, specifically in that sublime infinity evoked by Descartes in his proofs for the existence of God. For what is Descartes's God if not a positive infinity that guarantees the Cartesian system against the bad or negative infinity of error, a "good genius" set over and against the evil genius or *malin génie*? God can do this because He is not only an "infinite substance" (*Meditations,* IX-1, 35) but also because He is the first cause not only of "me who thinks" and the rest of the universe but also of Himself. He is at once the guarantor of the *cogito* and of the workings of the universe.[23] God is at once incomprehensible, because infinite, and absolutely comprehensive, once again, because infinite.[24]

But the proof of an infinite and perfect God, far from laying to rest the problem of error, only puts it into greater relief. For after the long Third Meditation proving the existence of God, Descartes is obliged in the Fourth Meditation to explain why, given the infinite perfection of God, the phenomenon of error, on the basis of which the entire Cartesian system seems to have been built, should exist at all. Suddenly, the notion of God, which should have put an end to error, now needs to be defended and protected from error. To maintain the perfection of God and the perfection of His creation, Descartes is constrained to deny the existence of error even in the faculty of human understanding (*intellectus, entendement*): "For through the understanding alone I neither assure nor deny anything, but I only conceive the ideas of things, which I can neither assure nor deny. Now, in thus considering it precisely, one can say that no error is ever found in the understanding, provided one takes the word, error, according to its proper meaning" (45). Acting as if it went without saying, Descartes offers no explanation as to what he thinks the "proper" meaning of the word "error" is, a semantic problem whose solution, as our reading suggests, is far from being "clear and distinct." In fact, if the word "error" can be said to be naming anything in Descartes's discourse, it is the lack or loss of what is supposed to be proper: epistemological impropriety, a wandering from the proper path. Like Montaigne's "idleness," the ambiguity of Cartesian error (im)properly names the deferral of the proper. There is never any error if one understands the word in its "proper" signification, but that is to say that there is never any error if there is a proper signification for it. There are no "proper" errors. There will only be error if it is improper. And it is as a certain kind of impropriety that error will be understood. Such a conclusion will only come, however, once Descartes has also excluded error from being a problem proper to the will (*voluntas*): "From all this, I recognize that the power of willing, which I have received from God, is not in itself the cause of my errors, for it is very ample and perfect in its kind; nor yet is it the power of understanding or conceiving: for since I conceive nothing save by means of that power God has given me to conceive, there is no doubt that whatever I conceive, I conceive it as it must be, and it is not possible for me to be deceived in this" (IX-1, 46).

But if error has been judged proper neither to the understanding nor to the will, where does error come from if not from their interaction?[25] "Whence then are my errors [*errores*] born? It can only be from this one thing [*nempe ex hoc uno quòd*]: the scope of the will being ampler and wider [*latius*] than that of the understanding, I do not contain it within the same limits [*non intra eosdem limites contineo*], but I extend [*extendo*] it also to things I do not understand, which things being indifferent to the will, it easily turns away [*s'égare; deflectit*] and takes evil for goodness, or falsehood for truth. And so it is that I make mistakes and that I sin [*que je me trompe et que je pèche; & fallor & pecco*]" (IX-1, 46; **VII, 58**). Given that the will holds over a wider (*latius*) domain than does the understanding, they cannot be contained within the same bounds (*non intra eosdem limites contineo*). Error occurs when instead of reducing the exercise of the will to the compass of the understanding, one "extends" one's judgments beyond the realm of the understanding to objects one does not understand. Once this happens, it is easy for the will, as it is indifferent to what it pronounces upon, to "turn away" (*deflectit*) from the true and the good. This solution to the problem of error, which Descartes offers with great confidence (*nempe ex hoc uno quòd*), is curious in a number of ways. Once again, there occurs a convergence between the moral and the conceptual similar to what happens at the beginning of the *Discourse* and in the dream. In the remaining pages of the Meditation, the commitment of an error, that is, the making of judgments on matters beyond the capacity of the understanding—an act implying a misuse of our God-given faculties—takes on the air of a sin, and more particularly of the sin of hubris: "For it is surely no imperfection in God that He has given the freedom to judge or not to judge upon certain things of which He put no clear and distinct perception in my understanding; but it undoubtedly is an imperfection in me not to use this freedom well, and recklessly to make judgments about things which I only conceive obscurely and with confusion" (IX-1, 48). An error is therefore an incontinence, a transgression, or an overstepping of the bounds of propriety. Descartes seems to have defined one sense of the word "error" by another; that is, a mistake is the result of a wandering (of the faculties), it is the inability to keep (them) within certain limits.

We do not need to repeat our previous argument about how the very metaphor of a topography of error is itself a way of containing that notion of error, a notion that, nonetheless, keeps intruding into Descartes's discourse even after so many attempts to do away with it once and for all.[26] The struggle could be followed right up to the final sentence of the sixth and last meditation: "But since the necessity of things to be done often obligates us to make determinations before we have had the leisure to examine these things carefully, it must be confessed that the life of a man is subject to many errors [*est sujette à faillir fort souvent; saepe erroribus esse obnoxiam*] in particular matters; and it is ultimately necessary to recognize the infirmity and weakness of our nature" (IX-1, 72; **VII, 90**).

In the course of this narrative of error, there is nevertheless one particular type of error, which is foregrounded and designated as "the chief and commonest error": "Now the chief and commonest error [*error*] that is to be found consists in my judging that the ideas which are in me [*en moi*] resemble, or conform to, things which are outside me [*hors de moi*]; for if I were to consider ideas only as certain modes or manners of my thinking without referring them to some other, external thing [*sans les vouloir rap porter à quelque autre chose d'extérieur; nec ad quidquam aliud referrem*], they could hardly give any occasion for error [*occasion de faillir; errandi materiam*]" (Third Meditation, IX-1, 29; **VII, 37**). The error is that of establishing *resemblances* between what is inside the subject (his ideas) and what is outside (things). These resemblances are furthermore understood as equivalences: one errs in believing that one's ideas not only conform but also apply to things, coincide with them. More than a simple relation of comparison, then, this structured error, as the positing of resemblances mistakenly perceived as identities, corresponds to the figure of a metaphor. Metaphor would be the "chief and commonest" error. But again, to pursue this denunciation of metaphor, Descartes is obliged to use metaphors, specifically the spatial metaphors that allow him to speak of what is "inside" or "outside" him.

Within this metaphorical scheme, metaphor itself is defined, true to its etymological sense of transferral (*meta-phora*), as the movement between inside and outside, an act of "referral" ("rapporter [les idées] à quelque autre chose d'extérieur" [IX-1, 29]; "ideas . . . ad quidquam aliud *referrem*" [**VII, 37**; my emphasis]), that is, a bringing or carrying back over (*re-ferre*). This referral or exchange between inside and outside is also a *materiam errandi,* an occasion for error or wandering. *Error* is the wandering over the border, the going over from one side to the other, the *metaphorein* between self and other. The eradication of error or metaphor seeks to establish a self-sufficient economy of the self, one that does not borrow from or engage in an exchange with what is brought over (*metaphorein*) from the other. But to institute this ideal economy, the self must mark itself off from all else, trace a clear and distinct line of demarcation between itself and what is other. The tracing of such a divider, however, already implies its transgression. To define an inside is by the same stroke to define or delimit an outside as whatever is *not* inside. Therefore, one who defines himself as an inside apart from that outside is, in the *act* of that definition, both inside and outside (or, if one prefers, neither inside nor outside, since one posits oneself as the origin of that opposition, that is, as what precedes it). The situation recalls the pun that is the title of Maurice Blanchot's book *Le pas au-delà,* in which the "step beyond" is taken at the same time that it is denied (the "not beyond").[27] In order to secure the inner sanctuary of the *cogito,* the subject must already be in "error."

Having failed to eradicate the problem of error through the literalization of the metaphor in his itinerant existence, does Descartes not, by enclosing himself in the mythic space of the *poêle,*[28] come to perform a curious enactment of the *pas au-delà*? The self-enclosure is simultaneously the inaugural step of another journey: through the metaphysical meditation he wanders from the *cogito* to the infinity of God, whose relationship to Descartes does not exclude that of resemblance: "But from the mere fact that God has created me, it is highly worthy of belief that He has in some way produced me according to His image and likeness, and that I conceive of this resemblance, which includes the idea of God, through the same faculty as enables me to conceive of myself" (IX-1, 41). And is there not also a certain resemblance between the spatial metaphors by which the subject is understood as an "inside" opposed to all that is "outside," the Cartesian separation of mind and body, and the situation of Descartes in the *poêle,* wherein he has closed himself off from the "outside"? And to what is the Cartesian anatomy, with its curious theory of the circulation of the blood as generated by the heart's production of heat, comparable if not the radiant warmth of the stove?[29] Is the *poêle* not a foundational metaphor as well as the physical and historical frame for the Cartesian invention of subjectivity? But the very establishment of such a metaphor already puts the inside of the subject into a relation with its outside, already gives it a *materiam errandi,* without which it could not constitute itself as "inside," as self. In the opening section of Part Four of the *Discourse,* the process of methodical doubt implicitly *empties out* all of the errors or unjustified "opinions" that are *inside* Descartes ("*in* my belief [*en ma créance*]," "the things that had *entered into* my mind [*les choses . . . entrées en l'esprit*]," VI, 31-32; my emphasis), but it is the very act of emptying the container that the mind is, that is, the very activity of doubting, or thinking, that constitutes the indubitable first ground of the truth for the subject.[30] So if the positing of an outside through the unbridling of the horse of error is allowed only in order to secure the inner truth of the subject of the *cogito,* the prior establishment and delineation of that inside necessarily presupposes an outside *in*herent to that inside.[31] To do without error, one must indulge in it.

Reemerging from his *poêle,* Descartes's subsequent travels could, then, appear to offer the prospect of a methodical flight from error: "Winter had not quite ended before I began again to travel. . . . during this time I uprooted from my mind all the errors which had been able to slip into it beforehand. Not that I imitated in this the skeptics, who doubt only for the sake of doubting and affect to be always undecided; for, on the contrary, my whole aim was to find assurance, and to cast aside loose earth and sand so as to reach rock or clay" (*Discourse,* VI, 29).[32] While left unnamed, Montaigne figures here as a negative model, as precisely he whose doubting practices Descartes is *not* imitating. Unlike his skeptical predecessor, whose movement would end up in something resembling quicksand, Descartes's travels allow him to "uproot" his errors but in such a way as to locate the solid bedrock below. Chief among the post-*poêle* journeys, and as if to exacerbate the parallel with Montaigne, was Descartes's trip to Italy, projected for as early as the end of November 1619, in the very aftermath of his dream and groundbreaking meditations. Seeking divine assurance, he hoped to gain in particular the aid of the Virgin Mary by undertaking a pilgrimage to her shrine in Loreto, a site visited not forty years earlier by Montaigne. Delayed for over three years, Descartes only left for the peninsula in 1623, after having sold off his inherited wealth.[33] As far as we know, Descartes kept no journal, and what little information remains to us about his trip has to be gleaned principally from allusions scattered throughout his correspondence. While the outline of his itinerary (leaving France via Basel and Innsbruck; passing through Venice, Florence, and

Rome; returning by Torino and Susa) would roughly replicate Montaigne's passage,[34] Descartes's impressions of Italy are decidedly negative. In a letter to Guez de Balzac (May 5, 1631), he vociferously complains about the climate: "I don't know how you can love so much the Italian air, with which one so often breathes in the plague, where the heat of the day is always unbearable and the cool of the evening unhealthy, and where the darkness of the night gives cover to thefts and murders" (I, 204). On more than one occasion, he actively dissuades his friend Mersenne from a projected trip south of the Alps: "Your trip to Italy worries me, for it is a very unhealthy country for Frenchmen; above all one must eat parsimoniously there, for their meats are too rich. . . . I pray to God that you may return from there contentedly" (November 13, 1639; II, 623). Following the skeptic's footsteps in the saintly destination of Loreto (although no proof exists that Descartes ever actually accomplished his pilgrimage there, once again in contrast to the elaborate painting of his family with the Virgin left behind by Montaigne as a votive offering and memento of his visit [*Travel Journal,* 141–42]), Descartes finds Italy hot, unsafe, and unhealthy.

Far from seeking the assimilation of Roman citizenship, Descartes takes up nearly permanent residence (broken only by three brief trips to France and the final, fatal move to the court of Sweden a few months before his death) in Holland, a country that stands in virtual opposition to Italy within his psychogeography. Not only is the Dutch climate deemed "healthy" by Descartes but, as he explains in the letter to Balzac, it is also the home of the philosopher's favorite heating device: "If you fear northern winters, tell me what shade, what fan, what fountain can as well preserve you from the discomforts of the heat in Rome, as a stove-heated room [*poêle*] and a great fire can keep you from being cold here?" (I, 204). The land of the *poêle* is a healthy one for the body of this thinker, whose own theory of the body, as we have noted, describes the circulation of the blood as an effect of heat transfer emanating from a central source, the heart. As the locale from which the drift of error can be mastered and converted into truth, the secure solitude of the *poêle* also pinpoints a high land (Holland) within the Lowlands, a Dutch oven of selfhood where Descartes seeks a refuge in which to write and from which to master the presentation of his public persona (first unveiled with the initial, anonymous publication of the *Discourse* in 1637). Resolving to "distance myself from all places where I might have acquaintances" (*Discourse,* VI, 31), Descartes discovers a land of comforting reversals where the hyperbole of constant warfare asymptotically attains a state of perpetual peace, and where the very fact of the population's crowded overabundance enables supreme solitude: "The long duration of the war has led to the establishment of such an order, that the armies that are kept up there seem to be used only in order to make the enjoyment of the fruits of peace all the more secure; and amidst the masses of this great people, extremely industrious and more concerned with their own business than curious about other people's, while I do not lack any conveniences of the most frequented cities, I have been able to live a life as solitary and retired as though I were in the most remote deserts [*dans les déserts les plus écartés*]."[35] We should not be surprised if, having found a proper home in a foreign place, Descartes should inscribe his signature into the last few words of this passage, which closes the third of six parts and thus stands at the very heart or hearth of Descartes's first published work, appearing eighteen years after his intial retreat into the *poêle:* "dans les DESerts les plus éCARTES." Des-Cartes, as his biographer Baillet spells his name, would seem to be born again (Re-né) as authorial persona from the mapping of certain spatial relations (Holland, the *poêle*) that delimit a warm and privileged interior from which the exterior can be progressively, methodically, appropriated as one's own. Such is, of course, the narrative of Cartesian science announced in Part Six of the *Discourse,* a narrative by which the systematic acquisition of knowledge that is certain will "thus make us as the masters and possessors of nature" (VI, 62).

Descartes's metaphorical economy of "inside" and "outside" thus both posits and denies (or contains) the outside. And if the figure of travel neutralizes the other that philosophy posits for itself or prevents that other from posing any serious threat to the philosophical system, recourse to such a metaphor also necessarily draws philosophy into a complicity with the literary, that is, with a radical other within itself. For the philosophy that represents itself as a voyage of discovery, or as a meditative journey from the obscurity of error into the light of truth, the risk is not that it will be called into question by what it discovers but by *how* it discovers, by the discourse it is obliged to use to discover what it discovers, by the very representation it gives of itself as a narrative of discovery.[36] The philosophical may be safeguarded by the literary, as Cartesian "error" confirms by leading back to the truth (of the *cogito*), but this shoring up of philosophy implicitly converts philosophy into a (literary) discourse among others: a particularly successful (and timely) story for a European age of newly found and putatively self-generated wealth at home and relentless expansionism abroad.

Chapter 3
Montesquieu's Grand *Tour*

*We burn with the desire to find a stable place and a final,
constant base upon which to build a tower rising to
infinity, but our entire foundation splits and the earth
opens onto the abyss.*

—Pascal

A View from the Top: *Voyage from Graz to The Hague*

In 1638, a year after the publication of Descartes's *Discourse on Method*,
there appeared another discourse, one written by a certain Yves Dugué,
the *Discours de la manière de voyager*. As Normand Doiron has argued in
a recent article, the appearance of this text (itself but a vulgarized translation of a German work) signals the rise of a subgenre derived from the
perception in seventeenth-century France of travel narrative as an accred-
itable genre of writing.[1] This new genre, actually a metagenre, which Doiron
calls the "art of travel," would take the form of a didactic treatise outlining
the rules by and manner in which one should travel. Such treatises would
prescribe who should travel and when, what baggage one should take along,
the company one should or should not keep, and the goals one should set.[2]
Just as Descartes's method would indicate the steps to take in pursuit of
one's mental itinerary, so the writers of these "arts of travel" would stipulate
the rules by which to move one's body in space. The domestication of *error*
thus becomes the common goal of travel literature and philosophy.
Grounded in the foundational security of a method (or *meta-hodos,* what
is alongside a road), solutions found in the one could have pertinence for
the other.

Yet in the course of traditional literary history, travel journals, like
diaries, notebooks, or letters, seem predestined to the ancillary role of
support or background material for the comprehension of a writer's accred-

ited masterpieces. Rare is the critic who would argue the superiority of Montaigne's *Travel Journal* over the *Essays* or who would read *The Charterhouse of Parma* in order better to understand the *Memoirs of a Tourist*. More commonly, the text of a travelogue is treated as an unproblematic document, a source of apparently empirical information with which to explain a writer's major production. Concomitantly, the claim that such writing was not destined for publication or does not match the aesthetic quality of a "finished" work is used to deny the possible validity—if not the frank necessity—of interpreting such material in terms of the text that it indeed is, whether finished or not, published or not.

Such is the temptation for that collection of notes and observations written a century and a half after Montaigne's trip to Italy by another Bordeaux nobleman, Montesquieu, and posthumously published as his *Voyage de Gratz à la Haye*.[3] Initially leaving Paris for Vienna in April 1728, Montesquieu traveled through Austria, Italy, Germany, and Holland until his departure for England in late October 1729, where he resided until his spring 1731 return to France. As for the extant travelogue, a good three-fourths of it describes Montesquieu's stay in Italy, with only a few scattered notes referring to his passage through other countries. Commencing abruptly in August 1728 and ending just as abruptly in October 1729, the sequence of notes chronicles neither the trip's beginning nor its end. Hardly the juvenalia of a gentleman's *formation,* this manuscript was written well after the publication of the *Persian Letters* (1721) and *Le Temple de Gnide* (1725) and prior to the composition of the *Considerations on the Causes of the Grandeur and Decadence of the Romans* (1734), *The Spirit of the Laws* (1748), and the *Essai sur le goût* (1757). Chronologically separating Montesquieu's literary production from his later theoretical and political works, the voyage can be seen to bring about the transition from belles lettres to political theory, from youthful frivolity to mature seriousness,[4] a view that conveniently forgets about Montesquieu's early scientific essays for the Académie de Bordeaux, on the one hand, and such late literary efforts as *Arsace et Isménie* (written sometime between 1734 and 1754), on the other hand. Some even credit the travel experience with effecting changes within Montesquieu's political thinking, such as a heightened skepticism toward the republican form of government or even the origin of his theories concerning the influence of climate on society.[5] The literal voyage doubles as intellectual odyssey, the empirical experience of which is deemed sufficient to explain a perceived change in style or thought, a change that could be emblematized by a text Montesquieu is reputed to have written during his voyage, the *Réflexions sur les habitants de Rome,* whose ostensible discussion of the contrast between ancient Roman "intemperance" and latter-day Roman sobriety seems to double the President's putative life change on the occasion of his peregrination. Montesquieu's travels to various foreign lands become the sociological equivalent of so many laboratory experiments, whose data then becomes systematized in the later political writings as the putative "triumph of the experimental method" in social science.[6] While it would be foolish to discount the manifest reprise of Montesquieu's on-the-road observations in his ulterior writing, such a critical perspective does nonetheless neglect the possibility that there may already be a theory or method that orients the practice of Montesquieu's traveling, that is, that there is an interpretation of the voyage in Montesquieu's *Voyage* which intersects with other interpretive practices of the writer.

That there is a method to Montesquieu's peregrinations is signaled about halfway through the manuscript when he writes: "When I arrive in a city, I always go up onto the highest steeple or the highest tower, in order to see the entire ensemble [*le tout ensemble*]" (I, 671). In a bold move that effectively levels the hierarchical relation between travel journal and political treatise, Jean Starobinski has read in the totalizing gaze from the tower a metaphor of Montesquieu's position as theorist in relation to his object of study in *The Spirit of the Laws,* namely the "entire ensemble" of human institutions. For Starobinski, the vertical perspective from on high implies both that "everything holds together, everything is connected" and that "the order of the demonstration matters very little."[7] Whence the celebrated disorder of *The Spirit of the Laws,* a disorder that, according to Starobinski, is but "the expression of this vertical gaze." The disorder is thus only an apparent one, Starobinski's project being to restore the text's hidden order, something that he can do by positing the contradictions in Montesquieu's text as the different moments of a dialectic.[8] And although such a dialectic implies a narrative through which a concept is arrived at, it is precisely this narrative aspect of thought that is denied by the totalizing gaze from above: "Montesquieu sees *everything* from the height of his tower; his gaze knows the distance from one point to another without having to follow out any pathways [*sans avoir aucun chemin à parcourir*]" (p. 40, emphasis added). Apparently, Montesquieu's dialectic is to be understood as so totalizing in its embrace that it neutralizes or annuls the very temporality of its movement through what Starobinski calls "a massive simultaneity" (p. 39).

To be sure, the belief in such a total vision is metaphysical to the extent that it remains blind to the narrativity of vision (what Louis Marin has called the "trajectory of the gaze [*parcours du regard*]").[9] In order to view the "entire ensemble," one must not only move one's eyes but also turn one's entire body around—or else risk missing part of the surrounding panorama. Now, this metaphysics of total vision is implicit to the kind of critical discourse practiced by Starobinski insofar as he supposes the notion of a unity or totality of the work; that is, that everything in the work coheres through a kind of organic logic. To find the possibility of such a totalizing view already inscribed in Montesquieu's text would thus legitimate Starobinski's critical perspective. We can then see in the image, which Starobinski develops at great length, of Montesquieu's all-encompassing view from the tower an image of Starobinski's own totalizing vision in his capacity as a reader of Montesquieu's entire discursive production.

But whatever one may feel about the pertinence of Starobinski's application of the passage from the travel journal to the wider work, his reading has the great merit of signaling Montesquieu's "desire to see" as a motivating force throughout. In the context of a travel journal, such a desire to see interestingly corroborates recent work on the social institution of travel in its most cultivated form—tourism, a practice whose visual dimension is rendered explicit by its synonym, "sightseeing." As opposed to the discoverer or the adventurer (who collects experiences), the tourist is a collector of sights seen. To sightsee is to see sights, to see what there is to be seen. As sociologist Dean MacCannell argues, sightseeing implies a semiotic activity wherein the tourist arrives at the tourist attraction via the intermediary of "markers." These are anything that point to the tourist attraction: maps, road signs, advertisements—signifiers to the sight's signified.[10] More significantly, the act through which the sight is seen implies an interpretive gesture whereby the tourist places every sight into a relation with the other sights seen as well as with the point of departure. It is through the construction of an imaginary universe that revolves around him that the tourist finds himself reintegrated into the society from which he left to go on his tour. As MacCannell writes, this integration requires "only that one attraction be linked to one other: a district to a community, or an establishment to a district, or a role to an establishment. Even if only a single linkage is grasped... this solitary link is the starting point for an endless spherical system of connections which is society and the world, with the individual at one point on its surface" (p. 56).

But if sightseeing thus implies an interpretive construct, it also becomes difficult to distinguish between such a vision of the world and a theory, especially when one recalls that the etymological sense of the word "theory," from Greek *theoriâ,* is that of a vision or spectacle. Theory, insofar as it assumes the rendering present to oneself of a conceptual schema (we say that we "see" something when we understand it), becomes a kind of sightseeing. Both theory and tourism imply a desire to see and to totalize what is seen into an all-encompassing vision, an ambition simultaneously served by an Enlightenment epistemology embedded in visual metaphors and the contemporaneous social ritual of the "grand tour."[11]

To return to Montesquieu, we find him practicing a very methodical form of sightseeing, his own brand of tourism requiring not only "un tour" (a tour) but also "une tour" (a tower). Montesquieu's "tourism" involves a vision both all-encompassing and from on high, from the top of the tallest tower. The best perspective on the city is the one that is literally superior. But the superiority of the view does not necessarily mean that its perspective is a sufficient one, that everything is seen from the vantage point of this ultimate *touriste*. A wider glance at the passage from Montesquieu, of which I, after Starobinski, have only cited the first half, reveals, however, that it is not a question of a single, all-embracing view but rather of a vision constituted in repetition: "When I arrive in a city, I always go up onto the highest steeple or the highest tower, in order to see the entire ensemble, before seeing the parts; and, upon leaving the city, I do the same thing, in order to fix down my ideas." There are at least three different views of the city: (1) the initial, elevated view of the "entire ensemble"; (2) the sight of the "parts" seen up close and one at a time in the order of a tourist's itinerary; (3) the repetition of the first view in order to "fix down [one's] ideas." Instead of a single perspective, Montesquieu's touristic method deploys a plurality of points of view.

Strictly speaking, there is never an absolute point of perspective from which everything can be seen. Every perspective is necessarily limited, mediated, and constituted by a certain opacity or distance of vision that can, at the limit, annihilate that vision. This distance constitutive of sight is exemplified by the position of Montesquieu on the tower. Here, it is only by seeing less—through the act of moving away from the object of vision in the ascent to the top of the tower—that one can see more, the "entire ensemble" of the area surrounding the tower, the *alentours de la tour*. The mediation through this perspective which is established is thus a kind of voyage, insofar as it involves a movement away from the object of sight.

Moreover, the play of perspectives articulated by travel can be seen to found an epistemology in complicity with exoticism, a complicity already exploited in the *Persian Letters,* published in 1721. Seeing and knowing refer to the same problem:[12] that of taking a distance sufficient to constitute the "proper" perspective on a given object of study. The truth the Persians are supposed to see is a "truth" revealed as a function of their foreignness or, if one prefers, of their extreme (cultural) distance from the French. They notice, says Montesquieu in the preface to the *Persian Letters,* "things which, I am sure, have escaped many a German who has traveled through France."[13] To pursue the same logic, though, blindness would be a function of cultural proximity. The same philosophic Usbek who so lucidly debunks all manner of Western mores is resolutely incapable of perceiving his own role as despotic oppressor of the women and eunuchs kept in the harem he rules back in Persia. The novel's final sequence of letters, detailing the brutal suppression of a revolt in the harem, and culminating in the eloquent anger of Roxane's suicide missive, remains unanswered by the globe-trotting prince to whom they are addressed. The empowering mobility of the latter's gaze thus finds its correlative in the veiled and immobilized status of the women kept back home. Indeed, one of the earliest forebodings of trouble in the seraglio occurs when the harem women go out on a trip into the countryside, where they say "we hoped to have greater freedom" (I, 196). Caught by a sudden storm while traversing a river, they face a choice between drowning or the dishonor of being seen outside the veiled boxes in which they are transported unseen and unseeing. Concludes Zachi, author of this letter, "What troubles journeys cause for women! The only dangers that men are exposed to are those which threaten their lives; while we, at every moment, are in fear of losing our lives or our virtue" (I, 196-97).[14] The philosophical insights gleaned by Usbek turn out to be as inescapably predicated upon his own blindness (or castration, to follow the other thematics of self-limitation registered in the *Persian Letters* by the figure of the eunuch) as upon the blindness he tries unsuccessfully to impose upon his subjects. As Montesquieu will later write in the preface to *The Spirit of the Laws,* "it is not a matter of indifference that the people be enlightened [*éclairé*]" (II, 230).

To return to the scene from his travelogue, it can be seen that the dialectic of vision and displacement remains a persistent concern of his. For if to ascend the tower is to see less in order to see more, one must by the same logic descend from the tower, that is, see less in order to see even more. The towering vision from the *tour* cannot do without a certain de-tour. It cannot do without the inferior, partial vision from down below of he who has descended from the tower to see the "parts" of the city because one cannot, in fact, see *everything* from the top of the tower. The detour into the city will, in any case, not be aimless, since it is already regulated by the preliminary sight of the "entire ensemble" from the tower. The view from on high should accordingly be the *first* view of the city: "When I arrive in a city, I always go up onto the highest steeple or the highest tower, in order to see the entire ensemble, *before* seeing the parts." The tower orients the traveler's movements, frames them and gives them a certain sense or *sens* (a meaning as well as a direction, what French tourist attractions designate as the *sens de la visite*). One could argue here that the view from the tower is of all the possible views of a city, the one that *cannot* be the first view, for one does not simply arrive in town perched on top of a tower. One must first enter a city by the "parts," that is, one must lose oneself down below, before one can even find the tallest tower or steeple—something not always as easy as all that.

Assuming, though, that such a monument can be located, the space of the city will be organized around the tower, *autour de la tour.* There will be no fears of being lost in the detours as long as one's coordinates can be situated in relation to that privileged point of reference that is the highest tower. The tower is the *oikos* that economizes the tourist's itinerary to the extent that the latter is bounded by an inevitable *re-tour* to the *tour.* As such, the foreignness of the terrain can be appropriated or rendered familiar through a glimpse whose elevated perspective is especially conducive to appraising the layout of a town's fortifications, an observation Montesquieu rarely fails to make on his visits.[15] This "visionary conquest" of Italy seems hardly innocent for someone who aspired at the time to a high diplomatic appointment and whose scanning activities proved suspicious enough for at least one French consul to write back to Versailles, asking if Montesquieu were not a spy sent out on a foreign mission.[16]

Even the combined vision of the entire ensemble and of the parts is not enough, though. Something exceeds this totality, something Montesquieu calls his "ideas," and which he needs to fix down [*fixer*] before leaving the city by viewing it again from the tower's initial vantage point. These ideas are themselves the product of the tourist's detour into the city, the return on his ambulatory investment. That intellectual *revenue* renders inadequate the inaugural view of the "entire ensemble," so that upon returning to the tower, we are not at all dealing with the same "entire ensemble." That these ideas need to be "fixed down" tells us that they are neither stable nor precise. Presumably, this rendering precise will occur through the repetition of the initial gaze, which will superimpose the new material of ideas over the previously scanned topography. These ideas are thus affixed to the landscape in an operation reminiscent of the *memoria* of ancient rhetoric, a practice we have already seen to be itself rooted in a projection of language as topography.[17]

Through the stereoscopy of a superior vision constituted out of the double distance (spatial and temporal) enabled by a second view from the tower, Montesquieu's touristic method gives rise to a literal theory, whose signified is the ensemble of ideas (what the mind's eye has seen), and whose signifier is the contour of the landscape (what the physical eye has seen). And here indeed can be found a striking parallel with the theoretical practice of *The Spirit of the Laws,* for in that work, Montesquieu's aim is not merely to construct an abstract theory of law but also to produce an exhaustive and methodical description of actually existing political systems. In other words, the illustration of Montesquieu's theoretical principles does not take place through the then traditional construction of a utopia in the style of a More, a Campanella, or even a Fénelon, but through the projection or reprojection of the theory back onto the world. The result is a kind of political topography made most evident in the celebrated passages on climate as an influence on social customs and forms of government. As if to underscore this politics of topography, maps were added to the text beginning with the second edition (1749). The map of the world becomes the signifier for the signified of theory and is thus, not surprisingly, entitled "Carte pour l'intelligence du livre intitulé *De l'esprit des loix.*" One should be able to understand the theory on the basis of the map. What is implied in such a cartography, however, is that the partitioning of the world is not innocent; on the contrary, it takes on a considerable political significance. Every geographical demarcation—coastlines, mountain ranges, rivers—has untold political consequences. Indeed, the very size of an area delimited by topographical factors has a determining influence on the nature of that government: as Montesquieu concludes in book VIII, chapter xx, large areas suppose despotism, medium-sized ones monarchy, and the smallest ones republicanism (II, 365). Republics are accordingly to be found in the ancient city-states of Greece and Italy; monarchies in the contemporary nation-states of France, England, and Spain; and despotisms in the vast empires of Persia, Turkey, and Russia. Montesquieu's formal systematicity in this regard is so inflexible that he is constrained, in the final chapter of book VIII, to argue the despotic character of the Chinese government over and against the Sinophilic tradition of the Jesuit missionaries, whose letters had spawned the popular contemporary stereotype of the "Chinese sage."[18]

Morality itself is inscribed by Montesquieu into the landscape, first in terms of the climatic opposition between cold and heat, but then even more egregiously by the opposition between north and south: "In northern climates, you shall find peoples who have few vices, a sufficient number of virtues, and a lot of frankness and sincerity. Draw near the southern countries, and you will think you have left morality itself far behind: the liveliest passions proliferate crimes; each person seeks to take advantage of everyone else in ways that favor these same passions" (II, 477).[19] Other conceptual oppositions spring from this same moral topography. In the north can be found activity, work, courage, masculinity, and freedom; in the south, one finds passivity, laziness, cowardice, femininity, and servitude. I doubt that there is any need here to insist upon the markedly ethnocentric and racist character of the geography proposed by Montesquieu—who undoubtedly considered himself to be a northerner, ensconced in a superior latitude.[20] We need to add, however, that it is precisely by projecting his political categories onto this topography that Montesquieu is able to indicate the *proper* place for each kind of government. Asia is thus found to be the place where despotism is "naturalized" (II, 296). Consequently, every existing government is the right one—including those that are despotic. The implication is that nothing should be changed, since things are as they should be, a manifestly conservative thesis. As Montesquieu states in the preface to *The Spirit of the Laws,* "every nation will here find the reasons on which its maxims are founded" (II, 230).

Montesquieu's putative impartiality does not keep him from granting great privilege to what is near (the theorist's homeland) as opposed to what is far. Everything is organized around the place where the theorist is found— perhaps we are now no higher than the tower of his home, the chateau of La Brède, near Bordeaux. This is to say that *The Spirit of the Laws* can be read in terms of a touristic theory insofar as it is a question of "fixing" a certain number of ideas to precise topographical references (which themselves only have value in relation to an ultimate point of reference, the *oikos* of a tower or the place of one's castle). If the elaboration of this theory takes place, it is because we are not at so high an altitude that everything below becomes undifferentiated, but at a medium altitude where only what is far away remains undifferentiated (Montesquieu's despotism, for example, is characterized both by its being far away—or "Asiatic"— and "uniform throughout" [II, 297]).[21] The situation of an intermediary height allows us to read a certain partiality in Montesquieu, a partiality seen in his distrust of the lowly populace who must be kept from taking "too much the upper hand" (II, 291). In his *Notes sur l'Angleterre,* he also cautions that if "the lower chamber became supreme" in England, that country would lose its freedom (I, 884). As for the election of parliamentary representatives, "all citizens, in the various districts, ought to have the right of voting at the election of a representative, except such as are in so low a state [*bassesse*] that they are reputed to have no will of their own" (II, 400). And if it is in the higher latitudes—that is, in the north— that all positive values, including liberty, are found, we should not be too surprised to learn that liberty "reigns" more in mountainous regions than in the plains (II, 532), the lowly plains being a terrain more associated with despotism. Despotism is not only the lowest form of government, it is also what is down below: "The danger is not when the state passes from one moderate to another moderate government, as from a republic to a monarchy, or from a monarchy to a republic; but when it falls and is precipitated [*quand il tombe et se précipite*] from a moderate to a despotic government" (II, 356). Despotism is effectively that into which one "falls" if the principles of a moderate government are not respected and begin to erode: "The rivers hasten to mingle their waters with the sea; and monarchies lose themselves in despotic power" (II, 364). While the value-laden opposition between "high" and "low" is, of course, a widely sanctioned and banal *topos* of Western thought, Montesquieu's systematic recourse to a scale of vertical value in passages such as these indicate the direction and force of the political discourse to be read in the theoretical fallout of his *tour*ism: "One only looks at the parts [*parties*] in order to judge the entire ensemble [*tout ensemble*]," he writes in the preface to *The Spirit of the Laws* (II, 230).[22]

Such corroborations of the homology between theory and tourism lead us back to Starobinski's vision of a theory in which everything is literally *in place,* fixed by the fiction of an all-seeing eye. But what are these ideas that Montesquieu brings back up to his tower? The expression "to fix down my ideas [*fixer mes idées*]" is a curious one, laconic, which points to the ambiguity of a double pun. For, in addition to the literal explication I have already proposed, the French verb *fixer* is not infrequently employed (in a usage already attested in the eighteenth century)[23] as a verb of vision usually translated as "to stare." Moreover, the etymological sense of the word, "idea," from Greek *idea*, is that of something "seen." An alternative reading of the expression *fixer mes idées* might be "to see what I have seen." In returning to the top of the tower, Montesquieu can see what he has seen. And it is in revising *The Spirit of the Laws* for a later edition, that is, "by fixing down my ideas yet again [*en fixant encore plus les idées*]," that Montesquieu is able to shed more light on his topic, to give "a new daylight upon all these things [*un nouveau jour à toutes ces choses*]" ("Avertissement," II, 228). The tourist's itinerary is only complete when he has seen not only the sights but also the seeing of the sights.

It is not difficult to see that what will constitutively elude the gazer's sight is the sight of his own gaze. Everything could conceivably be seen except for the sight of oneself seeing, and the attempt to catch up with that sight always leaves more to see. Interestingly, the bulk of Montesquieu's travel manuscript (remarkably devoid of events one could class in the realm of personal adventures[24]) is made up of the enumeration of sights seen, whether they be public monuments, famous or not-so-famous persons,[25] or those visual objects par excellence, works of art.[26] As Pierre Barrière has noted, "the great and master word is 'to see' [*voir*],"[27] and the most predictable sentence order begins with the anaphoric *j'ai vu*. It is as if the fact of the seeing prevailed over whatever was seen. A particularly significant moment occurs when Montesquieu revisits the city of Verona, stating that "I had the curiosity of seeing again what I had already seen in order to see the different impressions" (p. 798). What the repetition of the gaze reveals is difference, whether thought of as "ideas" or as "impressions." Hence, Montesquieu can write of his subsequent desire to see Paris again, "for I have not yet seen it."[28]

But that incremental difference, which prevents the accomplishment of a fully synoptic closure between a sight and its seeing, is in itself engendered via the spatial and temporal displacement that is travel, an activity that eludes a proper perspective. The sight of the voyage cannot do without a voyage of the sight, since one can only take a perspective on the voyage by taking a certain distance from it, a distancing that presupposes the continuation of the voyage, the prolongation of its course. This prolongation of the voyage can itself only be included in the perspective through recourse to another prolongation and so forth. The articulation of distance and repetition that gives rise to the tourist's theoretical mastery of the landscape cannot itself be mastered. The repetition of the view is already a repetition of what happens elsewhere, and, in fact, everywhere in Montesquieu's journey, if it is true, as he says, that when he arrives in a town, he goes "*always* up onto the highest steeple or the highest tower." Each town becomes the displaced repetition of every other. It is the *tour* itself (the supposedly immovable reference point or *oikos* upon which rests the economy of travel as touristic theory) which begins to travel or go "on tour," which is displaced in its repetition, repeated in its displacement. This "tour" of the *tour* engenders an infinity of perspectives, none of which can claim the superiority of an all-embracing view over the others. There is no tallest tower. Montesquieu's travel notes have no clear beginning or end: there is no terminus to his wanderings, no way to enclose them within the comfortable circuit of return signaled by a continuous narrative. The text remains a collection of disconnected fragments, often repetitious, full of inexplicable gaps and even capable of such chronological illogicalities as his arrival in Heidelberg on August 26, 1729, and his departure the day before.[29] Such a loose textual conglomerate is further exploded by Montesquieu's habit of writing his observations sometimes in his travelogue but at other times in other notebooks such as *Mes Pensées, Spicilège,* or the special one he uses to describe Florentine art (I, 923-65).[30] Narratively disordered, the very plurality of perspectives even seems to depersonalize the writing subject, as the *je* of the observer often dissolves into the *on* of a mere point of view. A case in point occurs when Montesquieu describes a visit to the Vatican (I, 686–93). The autobiographical narrative evoked by the opening, "I went today to see the galleries of the Vatican," a sentence whose announcement is bizarrely repeated for no discernible reason some six pages later, yields only an impersonal itinerary wherein the *on* who "passes" from one gallery to the next merely enumerates the artworks and other curiosities to be seen there—by *any* passing observer. Carrying to an extreme the Cartesian grounding of subjectivity in the Archimedean point of the *cogito,* the traveling subject is here reduced to the impersonal ascription of a mere *point* of view.[31]

It is surely no coincidence that Montesquieu should lay out his touristic method during that part of his text that pertains to his lengthy stay in Rome. For of all the cities visited by Montesquieu, Rome is the one most clearly *not* dominated by some central cathedral spire or other tall monument. The city of the seven hills offers a number of different perspectives, none of which is manifestly superior to the others.[32] Even though he spends nearly half his year-long Italian adventure in Rome (from January 19 through July 4, 1729), a stay broken only by a three-week excursion to Naples, Montesquieu's touristic theory cannot grasp Rome: "One is never finished seeing [*On n'a jamais fini de voir*]" (I, 695). And as Montesquieu's authorial persona is scattered through a perspectivism such that while abroad, he says, "I attached myself there just as to what is my own" (*Mes pensées,* I, 976), so Rome's multiplicity englobes all nationalities: "Everyone lives in Rome and thinks to find his homeland there" (*Voyage,* I, 676). The statement echoes the words written nearly 150 years earlier by that other Gascon nobleman who pursued a similar itinerary and who even went so far as to acquire an official document granting him Roman citizenship. The echo of Montaigne's characterization of Rome as "the only common and universal city" (*Essays* III, ix, 997) alerts us once again to the fact that Montesquieu's trip is already the repetition of many a French trip to Italy, a veritable *topos* spanning the history of the literature, from Du Bellay on up to Stendhal, Nerval, Gide, and others. In Montesquieu's century, among the most noteworthy travelers were Misson, Deseine, Montfaucon, Silhouette, Labat, De Brosses, Lalande, as well as Burnet, Addison, Gibbon, Smollett, and of course, Goethe.[33] Since "all roads" are proverbially said to lead there, Rome is everybody's home, and everybody wants to go there. The superimposition of itineraries means that one is also always seeing what others have seen, making Rome, the sight of so many sightings, the tourist attraction par excellence. It is truly the "eternal city" (I, 676), as Montesquieu can only say after (and before) so many others. The history of famous visitors to Rome produces a cultural sedimentation on a par with the traditionally mentioned geological sedimentation that physically superimposes the Rome of one historical period over another.[34] Rome is what one can never finish seeing because ever new layers of sedimentation cover over the layers below even as they point to the existence of those layers. The city is on the move, building upon itself in an upward direction as if to catch up with the tourist on his hypothetical tower: "One can make conjectures about how much the ground of the city has risen in Rome by the Colosseum, the Arch of Severus, the Tullian Prison (which is underneath a church), the Column of Trajan, that ones sees sunken into the ground by twenty feet. In general, all cities are moving upwards [*toutes les villes haussent*]: streets are paved over ancient pavement. Thus, in Rome, ancient paving stones are found twenty or thirty feet underground" (I, 706). Or is it that the tourist's path, in adding a further layer to the strata of so many visits to Rome, also makes him a part of the city's history, a bit of the sediment itself? Whence the universality of Roman citizenship, a condition Montesquieu freely assumes and appropriates, in contrast to Montaigne's anxious quest for the official document formally granting him civic status in the eternal city.[35] In her letters to him, Mme. de Tencin, for instance, addresses Montesquieu as "my dear Roman."[36]

As for Montesquieu's desire to see, the endlessness of things to see endlessly maintains the pleasure of seeing by denying the ultimate satisfaction of the desire to see everything. This is the aesthetics later formulated in his *Essai sur le goût (Essay on Taste,* 1757) and epitomized by none other than the sight of Saint Peter's in Rome: "As one examines it, the eye sees it grow bigger, and the astonishment increases" (II, 1256).[37] Not unsurprisingly, the basic premise of Montesquieu's aesthetics, first published in the article "Goût" in the *Encyclopédie,* lies in the desire to see more: "Since we love to *see* a great number of objects, we would like *to extend our sight, to be in several places, to traverse more space;* in short, our soul flees all confines, and it would like, so to speak, to *extend* the sphere of our presence: it is thus *a great pleasure for it to set its sight in the distance*" (II, 1244, emphasis added). The aesthetic experience is understood as a travel of the gaze, whose pleasure is guaranteed by an indefinite extending of the soul's "sphere of presence." Undisrupted by any of the displacement or repetition required by the limited vision of the tourist in his tower, this appropriative aesthetics of visual pleasure geometrically describes the (asymptotically unattainable) ideal of a pure, unobstructed view in every direction and with every point along its circumference equidistant from the ocular *oikos* of its center.

The Occidental Tourist; or, The Drift of History: *The Spirit of the Laws*

But this same pleasure can just as easily be reversed into the anguish poignantly expressed in the later books of *The Spirit of the Laws* by an aging Montesquieu gone blind from too much reading and painfully aware of the ways in which his vast subject matter—the totality of laws and human institutions—exceeds the purview of his theoretical gaze. Interestingly enough, the theorist's dilemma is thematized, once again, in terms of tourism: "I am like that antiquarian who set out from his own country, arrived in Egypt, cast an eye [*jeta un coup d'oeil*] on the Pyramids, and returned home" (II, 865). In this passage, the theorist sees himself as a tourist in the pejorative sense of someone who undertakes a great voyage only to take back a partial, superficial view of what he has seen. What he sees without really seeing (since it is only a glance, or *coup d'oeil*) is seen at the cost of a great effort, of an expense that ludicrously exceeds the revenue. It is equally to be remarked that this partial view is a view that looks out at the monumental height of the pyramids *from below.* We have strayed from the economy of a theoretical vision that sees everything from the height of its tower.

The image of the theorist as tourist returns a few pages later: "When one casts one's eyes upon the monuments of our history and laws, it seems that it is all open sea [*tout est mer*], and that this sea does not even have bounds. All these cold, dry, insipid and hard writings must be read and devoured" (II, 894-95). Here, the touristic vision sees not too little but too much, a situation evoking the disorientation of being set adrift in a boundless sea, which is none other than the infinity of text in which the theorist finds himself lost and engulfed. The vision is not only excessive, but its very excess is turned back against the spectator and erodes his position, so much so that in seeing too much he ends by seeing too little. The movement or travel of the vision no longer "fixes" anything down; rather, it is what erodes any possible point of reference, what undermines the economy of travel as method. This radical estrangement within erudition, warned against by Descartes in the *Discourse on Method,* is also signaled by the egregious mixing of metaphors in this passage. The casting of one's gaze upon the material to be read in Montesquieu's research on the laws oddly converts that material into a dauntingly boundless sea. The sea of erudition is then described as what must be not merely read, but "devoured."

That this feat of oceanic orality is as inhabited by the ghost of indigestion as the various mouths in Montaigne's "Of Cannibals" is made clear by the mythological allusion made in the passage's final clause: "All these cold, dry, insipid and hard writings must be read and devoured, in the same manner as Saturn is fabled to have devoured the stones." Montesquieu misreads the ancient myth. What Saturn devoured was his children, until his wife Cybele saved one of them, Jupiter, by substituting a stone for the child's body. The eating of this one stone (not the plural stated by Montesquieu) meant the subsequent rise of a powerful progeny who would one day overthrow Saturn and send him into exile in, of all places, Italy. Progeny, in fact, is very much at issue in a work whose epigraph, *prolem sine matre creatam,* celebrates an "offspring created without a mother." Circumventing the maternal, Montesquieu's authorial self-generation stems not, as in the case of his literary forefather Montaigne, from the expulsion of the *pierre* but from its ingestion. Not only must the *Essays* count among the textual monuments the author of *The Spirit of the Laws* has to "devour" to write his opus, but the placement of the passage that expresses the tourist's digestive disaster in the penultimate book (XXX) bespeaks Montesquieu's anxiety, and his personal investment in the concluding topic of *The Spirit of the Laws:* the historical origin of the French aristocracy in the innovations in Roman and Gallic law that helped organize the handing down of fiefs along patrilineal lines, eventually determining the privileged status of a landed nobleman—such as Montesquieu—born into hereditary wealth and power ("Our fathers, who conquered the Roman Empire," II, 380). Perhaps the infinity of perspective derives from the observer's positioning within his own field of vision, an unlocalizable location that undoes the fixity of an assured or objective point of view. The continuum of history blurs the putatively objectifying distinction between the writing subject and the geopolitical map set forth in *The Spirit of the Laws,* and situates the spectator of governmental forms *within* what he is observing.

Indeed, the category of history is precisely what erodes all kinds of boundaries in *The Spirit of the Laws.* However one considers the spatial setup of political possibilities, the diachrony of history is what inevitably must disrupt the pure synchronicity of the geographical projection, and if Montesquieu can be seen, in the eyes of many a critic,[38] to have "discovered" history, this discovery takes place through a concomitant denial of history. When Montesquieu speaks of history, what is most often implied is a kind of immanent teleology: the history of a nation is the unfolding or development of what is already inscribed within the founding conditions, or "principles," of that nation.[39] The end of a nation is thus already found in its origin: "I have laid down the first principles, and have seen the particular cases bend to them as if of their own accord; the histories of all nations are merely the consequences of these principles" (II, 229). Theoretically, everything one needs to know about a country should accordingly be deducible, in a manifestly Cartesian manner, from its map. On the other hand, a history that would remain identical to its origin would not be historical, would not be history.[40] In the eighth book of *The Spirit of the Laws,* Montesquieu is thus obliged to propose another kind of historical force, a sociopolitical clinamen referred to as the "corruption" of the founding principles, by which one form of government would "fall" into another. The exact source of such corruption remains somewhat unclear in Montesquieu and presents him with a number of theoretical problems. His dilemma is most acute in the case of despotism, which is a government defined as "by its nature corrupt" (II, 357), for how can what is already corrupted become corrupt?[41] More generally, the paradoxical consequence of the concept of corruption is that the pivotal founding principles are themselves revealed as fragile, precarious, and in need of preservation. The question raised at the end of the eighth book, then, is, how to conserve these principles. Montesquieu's answer is that "in order to preserve the principles of the established government, the state must be maintained in the size it already has; and that the spirit of this state will alter in proportion as it contracts or extends its limits" (II, 365). To change the size of a country is to change the principles of its government. It is to change everything given that the size of a country is one of the founding conditions of the state. To change the government is to change the map, and to change the map is to change the government. Geography is political and politics geographical. The map begins to move, but it is no longer the same map. A country changes its borders, but it is no longer the same country.

The diachronical geography that is historical change also provides the conceptual apparatus underpinning the entirety of Montesquieu's earlier *Considerations on the Causes of the Grandeur and Decadence of the Romans* (published in 1734, soon after his return from abroad), where it is argued that the very *expansion* of Roman power abroad is what triggered the demise of the Republic and precipitated the despotism of the Empire. As a cause of the fall into despotism, excessive expansion thus provides a spatial correlative for the temporalized "corruption of principles." As Montesquieu states in that work, "It was solely the great size of the republic that did it in" (II, 119). Rome's shifting frontiers thus propel it through all three of Montesquieu's governmental "natures," a historical metamorphosis that makes of it less the explicative paradigm of politics than its vanishing point, the unfathomable source of legal and social history, as inexhaustibly in need of interpretation as the traveler's Rome is of seeing: "One can never leave the Romans: thus still today, in their capital, one leaves the modern palaces to seek out the ruins; thus, the eye, after resting upon flowery meadows, loves to see rocks and mountains" (II, 414).[42]

But if history redraws the map, then history—at least since the demise of the Roman *imperium*—cannot be understood to be internal to one country (as if one could even begin to speak about the history of a nation without speaking of its relations with other countries).[43] History can only be conceived as the history of the relationships *between* nations, as the tracing of the lines that *describe* the map. It could probably even be shown that the notion of a nation-state is complicitous with that of its cartographical representation, to the extent that each is conceived as a positive entity and not as defined negatively by what is outside it.[44] One needs to understand history as the writing and rewriting of the map. What happens on the border exceeds the spatial entity that is defined by it (the fixity of the map, the "natural boundaries" of the nation-state).

What then takes place on the border? We can answer this question if we turn to that book of *The Spirit of the Laws* for which the map is supposed to serve as a reading aid, book XXI: "Of the Laws in Terms of their Relation to Commerce, Considered According to the Revolutions It Has Undergone in the World." What is proposed is a history of commerce, a history Montesquieu defines as follows: "The history of commerce is that of the communication of peoples. Their various destructions, and the flux and reflux of populations and devastations, form its greatest events" (II, 604). Obviously much more than a simple dialogic exchange between two societies, each of which conceived as a distinct entity, Montesquieu's "communication of peoples" describes the very ebb and flow of the border that separates them and defines them as separate entities. What Montesquieu calls commerce involves the "flux et reflux" of peoples, their intercommunication, in the sense that one speaks of the communication of liquids. Populations intermingle and flow into one another in a perpetual erosion of national distinctions. Thus Montesquieu can speak of the barbarian "inundation" of Rome (II, 526, 709, and *Persian Letters,* I, 335). But this communication is also what defines new social entities as it is a question of the "flux *and re*flux" of populations. Beyond the chronicling of mercantile laws announced by the title, Montesquieu's history of commerce, understood as the communication of peoples, takes as its object the very creation and destruction of nations, a history whose "greatest events" are nothing less than the vast migrations and transformations of societies. This history of commerce is, therefore, indistinguishable from history in general, with "commerce" or "communication" as its driving force. What, then, does Montesquieu tell us in this history of commerce, which presents itself as a history of the world? What are we told about in book XXI?

Boats. We are told all about them. Page after page is devoted to recounting the advantages and disadvantages to be found in various ways to build boats. We are told, for instance, that two boats, each of a different speed, do not accomplish their journey in a time proportionate to their relative difference in speed; that boats made out of wood travel faster than those made out of reeds; that boats with a wide and round bottom are slower than those with a deep and narrow hull that makes them lie low in the water; that large boats survive tempests with greater ease than small ones. Admitting the obsessive pull this topic has on his imagination, Montesquieu writes: "I cannot leave this subject" (II, 610). He then goes on to list the technical accomplishments achieved through boats, namely the voyages of discovery undertaken by the Greeks, the Romans, the Phoenicians, and others.

The inflation of the history of commerce into a history of the world seems to have deflated into a mere history of navigation. Need we take this conclusion, that history is contained in navigation, seriously? To the extent that it is consequent to a topographical theory of law, yes. For how can one understand the relationship between two geographically determined entities without having recourse to a certain concept of travel? Navigation would be what establishes this relationship, what puts it into a relation. The voyage institutes a relationship between two geographical entities, which, to the extent that they are thought through the differences of a distance in space, only exist in the wake of the voyage. In other words, there is no map before the voyage. It is the voyage that produces the map—

and produces it as what tries to map out or comprehend the voyage. The voyage defines and delimits the map by its trace at the same time that the map retroactively appears as what defines or contains the voyage within the limits it imposes. The map is what frames the movement of travel, giving it the legibility of a linear inscription within the longitudinal and latitudinal parameters set forth by the map. At the same time, the very establishment of the cartographic frame is itself an effect of the travel that plotted its coordinates, and that replots them with every succeeding journey. In other words, the voyage always exceeds the map, and by extension, exceeds any theory conceived in spatial terms as a map.

The privileging of navigational technology is also in keeping with what we have seen to be the preponderance of aquatic imagery to represent the dislocating effects of history. The population movements that make and unmake societies are compared to tides and floods. The corruption of monarchies into despotism is described as the flow of rivers into the sea. Even Montesquieu's most structural theory of history, that of the progressive unfolding of founding principles, cannot seem to evade the liquid metaphor: he concludes book I with the boast that if he can establish the principle of a government, "the laws would then be seen to flow as from their springhead" (II, 238). Phrases such as "intermediate channels through which power flows" (II, 247); "the force of the principle draws everything along with it [*entraîne tout*]" (II, 357), and "everything flowed from the same principle" (II, 361) punctuate the elaboration of his political ideas.[45]

In the penultimate chapter of book XXI, the tidal forces of commercial history acquire the catastrophic dimension allegorized by one of Montesquieu's favorite examples, one already discussed at length in his "Considérations sur les richesses de l'Espagne" (1728) and in chapter xvi of "Réflexions sur la monarchie universelle" (1734), namely, the paradoxical impoverishment of the Spanish economy by its very acquisition of gold from overseas. For Montesquieu, the problem lies in a fundamental miscomprehension by the Spaniards about the nature of wealth: "Gold and silver are a wealth based in fiction or signs. These signs are very durable and little subject to decay, as suits their nature. But the more they are multiplied, the more they lose their value, because they represent fewer things. The Spaniards, after the conquest of Mexico and Peru, abandoned their natural riches in pursuit of riches in sign, which degraded by themselves" (II, 646). Hence, the more gold they import, the more the Spanish exacerbate the inflationary spiral triggered by the exploitation of the American colonies: "The Indies and Spain are two powers under the same master; but the Indies are the principal, while Spain is only an accessory... the Indies always draw Spain toward themselves" (II, 648). Furthermore, this bad wealth found overseas is not gratuitous; it must be paid for: "To extract gold from the mines, to give it the requisite preparations, and to transport it to Europe, necessitated a certain expense" (II, 646). This expenditure is that of taking the gold out of American soil and bringing it to Europe—namely, the cost of transportation. This extra expenditure means, though, that the Spanish suffer not only from the effects of inflation but also from an incremental loss of profit. Since the real cost of transportation remains the same while the value of gold depreciates, the percentage of profits lost through the cost of transportation will necessarily increase until the mines become unprofitable (this loss of profit having nothing to do, of course, with the empirical amount of gold contained in the mine).

The Spanish economy is an economy of travel (which precisely does not succeed in economizing on that travel), in which nautical voyages are undertaken to bring wealth back to the homeland, to the *oikos*. The repetition of this travel, the insistent circling of its circular trajectory between Spain and the New World, entails an incremental loss such that the travel that once seemed profitable brings about not just some financial losses but eventually and inexorably the loss of the *oikos* itself, that is, the loss of the home *as* home. The undermining of the economy brought about by travel instigates the travel of the *oikos,* set afloat in a continental drift of cataclysmic proportions: "the Indies always draw Spain toward themselves." This setting adrift of the Spanish ship of state bespeaks a catastrophic end to the world history written in book XXI, a floundering manifestly in contrast with Roman stability: "Rome was a ship held by two anchors, religion and morality, in the midst of a furious tempest" (II, 361). Whence the ambiguity of Montesquieu's appraisal of the European explorations: at one moment, he writes that the great voyages of discovery have led Europe to "arrive at so high a degree of power that nothing in history can be compared with it" (II, 644), and at another, that these same voyages have brought about a decentering such that "Italy was no longer the center of the trading world" (II, 642).[46] And in a completely different context, he evokes the possibility of an eventual demise of the arts and sciences in Europe concomitant with their reestablishment in America in imitation of the revival of letters in Europe after their fall in ancient Greece (*Spicilège,* II, 1435-36). The voyage makes and unmakes economic prosperity, through a movement that is as unmasterable as the drift of continents in the erosive ebb and flow of history.

This erosive drift of history ultimately must implicate the writer himself.[47] Not only, as we have noted, is Montesquieu's name and class status a residual effect of the barbarian "inundation" of Rome that left the feudal system in its wake, but the very narration of the principled flow of political events also engulfs its would-be author:

I am running a long course [*Je cours une longue carrière*]; I am overwhelmed with grief and tedium. (II, 584)

The following subjects deserve to be treated more extensively; but the nature of this work will not permit it. I would like to flow down a gentle river, but I am carried away by a torrent. (II, 585; this is the opening paragraph of book XXI, on commerce and navigation)

When one casts one's eyes upon the monuments of our history and laws, it seems that it is all open sea, and that this sea does not even have bounds. (II, 894-95)

What costs most to those whose minds float amidst a vast erudition is to seek out their proofs in places that are not foreign to the topic. (II, 898)

So if, at the beginning of *The Spirit of the Laws*, the theorist positions himself at the source or fountainhead of the laws, that is, metaphorically in the high mountains, what springs or flows from this source ends by sweeping him right down into the sea. As opposed to Descartes's conversion of the watery depths of doubt into the firm ground of the Second Meditation, Montesquieu's method seems progressively to uncover more water below the apparent terra firma of his principles (history as *error*?). The theorist's high ground is eroded until its submersion in the boundless sea of erudition is desperately brought to a close by his recalling an earlier, perhaps more epic, nautical journey to every French philosopher's preferred destination: "*Italiam, Italiam* . . . I finish my treatise on fiefs at a point where most authors commence theirs" (II, 995).

The final lines of *The Spirit of the Laws* thus evoke the comforting *topos* of the end of the book as the end of the voyage, signified by the citing of the shout of Aeneas's shipmates upon spying the Italian coast, their place of destination. A telling note in the Pléiade edition of Montesquieu naïvely or inadvertently qualifies this shout as taking place "at the end of their long voyage" (II, 1540), an error all the more curious given that Montesquieu himself provides the book and verse number in a footnote (*Aeneid* III, 523). Far from marking an end to the travels and hardships of Aeneas and his company, the sailors' shout of joy is laden with irony, as the sighting of the Italian coast marks only a stage in Aeneas's voyage, not its end.[48] We are, after all, still only in the third of the *Aeneid*'s twelve books. Moreover, the very repetition by the sailors of the name of their destination ("Italiam, Italiam") already points to the bitter disappointment of its loss at the very moment of its sighting, and more generally to the loss of any kind of finality to or exit from the regimen of repetition that structures the voyage narrative as an unending series of episodes. And while the context of the shout does not exactly connote the ideas of a safe return or of an end to wandering, the very act of citing that line from Virgil as that which is to denote the end of the text only ends the text by continuing it, by referring us to the text of Virgil and an even wider intertext. The text is only closed by its opening onto more text. Such a maneuver is, in fact, what happens in the closing words of *The Spirit of the Laws:* "I finish my treatise on fiefs at a point where most authors commence theirs" (II, 995). While the line bespeaks a triumph over rivals, it also places Montesquieu's work in relation to the others: the continuation of the history of feudalism is to be found in these other writers. Now, while this continuation might seem secondary in relation to Montesquieu's work, it is also that which, as Montesquieu says in the penultimate paragraph, "I do not have the time to develop." The other writers' writings are at once what is comprehended by or within Montesquieu's superior grasp of the subject and what cannot be included in *The Spirit of the Laws* because of the author's own finitude.[49]

But within the framework of Montesquieu's patriarchal concerns, a certain shore has indeed been sighted: *The Spirit of the Laws* ends its legal history at the moment fiefdoms become hereditary. No longer a mere recompense for political or military service, the fief began to be considered a "genre" of commercial good and hence fell under the jurisdiction of civil law. The category of history, so erosive of Montesquieu's psychogeography in the central books of his opus, could at the work's close have led to a new ground on the farther side of the "boundless sea," not the high ground of an all-encompassing or encyclopedic gaze but the assurance of a "descent" rooted in the proper transmission of a plot of land from father to son: the baronies of La Brède and of Montesquieu. In keeping with the onomastics of Western feudal nobility, the propriety of the proper name has as its enabling condition the property of the land, a property that is also a patrimony. Indeed, Montesquieu's personal attachment to his name and patrimony, far from being the "very silly thing [*très sotte chose*]" he calls it in *Mes Pensées* (I, 989), was so strong that in order to preserve it and to "reestablish our family which is falling,"[50] he arranged for his younger daughter, Denise—said to have been unwilling—to marry an elder cousin of his: "What I had principally in view was to have heirs to my name."[51] In fact, the very last legal detail discussed in *The Spirit of the Laws* concerns the right of feudal lords to control the inheritance of their territorial holdings by deciding the marriages of their offspring: "Marriage contracts became in respect to the nobility both of a feudal and civil regulation" (II, 995). And here, at the end of Montesquieu's long textual peregrination down from the height of the theoretical springhead whence flow his principles and across the sublime expanse of historical drift, a new height is achieved in the solemn ritual of the marriage contract, which positions the lord's gaze at an altitude from which he can securely watch over his descendants: "In an act of this kind, made under the eyes of the lord [*sous les yeux du seigneur*], regulations were made for the succession, with the view [*vue*] that the fief would be serviced by the heirs" (II, 995). And if one of Montesquieu's principles is the axiom that "the laws are the eyes of the prince" (II, 315), then given the stakes of such a patriarchal surveillance, La Brède may not be all that far from Usbek's harem, whose proprietor incidentally remarks on the "bizarreness" with which the French "have preserved an infinite number of things from Roman law that are useless, or worse, and they have failed to preserve the power of fathers, which it affirmed to be the first legitimate type of authority" (I, 323-24). The error of history would be contained by a fidelity to Roman law under the watchful eye of patriarchy and its attendant narrative of genealogical descent. In *Mes Pensées,* Montesquieu anticipates his descendants not being able to look back up at him, immortally nestled in the monumental height of his reputation: "It will require all of their virtue for them to acknowledge me; they will see my tomb as the monument of their shame. . . . I will be the eternal stumbling block of flattery and I will cause embarrassment to their courtiers. Twenty times a day, my memory will be uncomfortable, and my unhappy ghost shall incessantly torment the living" (I, 1292). Unless, of course, such a phallic domination from beyond the grave would risk the same castrating self-limitations and blindness that it does in the Persian prince, or in the tourist on top of his tower—that is, the inexorable necessity of one's separation from "the parts down below"; or the spectre of the family that "falls" for lack of progeny, with or without arranged marriages: "I can believe that they will not destroy my tomb with their own hands; but undoubtedly, they would not raise it back up again if it fell to earth."[52]

But if the predicament of political theorist or feudal patriarch is thematized in terms of the quest for perspective, then our inaugural passage from Montesquieu's *Voyage* is not merely anecdotal, but rather engages persistent concerns throughout Montesquieu's work, with problems of vision and positioning as metaphors of dominance (whether textual, theoretical, political, or familial). What the passage does is dramatize this concern by proposing the image of the appropriate place for Montesquieu to mount his eyes, a *Mont-es-yeux,* if you will. And the fantasy of a towering theoretical vision could thus be read as the insistent inscription of the writer's proper name. The touristic method would operate as a kind of signature over the landscape, through which, as the framing process enacted by the organization of perspectives already suggests, the strangeness of the foreign land is rendered familiar. As Montesquieu writes in *Mes Pensées,* "when

I traveled in foreign lands, I attached myself there just as to what is my own" (I, 976). But if he "attaches" himself to the foreign country as if it were his own, could it be that the foreign land is appropriated, rendered proper to him, through a practice that mimes, in a distorted but rebuslike fashion, the proper name of Montesquieu?

That proper name, though, derives from the place name of the property or piece of land whose ownership certifies the nobleman's aristocratic status. What is the place called "Montesquieu"? According to the etymology proposed by Robert Shackleton, *Montesquieu* would mean a "wild or barren mountain."[53] *Esquieu,* however, is also an adjective from Old French, which, according to Godefroy, qualifies something as what has been either taken from or forbidden to someone. A *montesquieu* would be a forbidden mountain, forbidden for instance to agriculture and thereby barren, or forbidden to travelers because of its inaccessibility and therefore wild. "Montesquieu" would be a forbidden height, that is, both the height *and* its forbiddenness: the "mont des yeux" of which one is deprived or the "mont-esquieu" of theory as an impossible vision, as an inaccessible position. Would the heights of Montaigne, his compatriot and intellectual father, be too great to scale?

Or is the very failure to achieve such an all-encompassing vision from on high not the condition of Montesquieu's success as a critic of human institutions?[54] In seeking to establish the fixity of the political landscape, he ends up demonstrating its historical changeability, and hence the *possibility* of its being changed by those who become not merely the subjects but also the agents of history. It is in this sense that a provincial patriarch and nobleman, nostalgic for the preabsolutist glory days of the feudal aristocracy, could have become the father of modern social science and a precursor of the American and French revolutions, events whose radical newness was as often as not thematized by the return to Roman garb and custom immortalized in the paintings of David.[55]

Would not the proper name of Montesquieu then designate an improper place, one not readily appropriated? The scene of appropriation takes place elsewhere, in another place, in a foreign land—Italy, for example. The traveler is as at home abroad as he is away at home. This is the dilemma played out throughout Montesquieu's work and life and with myriad permutations and combinations along the twin paths of exoticism (in his travels and literary works) and internal emigration (the retreat from public life into the long solitude of his château), neither of which can lead to any absolute or final, much less definitively elevated, perspective. To repeat the lesson of Rome, "one is never finished seeing."

Chapter 4
Pedestrian Rousseau

*What serves to deceive others was for me the pathway
to truth.*
—Jean-Jacques Rousseau, *Emile and Sophie: or,
The Solitary Ones*

Pedagogy and the Teleology of Travel: *Emile*

One of the most consistent themes of travel literature in the Age of Discovery
is that of the pedagogical value of voyages for those who undertake them.
At least since Montaigne's "Of the Education of Children" (*Essays* I, xxvi),
travel has been grasped as literalizing the etymological sense of education
as an *e-ducare,* a leading out from received prejudices and customs. The
act of travel becomes pedagogically justified as "pleasurable instruction."[1]
The correlation is massively underwritten by the Lockeian epistemology of
understanding gained through accumulated sensory perception, by the cultural practice of the young gentleman's "grand tour," and by various strands
in the emergence of the novel, such as the picaresque, the *Bildungsroman,*
and autobiography, which tend to posit wisdom as a function of accumulated experience and to prescribe the formation of the individual through
his progressive contact with social, sexual, and cultural others. The educational value of voyaging, which, according to Montaigne, should take
place "at a tender age" (*Essays* I, xxvi, 153), becomes so pronounced in
Enlightenment thought that the *Encyclopédie* article "Voyage" features a
special subsection devoted to the particular "educational" sense of the word
(see the Introduction). As I have argued throughout this work, however,
any such "accumulative" theory of travel must posit a privileged point of
reference in relation to which the increment of profit (here, wisdom) can

be measured. The educational voyage is thus especially dependent upon its completion, upon the *return home* of the neophyte who sets out on the grand tour; otherwise, the value of its formative lessons may be lost or reduced to naught. In this regard, the self-discovery of Descartes in the wake of his wanderings is to be preferred to the ambiguous perspective of Montesquieu/Usbek, just as the continuous narrative progression toward clarity must prevail over a discontinuous set of insights, whose peak lucidity always risks a corollary fall into personal blindness and civic decadence. It is against this background that one can measure the rather different view of travel set forth in the era's most influential pedagogical treatise: Rousseau's *Emile* (1762). The final section of that work is headed by the title: "Of voyages," and once again, the concerns uttered under that rubric evince a demonstrable pertinence to other aspects of Jean-Jacques's varied and disparate opus, and more specifically, to that economy of critical nostalgia that circulates throughout it as the desire for an impossible return, as well as to his longstanding need as perpetual wanderer for some point of fixity.[2] As such, a close reading of that section should point in the direction of what underlies citizen Rousseau's ambulatory concerns.

Concluding the presentation of Rousseau's pedagogical ideas, the *topos* of education acquired through travel is thus the final phase of Emile's education; it is what is to complete his education before his final reunion with Sophie. Yet this last step in Emile's education is made to seem inessential. The voyage is only undertaken, in fact, after Emile has already been sufficiently educated so that the voyage will only have those effects intended by Emile's tutor. Emile's education is what allows him to undertake a voyage, at the same time as that voyage is all that remains for his education to be completed. On the one hand, if, as Rousseau tells us right at the beginning of *Emile,* "the first education is the one that matters the most,"[3] then we might conclude that the final lessons arrived at through Emile's trip must be those that matter the least. On the other hand, the deferral of the voyage until the last possible moment suggests the difficulty and seriousness of the lesson and attaches a certain importance to it, since Emile must be thoroughly prepared before engaging on this last leg of his schooling.

This ambiguity of the voyage's place within the pedagogical hierarchy is reinforced by an ambiguity in the moral value of traveling, an ambiguity beyond the tutor's ability to control unless it is put off until the last possible moment. The section entitled "Of Voyages" begins, in fact, by taking note of this problem in considering the voyage's ability to do either good *or harm* to the traveler, an alternative the very statement of which complicates the traditional pedagogical value of travel as an unquestioned benefit. Rousseau will finally conclude, though, that "voyages impel one's natural character toward its bent, and finish making a man good or bad" (IV, 832). Traveling merely completes a "natural" tendency, makes one's character definitive, defining therefore what has already been defined, although not definitively. How is this possible?

Rousseau begins by arguing that the question of the value of travel should not be posed in terms of whether or not voyages are good. Instead, he proposes that one think in terms of whether or not it is good that one *have* traveled. This immediately changes the issue from that of the value of the activity of the voyage to that of its end result. Value can only be obtained from travel once the trip is over, the implication being that travel can only be judged in teleological terms. One of the objects of this discourse on voyages will thus have to be the delineation of the proper *telos* of any traveling.

But instead of moving toward this end, Rousseau immediately embarks upon a detour that moves the topic of discussion from the value of trips to that of books: "The abuse of books kills knowledge" (IV, 826). The world of books is opposed, as in Descartes, to the book of the world, the latter neglected as a result of the proliferation of the former: "So many books make us neglect the book of the world" (IV, 826). But in the particular case of travel narratives, this obfuscation is exacerbated by a double mediation or veiling of the truth: "It is too much, in order to arrive at the truth, to have to pierce through the prejudices of the authors as well as our own. . . . This would be true in the situation where all travelers are sincere, only tell what they themselves saw or what they believe, and that they disguise the truth only through the false colors it takes in their eyes. But how must it be when you further have to unravel the truth from their lies and bad faith!" (IV, 827). Rather than spurring an inquiry into this complex epistemological problem, however, such an exacerbated mediation leads Rousseau to dismiss the entire genre of travel literature with the rather unsatisfying conclusion that "in the matter of all kinds of observations, one must not read, one must see" (IV, 827). He then drops the subject and returns to his initial question regarding the value of voyages in themselves after a parting shot at the decadence of contemporary society: "Let us then leave the vaunted resource of books to those who are made to be contented by them. . . . That resource is good for training fifteen-year-old Platos to philosophize in circles and for instructing company in the customs of Egypt or the Indies, on the faith of Paul Lucas or Tavernier" (IV, 827). Exotic knowledge gleaned from travel books (like wisdom in the Third Reverie) seems principally used for ostentation, whether it be that of the writer who wants to tell a good story or the reader who can retell the story in polite company to his or her own credit.

Why this detour, then, through the value of written accounts of voyages? Why should the pedagogical justification of travel entail a critique of travel literature unless there is some possibility of confusion between them? Why should the problem of travel immediately come up against a problem of texts? Perhaps it is because what is at stake is the ability to read a particular text, the "book of the world," which can only be read through travel (otherwise, "everyone keeps to his leaf" [IV, 826]). Travel, to pursue the metaphor, is what allows one to "turn the pages," an ability essential to any reading. But if travel is a type of reading, then reading travel literature only serves to superimpose another reading, which would get in the way of one's journey to "arrive at" the truth (IV, 827). This superimposition of texts, moreover, would make it difficult to distinguish between the two; or rather, to be precise, the reader of travel literature runs the risk of forgetting that what he or she is reading is but the text and not the trip itself.

We rejoin one of the persistent fears of Emile's teacher, that of the confusion between sign and referent: "In whatever study it may be, without the idea of represented things, the representative signs are nothing. Nevertheless, children are always kept to these signs without any of the things they represent explained to them. In thinking to teach a child a description of the earth one only teaches him about maps [qu'à connoître des cartes]; he is taught the names of cities, countries, and rivers that he doesn't conceive of existing anywhere else than upon the paper where they are shown to him" (IV, 347). To know only about maps ("des cartes") would be to fall into an epistemological error (that of Descartes?), for in contradistinction to the Cartesian grounding of truth in the self-evidence of intuition, Rousseau's pedagogy stresses an experientially oriented method of learning through the presentation of the thing in question, while deferring as long as possible the child's encounter with signs in general and with writing in particular. But we should not forget that in the above passage, the example Rousseau uses to illustrate the suspension of the referent is drawn from cartography, a field whose pretension is to the utmost precision in referentiality. A map is nothing, if you will, but a collection of points of references, and yet they remain just *points* of references, that is, empty signs, unless the user of the map is able to attach some other bit of information to it, whether it be from having seen the place, or pictures of it, or whatever. The map can only become meaningful if one already has some idea of that to which it refers. On the other hand, if one does not already know what the referent is, then the reference point loses its capacity to carry out fully the semiological function that cartography ascribes to it. The map becomes an aesthetic object in the same way as the tool missing its handle in Kant's famous example: both have been cut off from their purpose while continuing to indicate that they do have a purpose. That they do have a purpose, though, keeps them from being "pure" aesthetic objects in the Kantian sense—that is, having a purposiveness without a purpose.[4] Perhaps that is why maps, like archeological artifacts, are usually considered lesser aesthetic objects, and are placed in museums less often to be seen in their own right than as backdrop to "pure" works of art.

But if the structure of the map allows for the possibility as well as the eventuality of the suspension or undoing of its referential function, the same is *a fortiori* the case for travel narratives, with their proliferation of strange names and places. If travelers are or have been accused of lying—and this is not to excuse them of it—it is because the account of an exotic place suspends as it names its referent, because its implicit claim to veracity cannot be verified.[5] The names are empty signifiers, indefinitely available to whatever significations are chosen.[6] And it is because accounts of voyages are potentially unverifiable that there is such an attempt to verify them. One trip to the North Pole or the moon demands another, and each must bring back more "authentic" documentation of its itinerary by way of photographs, geological samples, and so forth.[7] But as this attempted verification takes place on the one hand, the voyage's potential unverifiability shunts the account of it, on the other hand, in the direction of the literary. Even basically believable or verifiable travel stories come to be read as literature (Xenophon, Marco Polo, Bougainville, Cook, and more recently Lévi-Strauss, to name only an obvious few). It is easy to see, then, why Rousseau should extend the same negative criticism to travel stories that he persistently addresses to literature. In the corrupt realm of culture, all recounted facts inevitably become tainted by the corrosive effects of fiction. The educator's principle, consistent then with the larger view of pedagogy in *Emile* as a resistance to the corruption that is societal culture, is that the knowledge to be gleaned from travel, if there is any, must be acquired directly and alone. Hence, Emile is to learn his way around not through maps but through the personal experience of his wanderings with his teacher (such as their famous outing to Montmorency). In the same way, if voyages are to be of value, it must be through one's own voyaging and not vicariously through another's account.

So much for the mode, but the content of what is to be studied through travel remains as yet unclear. In "Of Voyages," Rousseau rephrases his initial question in such a way as to make the end of travel clear: "Is it sufficient that a well-educated man know only his compatriots, or does it matter that he know men in general?" (IV, 827). Knowledge of humankind in general means surpassing one's particular perspective. The pedagogical function of travel has to do, it would seem, with overcoming ethnocentrism, and with the corresponding establishment of a general anthropology. But while Rousseau says that it is not necessary to know every man in order to know man in general, he also asserts that every nation has its "proper and specific character" (IV, 827), and just as this "proper character" can be deduced through the comparative observation of individuals, so can the character of man in general by observing different nations. There ensues a comparative study of the way various nations travel and what they gain or lose from it. Rousseau proposes that just as "the least cultivated peoples are generally the wisest, those that travel the least travel the best" (IV, 828). This is because, less concerned with "our frivolous inquiries" and "our vain curiosity," they pay attention only to what is "truly useful" (IV, 828). In contemporary Europe, only the Spanish—so Rousseau says—can claim this expertise (or lack of it), while the ancients are considered the masters at knowing how to profit from travel. This mastery is immediately qualified, however, by the assertion that "since the original characters of nations are being effaced from day to day, they are becoming for the same reason more difficult to grasp" (IV, 829). If the ancients were better ethnographers, it would have been because national characters were more sharply delineated in the past. On the other hand, the blurring of nationalities occurred precisely because of the activities engendered by and related to travel:

> As races become mixed and peoples fused into one another, one sees disappear little by little these national differences which once struck the observer at first glance. Formerly, each nation remained more enclosed within itself, there was less communication, less traveling, less in the way of common or opposed interests, less in the way of political and civil liaisons between nations ... great sea voyages were rare. (IV, 829)[8]

But then again as intersocietal distinctions were lost, anthropological observation was done "more negligently and more poorly" (IV, 831) because the instruction (in the study of man) derived from voyages became of less interest than the "object" of their mission: "When this object is a philosophical system, the traveler only sees what he wants to see: when this object is personal interest, it absorbs the whole attention of those who give themselves over to it. Commerce and the arts, which mix and blend peoples, prevent them from studying each other. When they learn the profits that can be reaped from each other, what more do they need to know?" (IV, 831). Modern travel is condemned by Rousseau because it has become only self-serving. Whereas "primitive" man, who is sufficient in himself and needs no one else, "does not know and does not seek to know countries other than his own" (IV, 831), modern man in his dependency on others descends to a kind of cannibalism: "But for us to whom civil life is a necessity and who cannot do without eating men, the interests of each one of us is served by frequenting the lands where one finds the most men. That is why everything flows into Rome, Paris, or London. Human blood is always sold at a better price in capital cities. Thus, only the great nations are known, and the great nations all resemble each another" (IV, 831). The invention of travel has resulted in the establishment of commerce as a cannibalism that destroys all national distinctions. Such a formulation can easily be rearticulated into the more received Rousseauist theses concerning the opposition between nature and culture, with travel clearly on the side of culture. In addition, Rousseau has extended the Montaignian critique of imperialism as a higher-order cannibalism onto that paragon of modern culture, the urban commercial center (the first example of which is none other than Montaigne's and Montesquieu's beloved Rome).

Yet Rousseau is not prepared to dispense entirely with travel: "There is quite a difference between traveling to see other lands and traveling to see other peoples. The prior object is always chosen by curiosity seekers; the other object is only ancillary for them. For he who would philosophize, it ought to be just the opposite. The child observes things until he can observe men. Man must begin by observing his fellow men, and then he observes things if he has the time" (IV, 832). The philosopher's journey is opposed to that of either the curiosity seeker or the child, and it alone is capable of making travel useful or valuable, because it is the only one correctly centered on the study of man: "It is bad reasoning to conclude thusly that travel is useless because we travel badly" (IV, 832). Traveling can be profitable but only for a particular kind of traveler belonging to a sort of moral elite: "[Voyages] are suitable only to men firm enough in themselves to hear the lessons of error without letting themselves be seduced by them, and to see the example of vice without being dragged into it" (IV, 832). The prerequisite for travel is a certain inability to travel: one must be stable or "firm" enough in oneself not to be "seduced" or carried away by the lessons of error, just as is the Ulysses who remains unmoved by Circe's charms in the frontispiece plate for book V in the first edition printing of *Emile*. The Cartesianlike self-groundedness of the would-be traveler rejoins Rousseau's earlier comments in the long tenth note to the *Discourse on the Origins and Foundations of Inequality among Men* (1755), where he suggests that only trained philosophers should be voyagers (III, 213ff.). For Rousseau, instead of travel being an access to philosophical wisdom, as it was for Montaigne or Descartes, it is the status of philosopher that makes one qualified to travel in a manner profitable to both self and society.[9] Were we to study "a new world" through the expert eyes of philosophers "we should learn thereby to know our own world" (III, 214). In the "happy times" of antiquity, ordinary people neither traveled nor engaged in philosophy, leaving both tasks to "a Plato, a Thales, a Pythagoras, [who,] impelled by an ardent desire for knowledge, undertook the most extensive voyages solely to instruct themselves, and traveled far in order to shake off the yoke of national prejudices."[10] Through the comparative study of cultural differences, philosophers are able to "learn to know men by their resemblances and their differences, and to acquire a universal knowledge which is not that of one century or one country exclusively, but being that of all times and all places is, so to speak, the universal science of the wise [*la science commune des sages*]."[11] So, if the Second Discourse corroborates the anthropological aim set for travel in *Emile*—namely, the establishment of a common concept of man—it further qualifies that intellectual pursuit, not as a wisdom common to all, but as a knowledge common to but also reserved for "the wise."

In short, the value of travel rests upon the proper training of the philosopher, that is, upon a question of pedagogy, which brings us back to *Emile,* where we remember that "voyages impel one's natural character toward its bent, and finish making a man good or bad" (IV, 832):

> Whoever returns from running around the world is upon his return
> what he will be the rest of his life; more of them return wicked
> than good, because more of them leave inclined to evil rather than
> goodness. In their voyages, badly raised and badly led youth
> contract all the vices of the people they frequent, and not one of
> the virtues with which these vices are mixed; but those who are
> fortunately born, those whose good natural character has been well
> cultivated and who travel with the true design of instructing
> themselves all return better and wiser than when they left. Thus
> will my Emile travel. (IV, 832)

If travel merely completes one's education and moral upbringing, albeit definitively, then only those who are well educated should travel. The well educated, though, are those who see the voyage as a way to continue their education ("who travel with the true design of instructing themselves").

The next paragraph qualifies, however, this ideal of pure self-instruction: "Everything which happens according to reason must have its rules. Taken as a part of education, voyages must also have their rules. Traveling for the sake of traveling is to wander [*c'est errer*], to be vagabond; traveling for the sake of instructing oneself is still too vague an object: *instruction which has no set goal is nothing*" (IV, 832, emphasis added). Now it seems that it is not enough to pursue one's education through travel. For Rousseau, to wander, *errer,* would be an error. It does not suffice to be a lover of knowledge, a philo-sopher, or even a lover of "Sophie" herself, such as Emile. Travel as education, like Montaigne's idleness, must be teleologically determined, although probably not as much so as the self-interested travel of the urban cannibal. The proper *telos* of travel that Rousseau then proposes is the study of one's civil relations with others, a surveying, after Montesquieu, of the political landscape, including the nature of the government under which one was born: "Now after having considered himself in his physical relations with other beings, in his moral relations with other men, he still has to consider himself in his civil relations with his fellow citizens. To do this, he must begin by studying the nature of government in general, the various forms of governments, and finally the particular government under which he is born in order to know whether it is suitable for him to be living under it" (IV, 833). Behind the disinterested study of various political systems that ensues in the next few pages lurks a motive of self-interest: the search for the most advantageous place to live. The purpose of embarking on the journey is thus to find a home. Emile is to leave home to find a home—the location of which, however, has already been determined, if the tutor has successfully implemented the precepts of "negative education": "Either I am deceived in my method, or he ought to answer me more or less in the following manner: 'To what do I fix myself? To remaining what you have made me be'" (IV, 855). Emile replies that he will fix himself by being fixed to nothing. The tutor elaborates: "Freedom is not in any particular form of government, it is in the heart of the free man; he bears it everywhere with him" (IV, 857). For the runaway from Geneva with a plebeian name,[12] freedom is—irrespective of one's location within Montesquieu's tripartite topology of republics, monarchies, and despotisms—wherever the free man happens to be; home is defined by one's current "coordinates." Yet, despite this disjoining of the feudal link between surname and place name, another kind of link to place is introduced by way of the "attachment" for one's place of birth, an attachment taking the form of a "duty" owed to one's birthplace: "So do not say: what does it matter where I am? It matters that you be where you can fulfill your duties, and one of these duties is an attachment for the place of your birth. Your compatriots protected you as a child, you must love them as an adult" (IV, 858). This politics of the birthplace as *oikos* conforms to the choice of religion suggested earlier by the Savoyard vicar in book IV of *Emile:* although religious experience is said to be particular to every individual, one should practice the faith into which one was born.[13] A curious privileging of the home is effected: it is best to stay home, although one must be equally prepared to leave it without regret. Emile's voyage is circular; he decides to stay where he is and to do what he is doing. The voyage succeeds in immobilizing him, in making him *choose* to stay at home. One sees why, for Rousseau, the value of voyages is not a question of traveling but of having traveled.[14]

Emile's trip is thus quite obviously a rite of passage; it completes his education and defines him as a full member of society (in his accepting the rights and obligations entailed in living within that society). It is through his trip that Emile acquires manhood. But this trip is a guided one, in which the tutor takes care that Emile does not spend too much time in cities ("where a horrifying corruption reigns" [IV, 853]) or run the risk of debauchery in the company of women. The tutor leads Emile on a guided tour designed to make sure he will stay at home. "If there be happiness on earth, it is in the refuge [azile] where we live that one must find it" (IV, 867). But this tour is itself only the final step in that other, more comprehensive guided tour which is Emile's education under the tutor's panoptic guidance and which is designed to keep Emile "natural." Travel thus names the risk of an excursion outside the pastoral patriarchy envisioned by Rousseau's tutor, a risk, however, that cannot be circumvented if the pedagogical project wishes not only to check on its own efficiency but also merely to claim the status of an education.

One of the principal strategies of the negative education is to keep the child "natural" by keeping him as close to the home as possible. Hence the importance of the mother as the only wet nurse and of the father as the child's teacher. What is considered "natural" in *Emile* is what is associated with the home—or the principle embodied in it (self-sufficiency, independence, innocence, etc.), when the subject makes himself his own home. But if the "natural" education ensures the primacy of the home, it is not surprising that travel should be restricted. To underwrite this avoidance of travel, however, requires recourse to its language. Very near the beginning of this voluminous work, a metaphorical topography is delineated that obliges the teacher to choose between the "route" of nature and that of its other (humanity, society, culture, art, etc.). Emile's education is seen as an alternative journey (one that stays "within" or does not stray "outside" the state of nature), or as a nonvoyage, the natural route being one in which the traveler stays put, anchored against the imperceptibly corrupting crosscurrents of cultural drift: "To form this rare man [the man of nature], what do we have to do? A lot, undoubtedly; it is a matter of preventing anything from happening. When it is a question only of going against the wind, you change tack; but if the sea is strong and you wish to stay in place, you need to cast anchor. Watch out, young helmsman, that your cable doesn't pay out or that your anchor doesn't drag along the bottom, and that the ship doesn't drift before you notice it" (IV, 251).

A problem ensues, though, for this reactive travel, to the extent that it is still a question of "forming" this "natural" man—that is, of entering into a temporal process, which, if any educational practice, even a negative one, is to succeed, must be negotiated in such a way that the student knows more afterwards than before. There is no need to insist here on the ingenious manipulation of Emile's character undertaken by the tutor to keep Emile "natural."[15] Rather, what I would like to point out, keeping in mind the topographical model of the educational situation, is that a certain traveling is needed in order to maintain its exclusion, that a certain accommodation with the outside must be made to preserve the inner domesticity of the home.

Emile's first geography lessons center on the position of the home (IV, 434-35). The location of one's home or of oneself already demands a certain departure from home, from self. One can only learn what home is by knowing what it is not. Even earlier, one of Emile's first lessons involved learning the disposition of objects and distances around him, a lesson that can only be learned through one's movement in relation to them: "Only through movement do we learn that there are things which are not us, and only through our own movement do we acquire the idea of spatial extension" (IV, 284). Travel occurs as part of a strategy designed to deny it, the explicit purpose of the literal voyaging at the end of Emile's education. The "natural" education involves a succession of voyages, then, each of which involves a return to home. An economy of travel is established that would seem to allow for the possibility of a more adventurous journey at each succeeding outing in Emile's education. The riskier voyages are not taken, however, until there is some certainty that their route will lead back to the home. It is not surprising, then, that the last two of these figural excursions should involve women and literal voyaging, the "transports" of eroticism and the *jouissance* of travel. These only occur when all else is "in place" and the strategy itself of leaving the home to find it can be made evident without risk. There would seem to be a prescribed succession to the sequence of these voyages such that should one fail in its aim, all the succeeding ones would fail too, assuming, that is, that they could still take place at all. Such a hypothesis is borne out by Rousseau's statement that the first lessons are the most important, since they determine everything that follows, and again by his assertion that voyages do not change a person's moral character but only confirm and reinforce what is already there. If the first steps are taken properly, all the rest follows, which of course recalls Rousseau's insistence that the mother be the child's wet nurse and the father his teacher. That neither of these prerequisites to the natural education is met by Emile already indicates that that "natural" education is a fiction, since not even in its exemplary case, that of Emile, can its constitutive conditions be met. The student is always already "unnatural," always already out of the home.

Even were its conditions fully met, though, the "nature" in question is less natural than cultural, namely, the *social* institution of the family, here already nuclear in structure. The security of the home is assured by its conjoining of patriarchal pedagogue, nursing mother, and *male* child, an arrangement whose beneficent pastorality is elaborately played out in the fourth part of Rousseau's novel, *Julie, ou la nouvelle Héloïse* (1760), by the idyllic triad of Wolmar, Julie, and Saint-Preux (the childishness of whom is, of course, not a function of age but of his excessive sentimentality and narcissistic self-indulgence). Now if the value of travel lies in the comparative study of "man" and his institutions (which leads the son to realize that there is no better place to be than the patriarchal home), the danger of travel is linked to contact with women, who epitomize for Rousseau that urban corruption and "cannibalism" whose metaphorization also evokes the phantasmic specter of the *vagina dentata*. The anxiety of travel, underscored by the need for the tutor's literal "guidance," is fundamentally a displacement of Rousseau's deep-rooted and well-documented anxiety about women and sexuality.[16] Women figure the potential disruption of the home and of its fundamental dyad of father and son, the preservation of which is indeed the ultimate aim of the "natural" education; hence, and despite the excoriation of mothers who do not breast-feed their children, the virtual disappearance of the mother herself, or even of any surrogates of her, from Emile's early training.

And at the other end of the pedagogical itinerary is found the perfect girl for Emile: the uneducated, decorporealized, and domestically enclosed Sophie,[17] the sense of whose name further bespeaks her allegorical reducibility to the abstract "wisdom" Emile is supposed to have acquired from his education. Even so, Emile's encounter with her is carefully mediated by multiple comings and goings, whose dangers are themselves curbed by the advent of Sophie as the privileged object of the student's affections. This double domestication, issuing in the final apotheosis of the patriarchal home blessed by wife and child, provides the narrative backdrop for Rousseau's pedagogical ruminations in book V. We first spy Emile and his teacher returning from Paris, where they had thought to find Emile's future wife. This being the obvious place *not* to find her given Rousseau's antiurban prejudice, the quest's failure at this point redounds to the pedagogue's benefit as he inveighs against the city as the the very locus of vice: "Farewell then, Paris, you famous city, city of noise, smoke and mud, where women no longer believe in honor nor men in virtue. Farewell Paris, we seek love, happiness, innocence; and we will never be far enough away from you" (IV, 691). Sophie is predetermined to be a country girl, and it is only after teacher and pupil have utterly lost their way "in valleys and in mountains where no path is perceived" (IV, 773) that they find her, in a place so remote that it reminds Emile "of Homer's time [when] one hardly traveled, and travelers were well received by all" (IV, 774). Setting up their residence at a half-day's foot journey away, the tutor is able to fine tune his pupil's affective investment by a carefully controlled schedule of visitation privileges. When, after several months of courtship, wedding proposals are finally made, the tutor whisks Emile off on a two-year-long grand tour, the ostensible purpose of which, as earlier noted, is to help Emile decide on his civic status by "deciding" to stay in the land of his birth, an outcome all the more predictable, of course, thanks to Emile's amorous as well as civic attachment (see IV, 853-55). His desire to return home to his beloved Sophie also preserves him from the temptations of the city and of other, less innocent women. As for Sophie, she does not accompany her husband-to-be on this trip or on any of his peregrinations, but awaits his return home, as the desexualized keeper of his hearth and intended mother of "his" children (the "proper destination" of women, writes Rousseau, IV, 698). Only in this way can the *oikos* be preserved from the detour or "perversion" that women signify in the Rousseauian universe. As such, Rousseau's celebrated desire for a return to nature is perhaps less a yearning for some pre-Oedipal maternity than a desire for that ultimate *point de repère*, the father, for whom Sophie is but an imperfect stand-in, one whose precarious substitutability can be seen to follow what Derrida has described as the "logic of the supplement."[18]

Oedipal Returns; The Law of Succession: *Emile and Sophie; or, The Solitary Ones*

If the pedagogical logic of successive voyages can be construed as a strategy to master the dangerous detour of otherness emblematized by women, another kind of succession is equally targeted by the tutor's method, namely, the son's succeeding to the father's place as ruler of the home. At the same time that Emile is able to go voyaging and gains the right to accept or renounce his citizenship, he also gains the right to accept or renounce "his father's succession" (*Emile,* IV, 833), the renunciation of which can be carried out simply by leaving the home and not coming back. The succession of travel in *Emile* leads to Emile's right of succession, that is, to the establishment of his own paternity, consecrated in the child he begets. Emile will then face the task of educating his child according to the precepts of *Emile,* all of which means that his own education is completed by his becoming a simulacrum of his father/teacher.[19] Fatherhood is fulfilled by making one's son another father, thus establishing a structure of repetition—although to the extent that the anterior term (the father) is considered superior to and has jurisdiction over the latter (the son), the relation remains more what the text itself calls "succession," a term implying not the discontinuity of repetition but a temporal continuity achieved by the positing of a first term as the cause or precondition for the second term. At the same time, the second term is seen to build upon or add to what is already implied in the first term. A result of this relation of succession is the son's dependency on the father. Emile still needs his tutor/father at the end of *Emile* as an advisor and as a model to imitate: "Stay the master of the young masters. Advise us, govern us, we will be docile: as long as I live, I will need you. I need you more than ever, now that my functions as a man are beginning. You have fulfilled your functions; guide me so that I may imitate you, and take a rest, it is time for that" (*Emile,* IV, 868). These are the final words of the text of *Emile.* As we shall see in the sequel, disaster arrives when the father abandons the *domus* (to the son).

The father, therefore, incarnates the good economics of the home as *oikos.*[20] Hence, it is not surprising that travel abroad should be seen as a denial of the father concomitant with a seduction by women. And if the right to voyage is concurrent with the right to renounce the father, the accomplishment of the voyage with the return home affirms in a positive fashion the son's relation to his father. The return home makes the son worthy of becoming a father in his own right, that is, of succeeding the father. The succession of father and son then plays itself out through the narrative of the prodigal son.

It is surely no accident that the only two works of literature the tutor allows to become a part of Emile's education, *Robinson Crusoe* and Féne-lon's *Télémaque,* both confront the question of the father in terms of the voyage. The story of *Robinson Crusoe* (1718) explicitly relates travel to the rejection of the father, for the hero's misfortunes at sea leading up to his shipwreck on the famous island where he remains a castaway for twenty-four years are consequent to his disobeying his father's advice and commands not to travel. This disobedience of the paternal law of the *oikos* is construed as sinful. It is only through establishing and maintaining a home on his island, by domesticating it, that Robinson Crusoe is able to redeem himself in God's eyes (through his conversion) and to learn the lessons of the father. *Robinson Crusoe* is thus easily read as an allegory of atonement for sins against (God) the father.

Fénelon's *Télémaque* (1699) offers the story of a voyage that is simultaneously a search for the father and the means by which the son acquires his maturity or manhood. This maturation is accomplished precisely through the son's imitation of his father's voyages. Télémaque must become worthy of his father by undergoing a series of adventures reminiscent of those in the *Iliad* and the *Odyssey.* Télémaque both gains wisdom in exchange for his pains under the tutelage of Minerva, the goddess of wisdom disguised as Mentor,[21] and learns to value his own father and homeland through the contrast provided by other fathers (kings) and countries. But if the end of Télémaque's travails is to make him a worthy successor to Ulysse through the establishment of a mimetic relation between them, what is Fénelon's work if not a text that attempts to be a worthy successor to the *Odyssey* by miming it (a mimicry, though, that also opens the text up to the long tradition of its parody, from Marivaux's *Le Télémaque travesti* [1736] through Aragon's *Les aventures de Télémaque* [1966])? This mimetic vertigo is further exacerbated by Rousseau's describing the voyage of Emile and his teacher as itself an imitation of *Télémaque,* one whose itinerary can accordingly be supplied by the reader: "So I make him read *Télémaque* and follow his route: we seek happy Salentum and the good Idomeneus made wise by dint of misfortunes. Along the way, we find many Protesilas and no Philocles. . . . But let us leave the reader to imagine our travels, or have them undertake these travels in our place, a copy of *Télémaque* in hand" (IV, 849). To make matters brief, in these texts, and on several different levels within these texts, the resolution of the son's relation to the father is effected through the former's imitation of the latter. The destiny of Emile is in emulation.[22]

Emile's negative education is thus predicated upon a law of parental succession, which is itself a law of resemblances that nonetheless maintains a hierarchy of the resembled (father) over the resembling (son). The son can only succeed the father if he can establish a relation of resemblance between himself and his father. But this states the necessity for the son of *making* himself like the father, of making what distinguishes the father part of himself, of internalizing his fatherliness. Thus the institution of the law of the father in such a way that it makes the son worthy of succeeding him, that is, of becoming a father in his own turn. And yet, this metaphorical process of internalization or incorporation, this institutionalization of the father through such ceremonies as rites of passage and tests of lineage, must take place without the father.[23] It is up to the son to prove himself worthy of succeeding the father, because it is only if the son succeeds in resembling the father that he can be the son. Paradoxically, one must move away from the father in order to come near him, and here we begin to return to the problem of travel in *Emile:* just as one must turn oneself into one's home, so must one turn oneself into (the image of) one's father, but both of these transformations can only be effected by leaving home and father. The succession to fatherhood has the structure of a voyage (as the succession of places defining an itinerary to or from a home) insofar as the father becomes the point of reference (*oikos* or home) for the stabilization or domestication of family relationships. The succession of travel can only take place because (or be understood if) there is a home; the law of parental succession can only be carried out if a father is posited as a *point* of reference. The education of Emile attempts to ensure a smooth succession in both by maintaining the privilege of home and father even if it means that one must assume for oneself the role of home and father. We need to consider, though, what happens in the absence of home or father.

In *Emile*'s moral topography, the self-sufficient and patriarchal home in the country is opposed to the perverse, cannibalistic, and feminine interdependence of city life. Self-sufficiency and enclosure characterize the ideal *domus* to the point that the (male) subject must be willing and able to assume that *oikonomic* self-sufficiency in himself should the *domus* be lost. The sequel to *Emile*, the unfinished novel *Emile and Sophie; or, The Solitary Ones* can be read as an allegory of the loss of the *oikos*. The success story of *Emile* turns out in the sequel to be illusory and precariously fragile. It takes little more than the tutor's absence and Emile and Sophie's move to the city for all the peace and security gained through the "natural" education to be lost. On the most general level, one could resume the plot of *Emile and Sophie* as follows: because Emile and Sophie have left the paradise of home, they fall into a series of misfortunes that leaves Sophie pregnant by another man and Emile a vagabond who eventually finds himself a slave in Algiers. The denial of home, of the teachings of *Emile*, of one's origins, of the father, lead to disaster morally, economically, politically, and even physically. One can easily read onto this narrative the typically Rousseauist plot of the fall of man from nature as it is elaborated most explicitly in the two Discourses. If one were to follow the allegorization of these narratives as voyages, one would be tempted to conclude that the economy of travel in Rousseau would be one of loss; such an assertion would seem to be borne out by the negative pedagogical principles of *Emile*, which would try to preserve the "natural man" from such loss and therefore from travel (even if it means undertaking voyages as a means of keeping them from taking place).

A closer reading of the function of travel in *Emile and Sophie* reveals something more complex, however; for it is the structural *necessity* of travel that is not considered in this first reading of the novel, which only considers the voyage as a contingent or accidental fall (that is, as an unwise but essentially unmotivated decision). Why do Emile and Sophie leave paradise in the first place? A combination of circumstances: the departure of the tutor, the death of close family members (Sophie's father, mother, and daughter). In short, the Edenic happiness of the home has been lost. Home is no longer quite home, and what stands in its place serves only as a reminder of its loss: "All the objects which reminded [Sophie] of [her family] worsened her sorrows" (IV, 885). The only way to preserve home is to leave it, and so Emile resolves to "remove [*éloigner*] her from these sad places" (IV, 885). The home is to be conserved by its denial, a movement suggestive of the Hegelian *Aufhebung* by the negation of the home leading to its dialectical resolution at a higher level, that of travel as home. Nevertheless, the voyage away from home does not lead in this novel to a dialectical resolution of the problem, as the denial of the home does not succeed in preserving it but only provides the momentary illusion of preservation: the home away from home turns out to be even less of a home than its predecessor, and the flight to the city only triggers new and more irreparable disasters. These disasters in turn occasion new flights, new voyages on the part of Emile. We can thus detect the basic narrative structure of *Emile and Sophie:* the recuperation of the *oikos* through the flight away from it, a recuperation whose success is at best ambiguous. The loss of the home is denied by the affirmation of its loss, an affirmation the very enunciation of which is supposed to relocate or reinstate the home. It is as if by casting oneself out of the home one were casting out of the home whatever was interfering with its homeliness. The problem is that it is still oneself who is being cast out. As such, this narrative structure of mediation through flight is not simply infinitely repeatable; it implicitly requires that it *be* infinitely repeated as each loss (of home) can only be repaired through a strategy entailing a further loss, which in turn leads to further loss and so forth. Thus the voyage that is supposed to regain the home only leads to greater and greater losses (from Sophie's initial sorrow over deaths in the family to Emile's final captivity), even if all these losses are supposed to be recovered in the final proposed reunion of Emile and Sophie "in a desert island [*une île déserte*]."[24] Emile's ex-ile is to be brought to a close by the recovery of the home in the form of a utopic insularity that can already be read in his proper name: Em*ile*.

Such a conclusion would assert a redemptive return that closes the spiral of loss. It is the positing of such a circular movement that allows for the undertaking of the journey as an economic bid for the recovery of the *oikos.* One only sets out on the voyage because there is some assurance of recovering what one has lost or will have lost. Jean Starobinski speaks of a "joy of return" in Rousseau's work wherein the grief of departure is accepted insofar as it is a step or detour toward the pleasure of return or reconciliation.[25] While this hypothesis may be correct on the level of theme, it ignores a more complex structure in the economy of travel as circular completion, as what is asserted in *Emile and Sophie* is the paradoxical notion of departure as an arrival. Such an assertion disrupts any possible economy of travel by an uncontrollable proliferation of departures and arrivals, and therefore inevitably states the impossibility of coming to any final destination, and hence of completing the story: *Emile and Sophie* remains an unfinished (and unfinishable) novel.

A particularly strong example of this indeterminacy of departure and arrival occurs when Emile sets out on his journey away from Paris after Sophie's confession of infidelity. There it is that Emile comes back to himself (*revenant à moi* [IV, 898]) while leaving. The departure is a return to the self, in this case to the Emile formed by the lessons of the tutor, an Emile both more "natural" and morally superior to the one putatively depraved by city living and female infidelity: "I quietly *left* the house resolved never to go back. Here ends my lively but brief madness, and I came back into my good sense [*je rentrai dans mon bon sens*]" (IV, 894, emphasis added). Eschewing madness by reentering the "good sense" Descartes claimed no one ever found wanting in oneself, Emile is able to regain both meaning and direction in his new existence thanks to the "force" of the education given him by the tutor. At the same time, it allows him to return to a moral purity associated with that period in his life. Thus his voyage is also an allegorized moral journey in which he finds goodness and truth after the detour of error. But this is to forget that the detour is constitutive of the return, as error is of truth. It is only because one has set out on the journey that one can return, and so the flight from home or self becomes a necessary moment or movement in finding either one. But if the departure is paradoxically an arrival, then arrival calls for the perpetual departure emblematized in Emile's subsequent vagabond existence.

On the other hand, if one leaves in order to arrive where one supposedly already is, then the departure has already taken place before one leaves. One is neither at the point of departure nor at the point of arrival, and so one needs to affirm a departure and define a point of arrival in order to maintain the economy of the *domus* and of the voyage, of the voyage as *domus*. To repeat a point already made, Emile and Sophie only leave home when home has left them (the departure of the tutor and the demise of Sophie's parents and child—their departure, that is, on "the great voyage" that is death). Emile complains of a "repose worse than agitation" (V, 894). As in the case of Montaigne's idleness, what one thought was rest turns out to be another motion, and one all the more threatening because it takes place in the supposed place of rest, the home. According to the logic we have repeatedly seen, that motion in the home can only be immobilized if one affirms the motion of travel by leaving the home, by embarking on a voyage. To affirm travel is to give oneself the illusion that the motion (of travel) is caused by and therefore under the domestication of the traveler—with the implication that one is also capable of stopping that movement entirely. But this logic can easily be reversed to show that if rest is to be attained through travel, then the notion of rest is only an aftereffect of the movement of travel. It is only because one is already in motion that rest can or need be posited as a goal. What Emile does not realize when he speaks of taking "a great step toward repose" (IV, 905) is that any step in that direction must involve a step away from it: to move toward a state of rest means that one has moved away from it, since one is now more than ever in a state of motion.

What I would like to suggest is that even if the *domus* could be preserved in its domesticity, there remains something inherently undomesticatable or unhomelike (*unheimlich*) in the home, something that could be called a "repose worse than agitation." What *Emile and Sophie* enacts is the problem, only surreptitiously posed in *Emile*, of the inherent instability of the home. It is as if the home could not itself even be itself. It needs to be defended and protected (i.e., maintained as home) through what we saw in *Emile* to be a theory of patriotic duty.[26] But if the home is weak and cannot be depended upon to fulfill its very function of being home, then Emile's tutor is right to insist that Emile be able to survive even without the home. What does the home lack such that it cannot be depended upon or cannot even survive independently as home? An answer might be found if we turn back for a moment to the place in *Emile* where the student recounts to his tutor what he has learned in his voyages:

In my travels, I searched if I could find some corner of earth
where I could be absolutely mine; but in what place among men
does one no longer depend upon their passions? All things
considered, I found that my wish was itself contradictory; for had
I nothing else to hang onto, I would at least hold onto the land in
which I had fixed myself: my life would be attached to this land as
the land of the Dryads was attached to their trees. I have found
that power and liberty were two incompatible words; I could only
be the master of a thatched cottage by ceasing to be master of
myself. (IV, 856)

An opposition is drawn here between mastery of the home (*power, master of a thatched cottage*) and of the self (*freedom, master of myself*). Each of these tasks precludes the other. A home needs to be maintained as home, and thus demands a certain "attachment" that ties the subject to it, impairing his liberty. It is only a home to the extent to which it is *made* to be one. On the other hand, any instability in the home means the same for the subject dwelling in it. Witness Sophie's infidelity. The home is unreliable because it makes the subject dependent upon it, that is, upon something else besides himself.[27] Like the women enclosed within it or encountered outside it, the home itself becomes a treacherous detour in the economy of a (male) self, desirous of an absolute immediacy and autonomy.

The solution would seem to be for the subject to declare himself his own home, which means that he becomes his own master. For Rousseau, this is clearly the morally superior goal, which Emile achieves paradoxically only at the moment he loses his civic freedom. "I am freer than before," he concludes while locked in a Barbary prison (*Emile and Sophie,* IV, 916). This conclusion is sustained through a Stoic morality, which accentuates the difference between self and world by leveling all external influences or coercions to the same "law" or "yoke" of necessity: "From these reflections, I drew the consequence that my change of state was more apparent than real, that if freedom consisted in doing what one wanted, no man would be free; for all are weak, all are dependent upon things and upon harsh necessity; that he who most knows how to want what necessity commands is the freest, since he is never forced to do what he doesn't want" (IV, 917). Such Stoicism, patterned after Montaigne and the third rule of Descartes's provisional morality, allows the self to assert its autonomy at the very moment it accedes to all that it cannot master. It is a mere question of desiring what is already the case, a logic already implied in Emile's desire to travel as a way to master a movement already underway. That such a logic should become so clearly formulated at the time of Emile's captivity may seem ironic, yet it is nonetheless a proposition characteristic of the Rousseau who requested that he be kept in "perpetual captivity" on the island of Saint-Pierre, and who stated elsewhere that he could be free and happy even were he locked in the Bastille.[28] The advantage of the morality of self-domestication is that it can adapt to any contingent circumstances while claiming that contingency as willed: "The time of my servitude was that of my reign, and never had I such authority over myself as when I bore the fetters of the barbarians" (IV, 917). This servitude gives rise to a pedagogical experience rivaling that of the tutor himself: "Their deviances were for me livelier instructions than your lessons had ever been, and under these rough masters, I took a course in philosophy much more useful than the one I took with you" (IV, 917). Why is this education "more useful" than the first, if not because it is not dependent on another's instruction? Emile learns philosophy by attaining the ideal of the autodidact. After this apprenticeship, he begins his rise in Algerian society as a parvenu, using only his own wits. Everything is to the subject's credit, his losses as well as his gains.

The same stance allows for a leveling of all geographical and cultural differences: Emile's adaptability is credited with making him "a man who feels in his place everywhere" (IV, 906). Emile is everywhere at home because he *is* his own home. The qualification of always being "in my place" corroborates this thesis: "Thus, I was always in my place" (IV, 913); "What did I do in being born if not commence a voyage which should only finish with my death? I perform my task, I stay in my place [*à ma place*]" (IV, 914). This last citation clearly states the paradoxical economy of travel as nontravel. In fact, travel can no longer be rigorously understood when all lands become one's homeland: "Everywhere I passed for a native inhabitant" (IV, 913); "In breaking the knots that attached me to my country, I extended it to include the whole earth" (IV, 912). It is interesting that the gap between the self as home and the entire world as home should be so small. It is as if the self being assured, all else could be domesticated. Rousseau thus follows the itinerary charted by Montaigne, Descartes, and Montesquieu.

Concomitantly, though, the problem of the self has become a topographical one: "In order to know the universe in every way that could interest me, it suffices for me to know myself; with my place assigned, all is found" (IV, 883). If the assignation of one's place founds self-knowledge, which in turn suffices for knowledge about the universe, then all knowledge devolves from the answer to the question "*where* am I?" (as opposed to "who" or "what am I?").[29] But if one finds oneself (to be at home) anywhere and everywhere, one only finds oneself wherever one looks. The self reduced to locating itself by its topographical position is a solitary one. No one else is there when one is everywhere. Perhaps this is the sense of the story's subtitle, *The Solitary Ones*. It seems that for Rousseau, to find or refind oneself is to find oneself alone, and it is this solipsistic implication of the topographical understanding of the self that is described most strikingly in the strange world of the *Reveries of a Solitary Walker,* which begins, "Here am I, then, alone upon the earth" (I, 995). The bleak world in which the narrator, Emile, finds himself at the beginning of *Emile and Sophie* thus prefigures that of the First Reverie. Both describe the world around the narrator as a nowhere in which it is difficult, if not impossible, to find one's bearings. The narrator of *Emile and Sophie* describes himself as being in a "land of exile" (IV, 882); in the First Reverie, the narrator says that he is "on this earth as upon a foreign planet" (I, 999).

But if in the First Reverie, this disorientation would seem to be domesticated through a recentering of the discourse onto the speaking subject, in *Emile and Sophie* the only point of reference the narrator can find is his old tutor, whom he addresses as both "master" and "father":

> But you, my dear master, do you live? Are you still mortal? Are
> you still in this earthly land of exile [*cette terre d'éxil*] with your
> Emile, or do you already with Sophie inhabit the fatherland of just
> souls [*la patrie des ames justes*]? Alas! wherever you are, you are
> dead for me, my eyes will never see you again, but my heart will
> incessantly be preoccupied with you. Never have I better known the
> value of your caring as after harsh necessity had so cruelly made
> me feel its blows and had taken everything from me except me. I
> am alone, I have lost everything, but I remain to myself, and

despair has not overwhelmed me. These pages will not reach you, I cannot hope that they do. Undoubtedly, they will perish unseen by any man: but it does not matter, they have been written, I collate them, I bind them, I continue to write them, and it is to you that I address them: it is to you that I want to trace these precious memories that nourish and break my heart; it is to you that I want to give an account of myself, of my feelings, of my behavior, of this heart that you have given me. (IV, 882)

If Emile is lost in a "land of exile," that is, away from the island or "île" he would love as "aime-île," the tutor is either also in this land of exile (in which case he is still "with" Emile and can be invoked), or already in "the fatherland of just souls," a periphrasis for heaven. But if the tutor is dead and in heaven, he is also in the "fatherland of the just," where as father he justly belongs. Given that the morality of the tutor cannot be put into question at the level of Emile's comprehension of him, and given that the tutor is called "my father" by Emile, then the tutor's location in "the fatherland of just souls" becomes a tautology to the extent that the just father is where he belongs, in the fatherland of the just. So if the tutor is dead and cannot be reached by Emile's discourse, it is because he is in his proper dwelling place, the safe home or isle of refuge which is *out* of (or not in) the ex-ile. The father is at home, where the son would like to be but is not.

But then, in a surprising move, it suddenly turns out that it does not matter to the son where the father is: "Wherever you are, you are dead for me, my eyes will never see you again." It does not even matter if Emile's words never reach the tutor: "These pages will not reach you, I cannot hope that they do. Undoubtedly, they will perish unseen by any man: but it does not matter, they have been written, I collate them, I bind them, I continue to write them, and it is to you that I address them: it is to you that I want to trace these precious memories." The father is therefore only there to fill the discursive position of addressee. Whether the message ever reaches the receiver or not is of less importance than that the message be addressed to him, in other words, that the enunciation of the discourse take place. In addressing the father, who as far as the speaker is concerned ("you are dead *for me*") is out of exile and back at the home to which the speaker has no hope of returning, the speaker's task seems less that of attempting a hopeless communication than of finding a point of reference toward which the discourse can be addressed and around which it can be articulated. The speaker's predicament, as textual as it is topographical, finds issue in the positing of a certain *oikos* (the father as interlocutor), a *foyer* around which the discourse can be domesticated within the safe confines of a communicative act produced by and under the mastery of the speaker. The father, then, is the fatherland in relation to which the speaker's discursive wandering can take place without fear of loss or infinitude. In other words, because there is an addressee, there can be an addressor who sends a message to him. The speaker can speak because there is someone to speak to. Rousseau's grounding of the possibility of discourse in the determination of the *addressee* would thus seem to reverse Descartes's discursive grounding in the place of the *addressor.*

This formulation of the problem suggests another, however, in which the subject of the discourse entirely eludes the necessity of an interlocutor for the constitution of his own subjectivity by positing the addressee as a fiction, albeit a necessary one.[30] It is this fictionality of the addressee, of the father, of the *oikos,* that Rousseau's text demonstrates at the very moment that those principles are invoked as origins. It seems to matter less that these terms exist than that they be posited as such, as points of reference in relation to which all else can be placed and thereby mastered. At the same time, such necessary or theoretical fictions pose what seems to be an insurmountable dilemma: How can the fiction be recognized as both necessary and fictive, for the fiction would only fulfill its function of domestication if it were denied as fiction, that is, if it were accepted as truth? In other words, one must act *as if* the fiction were true in order to make it work. A *necessary* fiction cannot be posited as fiction . . . and yet this is precisely what Rousseau's text works to do whether that fiction be called nature, origin, home, or father.[31]

To make of the father such a necessary fiction cannot be without consequences, though, for the law of succession that posits the father as the son's ultimate reference point. If it is up to the son to become the father in the latter's absence, does this not mean that the son either makes himself into the father or himself makes the father (a problem of self-engenderment not unlike that posed by the autobiographical project of Montaigne)? Is it not the son who, in the rite of succession, defines the law of the father not by defining himself as son but by defining his father as father? But if the father is only defined as such so that the son can constitute himself as son, then at the same time that the father is privileged (as origin, as law) he is denounced as a fiction engendered by the son. The son turns out to be the father of the father, but to say this is to upset the very law of succesion set up by the son as the rule of the father. Somehow, for the paternalistic pedagogue that is Rousseau (whose own father had abandoned him before he, in turn, had notoriously abandoned his children to a public orphanage), the father must not be denied the authority and anteriority attributed to him by the son, for it is those attributes that define him as father. Nor must the father appear as a fiction of the son, and yet this is what happens in *Emile and Sophie,* both when Emile addresses his tutor as his father (since we know from *Emile* that the tutor is *not* Emile's father) and when he addresses him regardless of his being alive or dead, or of his being able to receive the message or not. At the same time, however, that the rule of the father seems to become in Emile's discourse only a fiction enabling that discourse to take place, Emile's invocation of his "father" takes on a note of pathos as Emile credits his own abilities to withstand misfortunes to the pedagogical work of his "father." The relation of succession thus implies both a nostalgia or desire for the anterior term and an assertion of its loss. In terms of travel, a desire for a return (to the home, to nature, to the origin) is uttered at the same time as the impossibility of the return. In terms of Rousseau's pedagogical project, the "natural" education, as he himself admits, is "from its first steps already outside nature" (IV, 259).

Walking and Writing: *Confessions*

To recapitulate, the placement of travel within the succession of experiences that make up Emile's education not only bespeaks the latter's larger itinerary as being itself a voyage but also reveals in its successive displacements the workings of an Oedipal nostalgia, of an impossible desire to return to a (paternal) home that, like nature in the Second Discourse, no longer is, and no doubt never was, because it can only be posited after the fact and in the wake of its loss. This logic or movement of succession, which retroactively posits a first term (origin, nature, father) as the cause or temporal precondition of a second one (history, culture, son), is endemic not only to Rousseau's pedagogical and political theories but also to the genre of autobiography practiced (or even, some would say, invented) by him.[32] Rousseau's *Confessions* differ from the kind of self-portrait exemplified, for example, in the *Essays* of Montaigne by the desire to explain his life through the recounting of its events in the order in which they took place. The notion of succession allows, then, for the hypothesis that because a particular event took place in one's youth or childhood (the mother's death in childbirth, a broken comb, a stolen ribbon) any subsequent misfortunes are but the inevitable consequence of that event.[33] (Such moments are marked in the *Confessions* by the refrain, "Here begins the tale of my misfortunes," whose very repetitiveness begins to deconstruct the *post hoc, propter hoc* fiction of succession.)

The first of these "misfortunes" Rousseau describes in the *Confessions* is his birth itself, which brings about his mother's death, but the resultant motherless home also remains a marvelous object of nostalgia for a Jean-Jacques who remembers the warm closeness of a father whose sentimental bond to his son was grounded in the latter's resemblance to his lost wife and solidified by their joint reading of novels until late at night. This wondrously idyllic symbiosis between father and son is broken when Rousseau senior, embroiled with a French officer and threatened with time in prison, is obliged to flee Geneva and "expatriate himself [*s'expatrier*] for the rest of his life" (I, 12), leaving his son to the tutelage of his brother-in-law, who pensions the young Jean-Jacques in Bossy with the Lambercier family. The succeeding events of book I, culminating in the famous closing of the city gates of Geneva on the hapless adolescent out for a walk "not even dreaming of returning" (I, 41), progressively distance Rousseau from the paternal home, thus expatriating him into (what he considers) greater and greater misfortune. The subsequent books of the *Confessions* can thus be seen to constitute a vast journey, roughly broken between the vagabond years of his youth (books II–VII) and the unending series of flights from "persecution" in the aftermath of his sudden rise to celebrity as the author of the *Discourse* of 1751 (books VIII–XII).

Book II already plots out a psychogeography that enframes in general Rousseau's itinerant existence ("my ambulatory mania", [I, 54]) and that is commensurate with what was found in *Emile*. Pursuant to his expatriation from Geneva, Rousseau wanders about [*j'errai*] until he meets the woman he will later so affectionately call "Maman," Mme. de Warens, living in Annecy amidst the Savoy mountain peaks and valleys, not unlike the terrain where Emile finally locates Sophie. Not only does this Alpine terrain connote a maternal and rural innocence (erotically evoked in such images as his fantasizing "vats of milk and cream on the mountain-sides" [I, 58]) but it invigorates the young Jean-Jacques with an almost literal sense of superiority: "For me, it seemed lovely to cross the mountains at my age, and to rise superior [*m'élever au dessus*] to my comrades by the full height of the Alps [*de toute la hauteur des alpes*]" (I, 54).[34] This sense of elevation continues as Rousseau crosses over on foot into Italy, a traversal he cannot resist describing with the kind of imperialistic allusion typical of French travelers to the region: "To be traveling in Italy so young, to have seen so many countries already, to be following in Hannibal's footsteps across the mountains [*suivre Annibal à travers les mons*], seemed to me a glory above my years [*au dessus de mon age*]" (I, 58). Indeed, the entire experience is said to explain one of Rousseau's lifelong passions: "This memory has left me the strongest taste for everything associated with it, for mountains especially and for traveling on foot [*les voyages pedestres*]" (I, 59).

Rousseau's Alpine epiphany is brought to a sudden halt, however, by his arrival in Turin, the great city at the beginning of the Northern Italian plain carved out by the Po river. It is here that the young Swiss runaway has been sent in order formally to abjure his Calvinist faith in favor of Roman Catholicism. A most powerful set of boundaries is thus already sketched out as country meets city and mountain encounters plain, with the difference between religions redoubled by the difference between the French and the Italian languages. Small wonder that a high hill overlooking Turin should have provided the setting for the moralistic injunctions set forth by Rousseau in the *Profession of Faith of a Savoyard Vicar* (IV, 565), or that his spirited defense of that work against the attack spearheaded by Jean-Robert Tronchin's *Lettres écrites de la campagne* (1763) should have seized the moral high ground with its rejoining title of *Lettres écrites de la montagne* (1764). But if for the likes of Montaigne, Descartes, and Montesquieu, the Alps could only represent a nuisance, a geographical obstacle to be overcome on their way to cisalpine adventure, for Rousseau they are that from which there is literally nowhere to go but down: "My regret at reaching Turin so quickly was tempered by the pleasure of seeing a great city and the hope of soon cutting there a figure worthy of myself. For the fumes of ambition were *rising to my head*, and already I regarded myself as *infinitely above* my old position of apprentice. I was far from foreseeing that in a very short time, I should fall considerably *below* it" (I, 59; emphasis added). And indeed in this land of Piemonte, situated at the foot of the mountains, Rousseau only finds what he views as base and ugly. To his horror, he finds himself lodging with both cultural and religious others ("Jews and Moors," and all kinds of Catholic Italians) and sexual others (homosexuals, courtesans, "the greatest sluts and most villainous whores" [I, 60]). If for Montaigne the charm of Italy was not far removed from a blissful morbidity, Rousseau's peninsular experience is that of a fearful and perverse sexuality, which he discovers in himself as well as in others. Residing in Turin at the very same time as Montesquieu, who saw it as a rather dull town in comparison to the ludic excitement of Venice and Milan,[35] Rousseau undergoes one perverse misadventure after another (leaving him, as he says, "not my virginity, but my maidenhead [*non ma virginité, mais mon pucelage*]" [I, 108]), from his being the object of a homosexual passion, to his unconsummated adultery with Mme. Basile, to his exhibitionist antics, to the inception of his onanism. It is also during this time that he falsely accused the servant girl Marion of having stolen the ribbon he had himself pilfered, and so committed the heinous deed that would forever weigh on his conscience. And years later, during his sojourn in Venice, Rousseau's view of Catholic Italy as urban depravity was no doubt reconfirmed by his disastrous adventure with the courtesan Zulietta, the sight of whose malformed or "blind" nipple (*téton borgne*) leaves Rousseau impotent, as if the blinding absence of the maternal nipple triggered a return of his repressed fear of women: "I saw as clear as daylight that instead of the most charming person I could possibly imagine I held in my arms some kind of monster" (I, 322).[36] It is in Venice too that

Rousseau claims to have gotten the idea for making Emile fall in love prior to his departure on the grand tour, whose stereotypical destination was Italy. The governor of a young Englishman would have prevented the latter's corruption at the hands of a Venetian lady by the lad's prior engagement with an English woman, news of whom would have kept him true to her (*Emile,* IV, 853).

Georges May's celebrated analysis of Rousseau's relation to women as split between asexual blonds and overtly sexual brunettes[37] would thus seem to find a geographical corollary in the opposition between Switzerland and Italy. The third country in which the peregrinations described in the *Confessions* occur is France, where there is a conjugation of the two poles, rural tranquillity and Parisian decadence, blonds and brunettes, Mme. de Chenonceaux and Mme. de Larnage, Thérèse Levasseur and the Comtesse d'Houdetot. The *Confessions* end with Rousseau's departure for England, a country where no women at all figure in Rousseau's imaginary; there he was uniquely preoccupied by his shifting relations with powerful men such as David Hume, James Boswell, and even King George III.[38] What one could call Rousseau's "Carte du Tendre" is again amply played out in *La Nouvelle Héloïse,* where the rural sanctity of Clarens contrasts both with the corruption of a Paris dominated by "loose women" and with Milord Edouard's erotic misadventures in Rome. More significantly, the moral purity and "goodness" of that Swiss *topos* is secured by that sternest of Rousseauian father figures, M. de Wolmar, who panoptically stands behind the ethereal and blond Julie as the unquestioned ruler of Clarens and guarantor of the home.[39] That this ultimate return to the patriarchal home can only take place in or as a fiction reconfirms the logic of succession adumbrated by the traveling in *Emile* and its sequel.

To understand the *Confessions* as a kind of extended voyage narrative nonetheless also requires accounting for another kind of return. Rousseau's autobiography is not a travelogue, like those written by Montaigne and Montesquieu, whose notations were compiled while on the road or shortly thereafter; it is a narrativized sequence of recollections, written years later, that mimes the succession of events in Rousseau's life, their return in writing as the accumulated experience of the book's signatory. If travel, pursuant to the logic of succession, simultaneously posits a desire for a return and the impossibility of its realization, then in terms of autobiography, the dread detour of travel would correspond to what risks not coming back to the autobiographer's memory, to what escapes his consciousness: the moment of forgetfulness that is the temporal precondition for the *remem-brance* of a memory to occur as an event. This dilemma is explicitly discussed in a passage of book IV of the *Confessions* in terms of Rousseau's regretful failure to write a travelogue: "In thinking over the details of my life which are lost to my memory, what I most regret is that I did not keep journals of my travels" (I, 162). Because his travels were not written down at the time they took place, they can no longer be remembered. But if travel takes place outside of memory and writing, one thing *is* remembered: "Never did I think so much, exist so much, live so much, be myself so much—if I may speak in such a way—as in the journeys I have taken alone and on foot." Rousseau's voyages imply a moment of plenitude (of intellection, of being, of selfhood) that no longer exists. Hence the nostalgic desire to remember them and the frustration at not being able to. Not having been put into writing, these moments of epiphany can no longer be recollected except for the mere fact that they were moments of epiphany, and as such, deserving to be remembered.[40]

One further detail does stand out, though—these voyages were of a specific kind, namely "alone and on foot." The celebrated image of Rousseau as *promeneur solitaire* (solitary walker) surfaces in this passage and imputes a powerful immediacy to the act of walking alone: travel without the mediation of a means of transportation or even of companionship. Lacking the cultural as well as the physical elevation and chivalric ease a horse can give, or the protective enclosure found in boats and carriages, walking is the least socially prestigious mode of transportation, the most plebeian way to get around, but it is also the most independent and least reliant upon some vehicular means of propulsion that could bring about the traveler's downfall or standstill:

> I can conceive of only one means of traveling that is more
> agreeable than going horseback, and that is to go on foot. You
> leave when you want, stop at will, do as much or as little exercise
> as you want. You see the whole country; you turn off on the right,
> or on the left. You examine everything that pleases you, you stop
> at every lookout point. If I notice a river, I coast by it. A thicket?
> I go under its shade. A grotto? I visit it. A quarry? I examine the
> stone. Wherever it pleases me, I stay. The moment I am bored, I
> leave. I depend neither on horses nor on postilion. I have no need
> to choose finished roads or convenient routes. I pass wherever a
> man may pass; I see all that a man can see, and since I depend on
> no one other than me, I enjoy all the freedom a man can enjoy.
> (*Emile,* IV, 771-72)

Low, slow, and exposed but utterly self-reliant, the walker's apparent dependence on no power other than his own would seem to make him an ideal image for the autotelic fiction of an absolute return to oneself, for the positing of oneself as home, which is able to sidestep even the already very limited detour through fatherhood. Such unmediated bliss is nonetheless placed irrevocably in the past by the Rousseau of the *Confessions:*

"I traveled on foot only in my prime and always with delight. Duties, business and luggage to carry soon forced me to play the gentleman and to hire carriages; then gnawing cares, troubles and anxiety climbed in with me, and from that moment, instead of feeling as I once had only the pleasures of being on the road, I was conscious of nothing but the need to arrive at my destination" (*Confessions,* I, 59). If the adult world of horses and carriages has replaced the child's pleasure in walking, it is because the immediacy of the latter has given way to the mediatory injunctions of the former, which turns transportation into a mere means to an all-consuming end. This kind of teleology, already denounced by Rousseau in the "Of Voyages" section of *Emile,* is what the tutor resists when traveling with his young pupil:

> We do not travel then as couriers but as travelers. We think not
> only of the two endpoints, but also of the interval that separates
> them. The journey itself is a pleasure for us. We do not undertake
> it grimly sitting and as if imprisoned in a little, tightly closed cage.
> We do not travel with the ease and comfort of women. We do not
> deprive ourselves of the fresh air, nor the sight of the surrounding
> objects, nor the convenience of contemplating them to our liking
> when it pleases us. Emile never entered a post-chaise, and scarcely
> travels post-haste unless he is rushed. . . . When all you want to do
> is to arrive, you can dash in a post-chaise; but when you want to
> travel, you must go on foot. (IV, 771-73)

The nostalgia for walking bespeaks the subject's insertion within a social symbolic whose ideology of "arrival" is viewed by him as imprisoning, feminizing, suffocating, blinding, unhealthy, and disruptive of thought. But if this horsedrawn world thus encodes a metaphorics of castration, it also evokes that period of hurried carriage flights from arrest and persecution, when the urgent "need to arrive" at some safe place drove Rousseau after 1762 across wide stretches of France, Switzerland, and England. This also, interestingly enough, corresponds to the period of his dressing up in "Armenian" style, whose loose-fitting robes inscribed a certain femininity into his attire even as they allowed easier access for the catheter he needed to treat the urinary retention from which he suffered. Long convinced, up until the medical examination urged upon him by the Duke of Luxembourg, that he suffered from gallstones (*Confessions,* I, 571-72), Rousseau could also no longer stand to read his philosophical forebear and that lover of horse travel, Michel de Montaigne.[41]

In contrast to this world of sickness and melancholy, wherein one brings one's woes along with one's baggage, the youthful ambiance of walking appears healthy, emotionally uplifting, and morally liberating: "How many different pleasures one brings together by this pleasant way to travel! Not to mention firmer health and a more pleasant humor. I have always seen those who traveled in good, soft carriages to be distracted, unhappy, scolding or suffering and pedestrians to be always gay, light-hearted and content with everything" (*Emile*, IV, 773). In the *Confessions,* Rousseau adds: "The sight of the countryside, the succession of pleasant views, the open air, a sound appetite, and the good health I gain by walking, the free atmosphere of an inn, the disappearance of everything that makes me feel my dependence, of everything that recalls me to my situation—all this serves to disengage my soul, to lend a greater boldness to my thinking, to throw me, so to speak, into the vastness of beings, so that I might combine them, select them, and appropriate them as I will, without fear or restraint" (I, 162). We have here an enumeration of the positive qualities of walking: the successive contact with the aesthetic beauty of nature, improved respiration and appetite, good health, freedom, and the feeling of one's own independence. Basically, these can be broken down into three qualities— aesthetic pleasure, corporeal well-being, and self-sufficiency—which are gained through this type of travel. Freedom, independence, and good health are linked with a sense of the self's autonomy before a "natural" world reduced to an object of aesthetic pleasure. The stroller's sense of self-sufficiency, which throws him into the "immensity of beings," allows his soul to be released ("all this serves to disengage my soul") and his thoughts to become more "bold." Walking is further linked to the production of philosophical ideas (and therefore to the walker's status as a philosopher): "Walking has something that animates and enlivens my ideas: I almost cannot think when I stay in place; my body needs to be in motion for my mind to be there." As opposed to the corporeal stability required for Descartes's meditative journeys, Rousseau's locomotion of the mind can only be triggered by that of the body: "I can only meditate while walking; as soon as I stop, I stop thinking, and my head goes only with my feet" (I, 410). In fact, the philosopher has his finest hour in Rousseau as a contemplative walker: "To travel on foot is to travel like Thales, Plato, and Pythagoras. I have difficulty understanding how a philosopher can bring himself to travel any other way and to tear himself from the investigation of the riches that he tramples underfoot and that the earth lavishes for his gaze. . . . Your salon-dwelling philosophers [*philosophes de ruelles*] study natural history in their studies; they have all sorts of fancy goods, they know names and they haven't got an idea about nature. But Emile's study is richer than those of kings; this study is the whole earth" (*Emile,* IV, 772). The recurrence in this passage of the same three philosophers whom the Second Discourse named as examples of the kind of philosophical expertise travelers should have *before* setting out on their travels begs the question of what it takes to be such a philosopher, if it is not *already* to engage in a particular mode of travel, that is, walking. Would it not be the very immediacy of the walker within the walking environment and his all-encompassing view of it—"You see the *whole* country. . . . You examine *everything* that pleases you; you stop at *all* the lookout points" (*Emile*, IV, 772; emphasis added)—that ultimately brings home the lesson that one does not have very far to go, that home is where one is and that one's task is to retire into oneself (as in the Rousseauist refrain of "to go back into oneself [*rentrer en soi-même*]") rather than vainly attempting to arrive at something beyond it? Rejecting the equine world of the symbolic, Rousseau flees into the imaginary world of the solitary pedestrian, the impossibility of whose return to the pleasures of childhood is circumvented by the triumph of his fictional autonomy. Imaginarily "populating" this world with "beings after my own heart," as he writes in the third Letter to Maleherbes, Rousseau locates the source of his fictional works as well as of his philosophical ideas in the practice of walking.[42] As he writes in the *Confessions:* "I dispose of all nature as its master. My heart, as it strays from one object to another, unites and identifies itself with those which soothe it, wraps itself in pleasant imaginings, and grows drunk on feelings of delight. If, in order to fix them down, I amuse myself by describing them to myself, what vigorous brush-strokes, what freshness of color, what expressive energy I bring to them!" (I, 162). The charming objects and delicious feelings encountered during the walk through nature are thus "fixed" through an inner description ("describing them to myself"). Horizontalizing Montesquieu's visual "fixing" of the landscape by postulating its movement not as up to down but as outside to inside, Rousseau also implies an aesthetic efficacy to this "fixing," that is, to the subject's ability to produce a faithful representation to himself of the charming object through his recourse to metaphors of painting (brush-strokes, color). The representation is faithful (true to life) insofar as it renders present the life of the object (vigorous, freshness, energy) even though that presentation of the object's life is credited to the subject's demiurgic mastery: "What expressive energy I bring to them." Is it not this vitalistic power of representing the world to oneself, of "fixing" internally what is perceived externally, that is the source of the subject's pleasure in his solitary walks and what he later graces by the appelation "reverie"?

This power of representation is further stated to be characteristic of Jean-Jacques's writings: "All this, I am told, people have found in my works, although they have been written in my declining years. Oh, if only they had seen those of my early youth, those I sketched during my travels, those I composed but never wrote down."[43] Whatever the expressivity or vivaciousness of Rousseau's writings, they are nevertheless said to lack the vitality of his travel thoughts as old age lacks the vigor of youth. In accordance once again with the logic of succession that privileges the earlier but also irrecoverably lost term over its successor, the earlier "composed" but unwritten works are considered superior to the later written and published ones, even as the former implicitly appear as irretrievable as the latter are paler and less inspired: "Why do I not write them, you will ask? But why should I?, I reply. Why rob myself of the present charm of their enjoyment, to tell others that I enjoyed them once? What did readers matter to me, or a public, or the whole world, while I was soaring in the skies?"[44] If the unwritten works were not written, it is because the writing of them would have destroyed their obviously autoerotic charm. To state the subject's enjoyment would be to do away with it. As Rousseau notes in the Fifth Reverie, one can never say one is happy without placing oneself outside the state of happiness (I, 1046).[45] Furthermore, insofar as the subject's pleasure in his fiction is that of the sense of his own autonomy, it must be a solitary pleasure. If the pleasure is to be maintained, the fiction must be left uncommunicated, but then the pleasure of the fiction is such that it makes whatever remains outside of it inconsequential: "What did readers matter to me, or a public, or the whole world, while I was soaring in the skies?"

But there is another reason Rousseau gives in this same passage from the *Confessions* for not writing the walker's reverie: "Besides, did I carry paper with me, or pens? If I had thought of all that, nothing would have come to me. I did not foresee that I would have ideas. They arrive when they please, not when it pleases me. Either they do not come at all, or they come in a swarm, overwhelming me with their strength and their numbers. Ten volumes a day would not have been enough" (I, 162-63). The text of the voyage depends upon the absence of writing instruments and even of the intention to write. The *plume* as pen prevents the use of the *plume* as feather in the metaphorical flight of the subject's reverie, and thus also prevents the fulfillment of its inscriptional function as pen. The charm of the walk cannot be written down without a writing instrument, but it cannot even occur if there is so much as the threat of writing: "If I had thought of all that, nothing would have come to me."[46] The subject cannot foresee that ideas will come to him. It is, in fact, not up to him to produce fictions or ideas, to charm himself; rather, it is the ideas or fictions that come to him "when they please, not when it pleases me," that is, it is for him *to be* charmed. So the walker does not go to his reverie; the latter comes to him. All that he can do by his walk is to put himself in a position of receptivity vis-à-vis the reverie. Contradicting his assertions that his ideas are animated by his walking, the real promenade only begins when the *promeneur* has stopped moving: "The movement which does not come from without, then, is made within us" (*Reveries, I, 1048*). Such is the lesson of the Fifth Reverie, which attempts to prescribe the conditions for the occurrence of a reverie: "It is true that these consolations cannot be felt by all souls, nor in all situations. It is necessary that the heart should be at peace and that no passion should come to trouble the charm. Certain dispositions on the part of the man who experiences them are necessary; it is also necessary in the getting together of the surrounding objects. There is needed neither an absolute repose nor too much agitation" (I, 1047).

If and when the reverie occurs, it is overwhelming, as the *Confessions* note: "Either [ideas] do not come at all, or they come in a swarm, overwhelming me with their strength and their numbers. Ten volumes a day would not have been enough" (I, 162-63). Instead of too few ideas, there are now too many.[47] This situation in which the influx of ideas or the production of fictions is overwhelming in force and number turns the problem of writing into one of adequation. So even if the subject wanted to write down these unwritten but composed works, and even if his intention to write and the availability of writing instuments did not prevent the thoughts from being triggered, there would still be neither time nor place to write everything down: "Where could I have found time to write them? When I arrived, my only thought was for a good dinner. When I set out, I thought only of a good walk. I felt that a new paradise awaited me at the door; I thought only of going out to find it" (I, 163). The success of writing depends upon the sedentary just as the success of the promenade demands the lack of writing. So, if on the one hand the Rousseau of the *Confessions* regrets his not having written down his travel experiences so that he could remember them, on the other hand he explains how those experiences could never possibly have been written down, or even have taken place had an attempt been made to write them down. Once again, and following the same logic as evinced in Rousseau's thoughts on travel in *Emile,* the nostalgia for these moments of pleasurable insight is posited at the same time as the impossibility of their being retained.[48]

In any case, the urgency of retaining the lost charm of foot travel surfaces throughout the autobiographical works, for no matter how overwhelming the reverie may be said to be, it is nonetheless understood as having a value of presence: "Never have I thought so much, existed so much, lived so much, been myself so much" And it is not only the subject's presence to himself and his sense of mastery that are concerned. It is also essential to the philosopher because the reverie provides him with a stock of ideas that then defines him *as* a philosopher: "I never do anything except during my strolls, the countryside is my study" ("Mon Portrait," I, 1128). But if the walk provides the philosopher with ideas, then he is dependent upon the continued vitality of the walk's charm. This vitality, however, is on the decline, as evidenced by Rousseau's assertion that his current experiences do not compare with "those of my early youth." Given his logic of succession, that "vitality" or "presence" is no doubt always already on the decline, incomparably below the heights of his youthful Alpine hike to Turin.

The "Fall" of Jean-Jacques Rousseau: Second Promenade

In the *Reveries,* written at the very end of his life, Rousseau is especially haunted by the fear that these charming experiences will disappear altogether, leaving him with no possibility of consolation. Doffing his Armenian garb upon his return from England in 1767 and then reestablishing his residence in Paris in 1770, the sexagenarian Rousseau begins to assume his final identity as the "solitary walker," as if in a desperate reprise of the youthful strength and innocence he would have had prior to his "fall" into writing and celebrity and prior to the forming of a "universal conspiracy" against him. It is at this moment too that Rousseau decides to "fix down in writing" the "charming contemplations" that have filled his daily walks (I, 999). An attempt will be made to reconcile the irreconcilable categories of writing and walking, an attempt motivated by the economic desire to save those charming moments of reverie so that they can be reused by him for his own pleasure: "Each time I reread them will give back the pleasure I had."[49] This attempted economy of pleasure will be the *Reveries of a Solitary Walker:* "In order to fulfill the title of this collection, I should have begun it sixty years ago: for my whole life has hardly been more than a long reverie divided into chapters by my daily promenades" ("Ebauches des *Rêveries,*" I, 1163).

So if, on the one hand, the state of mind produced by walking, that is, the reverie, is the origin of the philosopher's discourse and the condition that makes him a philosopher or "contemplative soul," on the other hand, the only writing that can adequately retain those states would be one that thinks of itself *as* a "reverie" or a "promenade," both of which names have been used indiscriminately by tradition to refer to the divisions or chapters of the *Reveries of a Solitary Walker* [*Rêveries du promeneur solitaire*]. Each of these would accordingly take the form of a reverie or a promenade, a sort of excursion in or through writing, at the same time that it is supposed to bring back or preserve for future use the pleasure of the reveries.[50] But this double recuperation (mimetic and mnemonic) of the reverie in writing makes it difficult to distinguish between text, reverie, and promenade, since each term would refer to the others as well as to itself. The Second Promenade or Reverie being the only one in which a single promenade or reverie is recounted (as opposed to being evoked in the frequentive mode: his "reveries" on the island of Saint-Pierre in the Fifth Reverie, his walks through Paris in the Sixth and Ninth Reveries), that text should offer an exemplary articulation of the relations between text, reverie, and promenade, or if one prefers, between writing, thinking, and walking. To the extent that the Second Reverie also bears an uncanny resemblance in both theme and structure to Montaigne's essay "Of Practice," its analysis should also allow us to reach some conclusions on the specificity of Rousseau's place in the economy of travel.

The first paragraph of the Second Promenade resumes and elaborates upon some of the same themes as those found in *Emile* and in the *Confessions*. The "reveries" that "fill" Rousseau's *promenades solitaires* are associated with his being "fully myself and for myself, without diversion, without obstacle, and where I can truly say I am that which nature wanted" (I, 1002). The reverie is understood as a moment of plenitude, of self-possession, of the abolition of all differences in the self or between the self and itself, and it comes therefore to be associated with being in the state of nature. The thought that takes place in the reverie, insofar as Rousseau states, "I leave my head entirely free and let my ideas follow their bent without resistance and without trouble" (I, 1102), would be the natural state of thought (as opposed to the painful or analytical thinking from which the walk would provide an escape).[51]

Once again, there surfaces the desire to keep a written record or "register" of the walk, so that, as Rousseau says, he can describe to himself "the habitual state of my soul in the most strange position in which a mortal can ever find himself" (I, 1002). But the stakes involved in this recording of one's idle thoughts turn out to be considerably higher than that of self-analysis (for either a narcissistic or an analytical knowledge of the self) since it is the self's very existence that is at stake in its ability to contemplate itself. Given the subject's temporal predicament, to contemplate oneself means to *remember* what one was like in one's "true" or "natural" state, that is, to remember the (earlier) reverie. At the limit, the self would prolong its existence by remembering itself: "I would exist only through memories" (I, 1002). The necessity of sustaining oneself through one's memories is occasioned, we are told, by a "decline" in the reverie's strength associated with the loss of one's vitality. Thus the reverie as the creativity of the imagination (such as it was described in the *Confessions*) gives way to the reverie as remembrance (of former reveries).[52] It is this qualitative change in the reverie that now simultaneously allows for and renders useless the writing down of the reverie: "How keep a faithful register? In trying to recall to myself so many sweet reveries, instead of describing them I fall back into them again. It is a state which its memory brings back" (I, 1003). The problem is no longer that the moments of writing and daydreaming are incommunicable but that their communication takes place through a short-circuit which makes that communication superfluous. The mere desire to remember the reverie so that it can be written down for later remembrance is sufficient to plunge the subject back into the reverie. The desire to write the reverie is what brings it back, an effect that then makes the writing of it unnecessary. The reverie can now be remembered at will, if it is not remembrance itself.

What is implied in this revision of the reverie is the possibility of achieving a full self-sufficiency, since, as we have been told, the self can survive on memories alone. The other, earlier reverie as imaginative production still required a convergence of different factors ("Certain dispositions on the part of the man who experiences them" and "the getting together of the surrounding objects" [Reveries, I, 1047]) in order to take place. Now, the self is dependent only on its own memories, that is, on itself. These memories are said to constitute a store of "wealth" and "treasures" (I, 1003), the capital for one's self-perpetuation through reveries. This self-sufficient economy or autoerotic autarky is also described through an alimentary metaphor: "Losing all hope here below and finding no more food for my heart upon earth, I accustomed myself little by little to nourish it with its own substance and to seek all its pasturage within myself" (I, 1002). And in the famous peroration to the Seventh Promenade, the practice of collecting flowers is revealed to be an especially efficacious means of perpetuating the self through memory, Rousseau's own version of the loci of the classical ars memoria: "All my botany excursions, the different impressions of the locality of objects which have struck me, the ideas which they have called up in me, the incidents which are mixed up with them—all this has left me impressions which are renewed by the aspect of plants gathered in the same places. . . . but now that I can no more traverse those pleasant lands, I have only to open my herbarium, and soon I am transported there. The fragments of plants which I have collected there suffice to recall to me the entirety of that magnificent spectacle" (I, 1073). Here, the memory is fixed down by uprooting the plant that was fixed in the soil where the walker trod and by affixing it to a page in the herbarium, whose perusal in turn allows the reader to travel once more through all the times and places literally anthologized (from anthos + logia, a collection of flowers) within it.[53] What such a local memory makes possible is a self-transporting for a henceforth immovable or sedentary self, a transporting of the self to itself, that is, to what is found in the places that are recalled by the flowers: the self itself. As J.-B. Pontalis has astutely observed, "for Rousseau, places are so many figures of himself."[54]

Whether self-sufficiency is metaphorized as herbarium, as treasure chest, or as autocannibalism, what is implied is a return to the self, the return of the self to itself exemplified in the Rousseauist injunction, "Go back into yourself," which appears in the Second Reverie as "the habit of going back into myself" (I, 1002). Such a reentering into oneself posits the self as the identifiable space of a home, whose temporal continuity is assured by the reverie's function as *re*membrance: the self can define itself as alive as long as it can live off its memories, that is, by a perpetual return unto itself. But if what defines the self's existence can be reduced to the functioning of a structure of return or autosuccession, then we see implied a notion of the self as the aftereffect of that structure, even though it must also proclaim itself the origin and end of the cycle of return. Such a definition of the self is structurally indistinguishable from the notion of a transcendental home or *oikos*. This congruence of the notions of self and home can be seen to organize the ensuing narrative of Rousseau's walk and accident, and to provide retrospective confirmation of the ethics proposed in *Emile* of the self as home.

Insofar as it is a narrative or *récit,* that account of one of Rousseau's *promenades* is the return in writing of a memorable event in Rousseau's life: an accidental and nearly fatal collision with a dog during a walk in the outskirts of Paris, near Ménilmontant, on October 24, 1776. To the extent that what is remembered is the trip back home after the accident, what the text recounts then is not just a return, but the return *of* a return, which itself *qua* return (*retour*) requires that there be a prior detour (*détour*): "I took a detour to return via the same meadows by another path" (I, 1003). Another kind of detour is presaged by Rousseau in regards to the effect this event has on his thinking: "An unforeseen accident came to break the thread of my ideas and to give them for some time another direction" (I, 1003). The text, moreover, places a detour before the description of the accident itself, a detour given over to recounting the pleasures of return. Among these, we might count the collecting and recognition of flowers ("whose aspect and classification, which were familiar to me, nevertheless still gave me pleasure" [I, 1003-4]); Rousseau's refinding despite his accident of his rare *cerastium aquaticum* "in a book which I had on me" (I, 1003); the remembrance of the past ("I recapitulated the movements of my soul since youth" [I, 1004]); as well as an extended analogy between the autumn landscape and his own situation "at the decline of an innocent and unfortunate life" (I, 1004).

In this last case, the entire topography becomes a metaphor of the self such that Rousseau can see himself mirrored in what he sees. This metaphorizing of the landscape by bringing the "ensemble" of observed phenomena back to himself is also what effects the return to himself of himself, unlike the elision of the self that occurs in Montesquieu's topographical vision. The explication of the analogy between himself and the landscape brings Rousseau's thoughts back to himself. It is then that he *re*capitulates "the movements of my soul since youth, and during my mature age, since I have been sequestered from the society of men, and during the long retreat in which I must finish my days. I returned with pleasure over all the affections of my heart" (I, 1004). The movement of the reverie is that of a return to the self (through the detour of the contemplation of nature) which constitutes that self as a single entity, which can be grasped in all of its multifarious manifestations both metonymically (in relation to the different moments or temporality of his existence) and metaphorically (in relation to the external world, which is reduced to a specular image of himself). The self produced by such a totalization would seem to be the very image of self-sufficiency (since literally *everything* is included in it), but this entire production is itself to be retained by the self for later use as Rousseau prepares himself to remember his reveries "sufficiently to describe them" (I, 1004). The whole experience, like the collecting of flowers, is brought back to the self, back to the home, where it will be reserved for the time when the self's imagination will have declined and it will have to subsist solely on its memories. It is in his latter situation that we find the narrator at the beginning of the *Reveries;* he is now precisely returning to what was stored up at the time the reveries took place. In other words, the Rousseau pictured in the narrative of the reverie, who sees himself in the autumn of his years, is one who is storing up for the analogous winter, in which we presume the narrator already is. So Rousseau returns from his foraging expedition, like a successful hunter: "I was returning very content with my day" (I, 1004).

But this last return is to be delayed by another detour, whose repercussion will not be felt, as Rousseau says, until "I came back to myself [*je revins à moi*]." In other words, the detour cannot be grasped as such until it has been brought back in or by the movement of the return. Cognition will only take place as recognition, a play on words warranted by the gap in the story between the moment prior to the accident and Rousseau's return to consciousness afterwards:

> I judged that the sole means that I had to avoid being thrown down to earth was to make a great leap, so that the dog should pass under me while I was in the air. This idea, more swift than lightning, and which I had not even the time to reason out or to execute, was the last before my accident. I did not feel the blow, nor the fall, nor anything of what followed, up to the moment when I came back to myself [*où je revins à moi*].
>
> It was almost night when I regained consciousness [*quand je repris connaissance*]. (I, 1005)

The gap between paragraphs acts as a sign pointing to the gap in Rousseau's consciousness, the gap that functions as the absent center of his narrative, the grand *trou* at the center of his not-so-grand *tour*. The purpose of the narrative is then to fill in that absence by returning to it (by remembering it or *reciting* it as a *récit*), by placing it within the successive movement of the return. But this is to forget that the *récit* is itself the *récit* of a return, the exemplary return of Rousseau to himself, which, as it happens, and true to the shades of Montaigne, is parallel to the return of himself to his home. The "I came back to myself [*je revins à moi*]" is curiously replicated in a "I came back home [*je revins chez moi*]." This replication, however, is not a contingent mirroring or metaphorization of one return in the other. Rather, the return to self and the return home are read as being *the same return*. Forgetting who one is and where one is seem to be conflated into the same problem: "I did not know who I was nor where I was [*ni qui j'étois ni où j'étois*]" (I, 1005). Similarly, it is through the establishment of topographical reference points that both the home's location and the self's name can be rediscovered: "They asked me where I lived; it was impossible for me to say. I asked where I was; they said, *à la haute borne;* it was as if they said to me: *on Mount Atlas*. It was necessary for me to ask successively the country, the city, and the neighborhood where I was. Still this did not suffice for me to recognize myself. It was necessary for me to walk the whole distance from there to the boulevard in order to recall my home and my name" (I, 1005-6). Refusing to take a cab for fear of catching cold and true to his ambulatory preference, Jean-Jacques is brought back to self and home under the assured self-propulsion of his legs, the supremely self-retrieving act of walking.

It is tempting to read the particulars of this event as a virtual parody of Montaigne's horse accident.[55] Whereas Montaigne is hit by a "powerful workhorse [*puissant roussin*]" (II, vi, 373), Rousseau is knocked over by a large dog in the retinue of a carriage, whose horses are just brought to a halt before they would have trampled on the writer's body: "The carriage to which the dog belonged followed immediately, and would have passed over my body if the coachman had not reined in his horses upon the instant" (I, 1005). But if a strong tug on the bridle saves Rousseau's life, the impact of the dog, whose designation as a "huge Great Dane" (I, 1004-5) already invites comparison with a small horse (especially for someone on foot such as Rousseau, as distinct from the mounted Montaigne), sends him flying literally head over heels. Unable to find his footing, in a reverse image of the submerged Descartes at the beginning of the Second Meditation, Rousseau finds solidity again, not at the rocky bottom of a watery abyss out of which he can then climb, but in the rough paving stone upon which he lands head first, specifically with his upper jaw: "The dog . . . had leapt upon my two legs, and striking me with its mass and speed, made me fall head foremost; the upper jaw, bearing the whole weight of my body, struck upon a very hard pavement, and the fall was the more violent because, the road being downhill, my head was thrown lower than my feet" (I, 1005). The severity and extent of the fall are said to be aggravated by Rousseau's already proceeding downhill ("on the descent from Ménil-montant"), although when he does land he is said to be at a place called *la haute borne,* figuratively speaking, the upper limit. But he had already seen himself "at the decline," as we remember, when he had contemplated his life in the landscape seen from the top of "the heights of Ménil-montant" (I, 1003), a place at that time just outside the Paris city walls and today incorporated into the city's 20th arrondissement, a place whose name means "the house uphill." Indeed, the location of Rousseau's outing situates him in the hills overlooking Paris from the northeast, in the vicinity of the soon-to-be-founded cemetery of Père Lachaise, whose spectacular view of the entire city was to be illustriously rendered by Balzac in the famous concluding scene from *Père Goriot.*[56] Rather than "fixing" his ideas on the city from that height as Montesquieu might have done, Rousseau could see only himself in the autumnal ambiance of falling leaves and declining temperatures.[57]

Perhaps it is this pre-Romantic collapsing of the distinction between subject and object (or more precisely, the reduction of all objectivity to an absolute subjectivity whose self-sentient autonomy exudes a feeling of oneness with the world) that allows Rousseau to experience his injurious fall as a genuine rebirth, and not, as it was for Montaigne, an appropriation of the liminal experience of death. Like Montaigne, though, and unlike Descartes, Rousseau's utter disorientation in the wake of his accident is seen to be a pleasurable experience: "I perceived the sky, some stars, and a little grass. This first sensation was a delicious moment. I did not feel anything except that of being there. I was born in that instant to life" (I, 1005). What is "delicious" is the sensation of firstness ("this first sensation"), of origin, or birth, yet what gives pleasure to Rousseau is less the originality or firstness of this moment of birth than the sensation of being in a state prior to the distinction between self and other, and prior to spatial and temporal distinctions, a state, in sum, prior to difference: "It seemed to me that I filled with my light existence [*ma légère existence*] all the objects I perceived. Entirely given up to the present moment, I did not remember anything; I had no distinct notion of my individuality, not the least idea of what had happened to me. I did not know who I was nor where I was. I felt neither evil nor fear, nor worry. I saw my blood flowing as I might have looked at a brooklet [*comme j'aurois vu couler un ruisseau*], without even dreaming that this blood in any way belonged to me" (I,

1005). While plenitude and pleasure are sustained in this primal indifferentiation, what appears to Rousseau in this moment of self-presence and rebirth, of the absolute return to home, is a part of himself not thought of as belonging to himself. This expropriated part of himself is a stream of blood, a *ruisseau de sang,* from which we can derive the phantasmic signature of a *"rouge* rui*sseau"* or *"rousseau."* What is most proper to Rousseau (whether his blood or his proper name) is not seen as proper. Yet this expropriation of the self is simultaneously understood as the greatest self-appropriation. Never is the self more itself than when it is not, than in the aftermath of this catastrophic walk.[58] Rousseau's greatest loss is his greatest gain, what is most (im)proper to him. But if Rousseau's pleasure is in this state of indifference (the indifference, for instance, with which he is able to watch himself bleed), then the return of difference would imply a loss of pleasure even though it is, as we have seen, only through the reintroduction of spatial, temporal, and linguistic differences that Rousseau can indeed return to self and home, or even remember his name. To speak, then, of a pleasure of return (à la Starobinski) becomes highly problematic in relation to a discourse like the Second Promenade (or, as we saw earlier, the sequel to *Emile*), in which different returns are at stake such that a return somewhere is a departure from somewhere else. Is Rousseau, in other words, more "himself" and more "at home" in the wake of his accident or upon returning to his domicile? Without an easy answer to this question, one must conclude either that not all returns are pleasurable or that returns are not all that pleasurable.

For Rousseau, as for Montaigne, the narrative of the return home is succeeded in the text by the writer's reflection on the image of himself as already dead, a reflection that ultimately bears upon the question of the property of his text as well as of his body, upon the question of his signature. While Montaigne appears as dead *to himself* in the image of the text as *écorché,*[59] Rousseau discovers to his horror that it is *others* who consider him dead: "Public rumor had it that I was dead of my fall; and this rumor spread so rapidly and so obstinately, that over two weeks after I learned about it, it was being spoken as certain fact by the queen and the king himself" (I, 1009). The literal disfigurement of his face on account of the accident ("Four teeth were bent back in the upper jaw, the whole of that part of the face which covered it extremely swollen and bruised" [I, 1006]) is less distressing than the story's mutilation in the mouths of others: "In a few days, this story spread about Paris, so changed and disfigured [*défig-urée*] that it was impossible to recognize anything of it" (I, 1006-7). As the story travels through the city, Rousseau's pleasure in not being able to recognize the distinction between subject and object in the *rouge ruisseau* of his blood turns to dismay at having to recognize not only his subjectivity's lack of autonomy but also the determination by others of what seems most his. Not only is he pronounced physically dead by "public rumor," but the subsequent announcement of a subscription fund for the publication of his posthumous works reveals the expropriation and disfigurement even of his textual production: "A subscription had been opened at the same time to print the manuscripts which might be found in my house. I understood by this that a collection of fabricated writings were being kept ready expressly for the purpose of attributing them to me after my death; because to think that anyone would print faithfully any of those which would be actually found, was a stupidity which could not enter into the mind of a sensible man" (I, 1009). While the postaccident bliss of indifferentiation and the pleasurable reverie may offer the triumph of an imaginary that can reduce or "fix" all externality into a metaphor of the interiorized self, the symbolic authority of the external,—that is, the social—world would seem to have "fixed" Rousseau's image ahead of time and beyond any possibility of self-determination on his part. For Jean-Jacques, his return "home" from his accident on his way down into the corruption of the city, after having found joy in the height of the country, only underscores the extent of his exile from the very society he inhabits. His text, as well as his body, can only survive (or so it would seem, and once again following in the steps of Montaigne) at the cost of its disfiguration.

Even the validity of his signature, that inscriptional act that would seem to authorize one's text as one's own, as whole, and as proper to its author's intent, is called into question by Rousseau's postaccident dealings with Mme. d'Ormoy. Bearing a name that uncannily juxtaposes wealth (*or*) and self (*moy*), Mme. d'Ormoy was the author of *Les malheurs de la jeune Emélie, pour servir d'instruction aux dames vertueuses et sensibles* (1777), a book written, she would have told Rousseau, for "the reestablishment of her fortune" (I, 1007). Obviously inspired by Rousseau's *Emile,* Mme. d'Ormoy's book was also, whether wittingly or unwittingly, contrary to the view of woman portrayed in the former, not only for its treatment of women's education but also for its being written *by* a woman. In book V of *Emile,* Mme. d'Ormoy could have read: "I would a hundred times still prefer a simple and coarsely educated girl, than a knowledgeable and witty girl who would set up in my house a literary tribunal of which she would make herself the presiding judge. A woman of wit and intelligence is the scourge of her husband, children, friends, servants, and of everybody. ... Every lettered girl will remain an old maid her entire life, when there are only sensible men upon the earth" (IV, 768). And in response to her gifts, visits, and requests for support from him for her novel, Rousseau could only remain unmoved: "I told her what I thought of women authors" (I, 1007). His suspicions about her were brought home upon the publication of her book, to which was appended a compromising note about kings and their ministers whose inclusion in the volume created a *succès de scandale*. Reflecting upon Mme. d'Ormoy's visits, Rousseau concludes that "all this had no other goal than to dispose the public to attribute the note to me, and consequently the censure that it might draw down upon its author" (I, 1008). Fearful of the appropriation of his name by a woman who was not merely urban and seductive but also a writer, Rousseau decides to "destroy the rumor" about the appended note by himself writing a note to Mme. d'Ormoy whose incipit was none other than his name: "'Rousseau, not receiving any author at his home, thanks Madame d'Ormoy for her kindness, and prays her not to honor him any more with her visits'" (I, 1008).

Once again, the detour of woman as emblematized by the episode with Mme. d'Ormoy is negotiated by a return to the father, but this time, wrote Rousseau, "I went further [*j'allai plus loin*]" (I, 1009). By hyberbolizing the universality of the conspiracy against him, he takes its direction out of the hands of any particular men or mere mortals and attributes its (to his mind) prodigious efficacy to the will of none other than God the Father Himself. God acts, then, as the final referent, the *haute borne* that provides an upper limit to the delirium of paranoid interpretation: "This idea, far from being cruel and lacerating to me, consoles me, calms me, and helps in resigning myself [*à me résigner*]" (I, 1010). The notion of God allows for repose from the movement of interpretation, which was constantly having to explain away "so many bizarre circumstances" or "the singularities of this epoch" (I, 1007), since it allows for the explanation of all possible contingencies or singularities, their return into a comfortable and comforting order. As such, the positing of God as the ultimate explanation of his woes puts an end to Rousseau's discourse, compositionally bringing the promenade to a close: "God is just, He wills that I should suffer, and He knows that I am innocent. There is the motive of my confidence; my heart and my reason cry out that it will never deceive me. Let men and destiny do what they may; let us learn to suffer without complaint; everything must in the end return to order, and my turn will come sooner or later [*tout doit à la fin rentrer dans l'ordre, et mon tour viendra tot ou tard*]" (I, 1010). If God is just, it is because he exercises just *re*tribution; that is, He is the guarantor of a just economy in the circulation of human success. But if God guarantees the return to order, it is because He is nothing more in Rousseau's discourse than the principle of return itself. God as the paternal law of return states that "everything must in the end return to order." In this ultimate grand tour of the divine eschatology, Rousseau's turn (*mon tour*) will come "sooner or later."

The telos of the traveler's journey is thus proleptically secured, not by the instructional prophylaxis set forth in *Emile,* but by the divine order of a predestination. Such a Christian allegory can also do for Rousseau what his narrative of the historical fall from nature into culture could never do— namely, engineer the return of the innocence and happiness that was lost. As both absolute origin and absolute end, as the fundamental *oikos* from which all divagation can be measured, God allows for a way around the logics of succession and supplementarity that lead Rousseau ever further away from himself, and humanity ever further away from the state of nature. As Julie writes to Saint-Preux, God is "the Being for whom time has no succession nor space any distance" (*La Nouvelle Héloïse,* II, 673). Yet if God turns out to be the ultimate *point de repère* in this discourse which talks of nothing but return, that point of absolute return can only be posited through an act of faith, a "profession of faith" if you will. It is an act of faith because the positing of this transcendental point of reference, to the extent that it is governed by the deontic modal *devoir,* cannot assure that there *is* such a place of return, only that there ought to be one. In more general terms, for there to be any such thing as a point of reference or of return, that point can only function in its referential capacity if and only if it is not immediately present, that is, if it is not here and not now. One's bearings can only be set by something spatially and temporally *distant.* That one can refer to a point of reference already states that it is far away or in the past or in the future. There is a referent but it is always already absent. Such an absent referent is Rousseau's God, a principle of return situated at an unspecified moment in the future: "Everything *must* in the end return to order, and my turn will come sooner or later." The return can only be had on faith, on the faith that there will be a return. On the other hand, a reference point is not merely a fiction, since it does in fact exist by reason of its being posited. A point of reference exists the moment reference is made to it. It exists *because* it is referred to. A reference point is then paradoxically both real and a fiction, both found and lost. What Rousseau's God points to is the theological character of all points of reference, of the *oikos* (whose gods, the penates, as we remember, were rescued from burning Troy by Aeneas in order to assure the return of the home in another place, the New Troy that he would found in Rome).[60] But if the believer must then be said to create God by his very belief in Him, then God plays the same ambiguous role (a progenitor who is the "progeny" of its progeny) as that of the father in *Emile and Sophie.* God is God the Father, the ultimate *point de repère* and a necessary fiction, a supreme addressee who hears the victim's every woe and whose invocation grounds the writer in his text, giving him the security of an ultimate end and purpose to his discursive meanderings, a *topos* of solace and return.

His faith affirmed that there will be a return, Rousseau can then "resign himself" to whatever further misfortunes may befall him: "This idea, far from being cruel and lacerating to me, consoles me, calms me, and helps in resigning myself [*à me résigner*]" (I, 1010). To resign oneself to something, though, is to give up one's claims to mastery or ownership, to deny one's authorship. To re-sign is paradoxically not to sign. *The Reveries of a Solitary Walker* remains an unsigned work, one not bearing the writer's signature, not simply and contingently because of the death of its author prior to the work's completion, but because its publication and concomitant ascription of a signature could only take place henceforth, within the writer's imaginary, as an act of God.[61]

Having already signed in blood on the pavement of *la haute borne,* Rousseau would seem to find more solace in the return to indifferentiation, or in the indifference that is resignation, than in what for him are the undoubtedly "crueler," more "lacerating" (*déchirante*), and disfiguring effects he suffered from signing his name in ink and on the cover of books. Either way, however, the affixing of the name as the mark of appropriation implies a simultaneous expropriation, a disappropriation. While the gain of presence is paradoxically acquired through the loss of blood and consciousness, the fame of authorship is haunted by the limitless fear of deceit and betrayal. Even when the ensuing paranoia is put to rest by faith and trust in God, the promised return to normalcy is offered only in exchange for one's "resignation," as if one could be for oneself only by being for another. One can only be present (or absent) to oneself as other, when one is not "chez soi" through the deferral of memory or writing. Likewise, the return home can never be fully sure of its point of arrival, whether it be Geneva, the Island of Saint-Pierre (scene of the idyllic Fifth Reverie), Ménilmontant, his residence in the rue Plâtrière of Paris, or Ermenonville (the place of his death a few weeks after his final relocation).[62] In other words, the promenade can never *fully* return as reverie, which, in turn, can never *fully* return as text. Each return implies a disappropriation that takes away as much as it gives, making the assignment of the *oikos* an inescapably retrospective and fictional gesture, one caught in the endless revisionary process of what Freud calls *Nachträglichkeit.*[63] As such, and despite the best efforts of Emile's tutor, there can be no final end to wandering, no ultimate destination or telos to travel.

Such revisionism also marks, however, Jean-Jacques's differences from the other philosophical writers studied in this volume. Despite following in their footsteps, Rousseau rejects the trope of philosophical wisdom as an accumulated effect of foreign travel in favor of the apparently more elitist notion that only those already in possession of philosophical knowledge be allowed to undertake voyages. To the extent, though, that this expertise is acquired not through book-learning but through the simple experience of walking, which places a suitably sensitive subjectivity in a relation of immediacy with the world he traverses, Rousseau democratizes the philosopher's tour by implicitly allowing anyone who stumbles while out for a walk to claim great thoughts. Certainly this is the legacy of Rousseau as it was appropriated by the Romantics, whose generation also saw the invention and rise of the word "tourist," applied not to the aristocratic followers of the grand tour but to the new breed of bourgeois adventurers in sentimentality such as Stendhal (whose 1838 *Mémoires d'un touriste* first gave legitimacy to the word in French). As such, it is not the equestrian Montaigne, as Charles Dédéyan would have it, but the pedestrian Rousseau who should be called the first tourist.

In revising Montaigne, Descartes, and Montesquieu, Rousseau also marks his debt to them, emulating, for example, Montaigne much as Emile does his tutor, or Télémaque Ulysse, or Montaigne his father. For their accidents to offer such similarities is not just a bizarre coincidence but also the sign that for neither Montaigne nor Rousseau can that moment of utter self-(dis)possession be construed as one's own. No doubt Rousseau read Montaigne's text and was consciously or unconsciously informed by it in constructing the narrative of his own accident, yet the fact of such an influence is complicated when the constitutive detour that is travel is inversely understood—as it is from the watery depths of Descartes to the airy heights of Montesquieu, on horseback with Montaigne and on foot with Rousseau—as determinant of filiation itself. One cannot simply say, for instance, that Rousseau is the successor of a tradition of the voyage, the father of which tradition would be Montaigne, without making of that very tradition precisely the kind of voyage of filial succession described in the writings of Montaigne, Descartes, Montesquieu, and Rousseau. Moreover, the question of intertextual appropriation is not an innocent one when the travel narrative assures the transitional smoothness of a patrilinear succession whereby the son can eventually come to occupy the place of the father. If the signature that is the writer's particular mode of travel would seem to convert the banal trope of the voyage into something he can call his own, the anxieties associated with that signature, as revealed most overtly in Rousseau, point to the dread detour that the detour of travel is meant to circumvent: namely, woman, whose difference is as unmasterable for the male philosopher as the *oikos* is unstabilizable for the traveler. As such, even the names (as)signed to the texts of Montaigne, Descartes, Montesquieu, and Rousseau can be shown to be caught in the drift of an appropriation that is, at some point and at some time, also and inevitably a disappropriation.

Notes

Introduction: The Economy of Travel

1. In fact, the very movement between the voyage and other *topoi* itself suggests a reading of the history of literature as a voyage. For one of these *topoi* or stopping places on this itinerary to be what signifies that journey as a whole cannot be without consequences. As we will see, the motif of the voyage is an exemplary locus of literary self-reflection.

2. Louis de Jaucourt, "Voyage," *Encyclopédie ou dictionnaire raisonné des sciences, des arts et des métiers par une société de gens de lettres* (Neufchâtel: Samuel Faulche & Compagnie, 1751–65), XVII, 476.

3. Extensions of the concept of economy have been a key feature of much recent French critical discourse, since at least Georges Bataille, *La part maudite* (Paris: Minuit, 1949), especially the section entitled "La notion de dépense," initially published in 1933. For an incisive analysis of Bataille's notion of economy, see also Jacques Derrida, "From Restricted to General Economy: A Hegelianism without Reserve," in *Writing and Difference,* tr. Alan Bass (Chicago: University of Chicago Press, 1978), 251–77. Among others in this tradition, see especially: Jean-Joseph Goux, *Symbolic Economies: After Marx and Freud,* tr. Jennifer Curtiss Gage (Ithaca, N.Y.: Cornell University Press, 1990), and *Les monnayeurs du langage* (Paris: Galilée, 1984); Jean-François Lyotard, *Economie libidinale* (Paris: Minuit, 1974) and *Des dispositifs pulsionnels* (Paris: Union Générale d'Editions, 1973); Jean Baudrillard, *For*

a Critique of the Political Economy of the Sign, tr. Charles Levin (St. Louis, Mo.: Telos Press, 1981); Gilles Deleuze and Félix Guattari, *Anti-Oedipus,* tr. Robert Hurley, Mark Seem, and Helen R. Lane (Minneapolis: University of Minnesota Press, 1983) and *A Thousand Plateaus,* tr. Brian Massumi (Minneapolis: University of Minnesota Press, 1989). In a more sociological vein, see Pierre Bourdieu, *Distinction: A Social Critique of the Judgement of Taste,* tr. Richard Nice (Cambridge, Mass.: Harvard University Press, 1984); and in regards to literary history, Marc Shell, *The Economy of Literature* (Baltimore: Johns Hopkins University Press, 1978), and *Money, Language, and Thought: Literary and Philosophical Economies from the Medieval to the Modern Era* (Berkeley: University of California Press, 1982).

4. Jean de La Fontaine, "Les deux pigeons," *Oeuvres complètes* (Paris: Seuil, 1965), 140. The poem was first published in 1679.

5. François-Marie Arouet de Voltaire, *Candide, ou l'optimisme* in *Oeuvres complètes,* ed. Louis Moland (Paris: Garnier Frères, 1877–85), XXI, 137–218.

6. Dean MacCannell, *The Tourist: A New Theory of the Leisure Class* (New York: Schocken Books, 1976); see also Jonathan Culler, "The Semiotics of Tourism," *American Journal of Semiotics* 1, no. 1–2 (1981), 127–40, and my "Sightseers: The Tourist as Theorist," *Diacritics* 10 (Winter 1980), 3–14. For more properly ethnographic discussions of the journey as a mode of cultural, or even political, empowerment, see Claude Lévi-Strauss, *Tristes Tropiques,* tr. John and Doreen Weightman (New York: Atheneum, 1973), 26–34; and Mary W. Helms, *Ulysses' Sail: An Ethnographic Odyssey of Power, Knowledge, and Geographic Distance* (Princeton: Princeton University Press, 1988).

7. The most celebrated account of the Spanish conquest is Bartolomé de Las Casas, *Brevissima relacion de la destruycion de las Indias* (Seville, 1552). For the influence exerted on early European liberal attitudes toward colonialism by Las Casas's horrifying descriptions of Spanish atrocities, see Michèle Duchet, *Anthropologie et histoire au siècle des lumières,* rev. ed. (Paris: Flammarion, 1977), 94–95, 149–54. See also, on the "discovery" of the "New" World, Edmundo O'Gorman, *The Invention of America: An Inquiry into the Historical Nature of the New World and the Meaning of Its History* (Bloomington: Indiana University Press, 1961); J. H. Elliott, *The Old World and the New, 1492–1650* (Cambridge: Cambridge University Press, 1970); Tzvetan Todorov, *The Conquest of America: The Question of the Other,* tr. Richard Howard (New York: Harper and Row, 1984), and Mary B. Campbell, *The Witness and the Other World: Exotic European Travel Writing, 400–1600* (Ithaca, N.Y.: Cornell University Press, 1988), especially 165–266. A crucial recontextualizing of Las Casas and the subsequent notoriety of the Spanish conquest can be found in Roberto Fernández Retamar's brilliant and moving "Against the Black Legend," in *Caliban and Other Essays,* tr. Edward Baker (Minneapolis: University of Minnesota Press, 1989), 56–73. Unlike other critics of Las Casas, Retamar is less interested in disputing the numerical accuracy of the atrocities alleged by Las Casas than in exposing the racism that has inspired his northern European readers, who fail to perceive that the earliest criticism of Spanish colonialism was itself Spanish in origin. On the other hand, this oppositional voice turns out to be virtually absent from the perhaps quieter but no less efficient genocide carried out in North America (and elsewhere) by English, French, and Dutch colonialists. On early French colonialism and reactions to the Spanish conquests, see Charles-André Julien, *Histoire de l'expansion et de la colonisation française I: Les voyages de découverte et les premiers établissements* (Paris: PUF, 1948); and Tom Conley, "Montaigne and the New World," *Hispanic Issues* 4 (1989), 225–62.

8. *The Poetics of Aristotle,* ed. and trans. S. H. Butcher (London: Macmillan, 1936), 31.

9. *La syntaxe narrative des tragédies de Corneille* (Paris: Klincksieck, 1976). See also his more recent *Poetics of Plot* (Minneapolis: University of Minnesota Press, 1985) and *Fictional Worlds* (Cambridge, Mass.: Harvard University Press, 1986).

10. *L'invention du quotidien I: Arts de faire* (Paris: 10/18, 1980), 206. While de Certeau's statement may sound excessive out of context, one can find considerable support for his hypothesis in theoreticians of narrative, who almost invariably draw on the voyage as either the model narrative or the model for narrative. Witness Georg Lukàcs for whom the novel is the form that expresses "transcendental homelessness" (*Theory of the Novel,* tr. A. Bostock [Cambridge, Mass.: MIT Press, 1971], 41 and passim). As for the system of character functions put forth by Vladimir Propp, it is possible to read the entire sequence of functions as constituting a journey begun by the very first function, the departure of someone from the home, and ending when all the complications surrounding the hero's return home are resolved: *Morphology of the Folktale,* tr. L. Scott, rev. Louis A. Wagner (Austin: University of Texas Press, 1968). A literary historical argument concerning the relation between the early modern vogue for travel literature and the rise of that most elaborate of narrative genres, the novel, is made by Percy Adams in *Travel Literature and the Evolution of the Novel* (Lexington: University Press of Kentucky, 1983).

11. No doubt the most eloquent expression of the imbrication between text and travel remains Michel Butor's "Le voyage et l'écriture," in *Répertoire* IV (Paris: Minuit, 1974), 9–29. Similar insights can be gleaned from Louis Marin, *Utopiques: Jeux d'espace* (Paris: Minuit, 1973); Normand Doiron, "L'art de voyager: Pour une définition du récit de voyage à l'époque classique," *Poétique* 73 (1988), 83–108, and "De l'épreuve de l'espace au lieu du texte: le récit de voyage comme genre," in Bernard Beugnot, ed., *Voyages: Récits et imaginaire, Biblio 17* 11 (1984), 15–31; also, Bernard Beugnot's preface to this same volume, ix xvi; Gilles Deleuze, *Proust and Signs,* tr. Richard Howard (New York: Braziller, 1972); Roland Barthes, *S/Z,* tr. Richard Miller (New York: Hill and Wang, 1974), 105; Michel de Certeau, *L'invention du quotidien,* 171–227.

12. Such a critique of metaphysics is the one offered by Jacques Derrida, and the entire corpus of his work could be cited in this regard. In reference to the argument I am trying to make here, suffice it to mention in particular *Of Grammatology,* tr. Gayatri Chakravorty Spivak (Baltimore: Johns Hopkins University Press, 1974), and *Speech and Phenomena and Other Essays on Husserl's Theory of Signs,* tr. David Allison (Evanston: Northwestern University Press, 1973).

13. A variant of the *relation de voyage* is that of the voyage recounted through letters. Here, the steps in the voyager's itinerary are brought back or related to the addressee (stereotypically positioned at the traveler's point of departure) in the concrete form of the missives marked by their changing dates and place names. The dateline thus designates its addressor's progress even as it measures the distance the letter itself must retrace on its way back to the addressee. La Fontaine's *Relation d'un voyage de Paris en Limousin* (1663) and Mme. d'Aulnoy's *Relation du Voyage d'Espagne* (1691) exploit this possibility, as do, albeit in a very different register, the *Lettres édifiantes et curieuses de Chine* (1702–76), compiled and edited by Jesuit missionaries. The device is also widely exploited precisely to obtain an (often facile) effect of cultural and geographical alienation in such eighteenth-century exotic novels as Montesquieu's *Lettres persanes* (1721), Poullain de Saint-Foix's *Lettres turques* (1730), and Mme. de Graffigny's *Lettres d'une Péruvienne* (1747).

14. On the translation or transformation of topography into topic as it relates to the constitution of narrative, see Louis Marin, "Du corps au texte: propositions métaphysiques sur l'origine du récit," *Esprit* 423 (1973), 913–28.

15. Such a minimal voyage narrative is the one left behind by Jean-Jacques Rousseau as a "Road Notebook," dated 1754, whose text can be cited in toto:

Dined Sunday on the grass close to Hermance.
Slept at the château of Coudrée.

Dined Monday on the grass close to Ripailles.
Slept at Meilleraie.
Tuesday slept at Bex.
Dined at Pisse-Vache.
Slept at Saint-Maurice.
Dined at Aigle.
Frugal meal offered out of hospitality.
Is there not something Homeric about my voyage?
Dined Tuesday at Villeneuve.
Slept at Vevai.
Dined Wednesday at Cuilli.
Slept at Lauzanne.
Dined Tuesday and slept at Morges.
Dined Friday at Nion and slept at Eaux-Vives.

The place names for meals and overnight rests describe an itinerary around the most celebrated of Swiss lakes, an *excursus* whose circle can be closed by the addition of the implicit point of departure and return, the city of Geneva. The only nondesignative sentence raises the question of a Homeric allusion putatively capable of dignifying this modest outing. This text, if it can be called one, is then placed back into the literary tradition of epic travel, comfortably anchored in the name of its inaugural poet, even as Rousseau's Alpine odyssey brings him back home to the "living waters" (Eaux-Vives), not of Ithaca, but of Geneva.

16. Such a marking would extend even to so-called unmarked places, which are nonetheless marked as unmarked. Cf. Barbara Johnson, "Quelques conséquences de la différence anatomique des textes: Pour une théorie du poème en prose," *Poétique* 28 (1976), 465.

17. The topological conception of language can be as explicit as in Ludwig Wittgenstein's metaphor of language as a city (*Philosophical Investigations,* 3rd ed. rev., trans. G. E. M. Anscombe [New York: Macmillan, 1958], 8) or as implicit as the spatial metaphors endemic to structural theories of language with their horizontal and vertical axes of signification, positions of the speaking subject and synchronic projections. Indeed, the very notion of language as a structure implies its conceptualization as a space.

18. Cicero, *Topica,* tr. H. M. Hubbell (Cambridge, Mass.: Harvard University Press, and London: Heinemann, 1960), 382; translation modified.

19. For a detailed discussion of *memoria* as well as of the use of topography as a memory aid in general, see Michel Beaujour, *Miroirs d'encre: Rhetorique de l'autoportrait* (Paris: Seuil, 1980), 79–168; and Frances Yates's classic, *The Art of Memory* (Chicago: University of Chicago Press, 1966).

20. César Chesneau Du Marsais, *Traité des tropes ou des différents sens dans lesquels on peut prendre un même mot dans une même langue* (Paris: Le Nouveau Commerce, 1977), 7, my emphasis. Cf. Quintilian: "A trope is the advantageous removal [mutatio] of a word or a discourse from its proper signification over to another. . . . Now, a name or a word is transferred from that place in which it properly is [*ex eo loco in quo proprium est*] into another place, where either the proper name is in default or an improvement is made upon the proper term as a result of this removal [*tralatum*]." *Institutio oratoria* 8.6.1–8.6.6, ed. M. Winterbottom (Oxford: Clarendon Press, 1970), my translation and emphases.

21. Roland Barthes, "The Old Rhetoric: An Aide-Mémoire," in *The Semiotic Challenge,* tr. Richard Howard (New York: Hill and Wang, 1988), 88, Barthes's emphasis.

22. Aristotle, *Poetics,* ed. and tr. Butcher, 77. Cf. Jacques Derrida, "White Mythology," in *Margins of Philosophy,* tr. Alan Bass (Chicago: University of Chicago, 1982), 231 and

passim. On the attempt to establish a hierarchy of tropes, see Hans Kellner, "The Inflatable Trope as Narrative Theory: Structure or Allegory?" *Diacritics* 11 (Spring 1981), 14–28.

23. On the complexity of the problems posed by such metaphors of metaphor, see Richard Klein, "Straight Lines and Arabesques: Metaphors of Metaphor," *Yale French Studies* 45 (1970), 64–86.

24. Derrida, "White Mythology," 241.

25. An argument similar to the one I have made concerning the ambiguous entrapment-liberation in travel and in critical thought could also be advanced in relation to that political doctrine which came to full fruition with the Enlightenment, namely, liberalism. The liberal's position has traditionally been that of the bad faith of supporting progressive reform only to the extent that such reform does not jeopardize his or her own privileged status. On the other hand, liberal largesse must at least make the gesture of what it claims to be doing if it is not to be immediately unmasked as hypocritical imposture. To an extent that remains to be determined, the liberal must support the very reforms he or she dreads, and one might offer by way of an emblem the famous night of August 4, 1789, when the French nobles in the National Assembly vied with one another to give up as many of their feudal privileges as possible. There is room here for a study of the historical relations between critical thought, travel literature, and liberalism. On the events of August 4, see Jean-Pierre Hirsch, ed., *La nuit du 4 août* (Paris: Gallimard/Julliard, 1978).

26. The historical importance of the literature of exploration for the development of French critical thinking has been variously argued since Gustave Lanson's influential essay, "Le rôle de l'expérience dans la formation de la philosophie du XVIIIᵉ siècle en France," *Revue du Mois* (1910), 4–28 and 404–29, rpt. in *Essais de méthode de critique et d'histoire littéraire,* ed. H. Pèyre (Paris: Hachette, 1965); see also, in this tradition, Geoffroy Atkinson, *The Extraordinary Voyage in French Literature Before 1700* (New York: Columbia University Press, 1920), *The Extraordinary Voyage in French Literature From 1700 to 1720* (Paris: Champion, 1922), and *Les nouveaux horizons de la Renaissance française* (Paris: Droz, 1935); Gilbert Chinard, *L'exotisme américain dans la littérature française au XVIᵉ siècle* (Paris: Hachette, 1911), and *L'Amérique et le rêve exotique dans la littérature française au XVIIᵉ et au XVIIIᵉ siècle* (Paris: Droz, 1934); Paul Hazard, *La crise de la conscience européenne, 1680–1715* (Paris: Boivin, 1935), especially chapter one: "De la stabilité au mouvement," 3–25; René Pomeau, "Voyage et lumières dans la littérature française du XVIIIᵉ siècle," *Studies on Voltaire and the Eighteenth Century* 57 (1967), 1269–89; Henri Pèyre, "Reflections on the Literature of Travel," in *Travel, Quest, and Pilgimage as a Literary Theme: Studies in Honor of Reino Virtanen,* ed. F. Amelinckx and J. Megay (Ann Arbor: Society of Spanish and Spanish-American Studies, 1978), 7–23. On the correlation between scientific progress and the aesthetic gaze as articulated in early modern travelogues, see Barbara Maria Stafford, *Voyage into Substance: Art, Science, Nature, and the Illustrated Travel Account, 1760–1840* (Cambridge, Mass.: MIT Press, 1984). For a rendition that insists instead upon the function of voyage literature as an expression of bourgeois class consciousness, see Erica Harth, *Ideology and Culture in Seventeenth-Century France* (Ithaca, N.Y.: Cornell University Press, 1983), 222–309. Other recent critics who likewise insist on the ideological complicities between travel narrative and the legitimation of colonialist aspirations include Michèle Duchet, *Anthropologie et histoire au siècle des lumières;* Michel de Certeau, "Writing vs. Time: History and Anthropology in the Works of Lafitau," tr. J. Hovde, *Yale French Studies* 59 (1980), 37–64, and *The Writing of History,* tr. Tom Conley (New York: Columbia University Press, 1988), 3–5, 215–48, and passim; and Georges Benrekassa, *Le concentrique et l'excentrique: Marges des Lumières* (Paris: Payot, 1980), 91–153, 213–24, 239–84; and, of course, Edward Said's monumental *Orientalism* (New York: Random House, 1978).

27. Charles Dédéyan, *Essai sur le Journal de voyage de Montaigne* (Paris: Boivin, n.d.), 35, 215.

28. Among many possible examples, see Derrida's deconstruction of the ethnocentrism that lies beneath Lévi-Strauss's putatively benevolent attitude toward the Nambikwara Indians he studies (*Of Grammatology,* 101–40). The range of historical possibilities for the critique of Western representations of otherness can be gauged by a number of recent works whose various subject matters span the gamut from the ancient to the modern world: François Hartog, *The Mirror of Herodotus; Representations of the Other in the Writing of History* (Berkeley: University of California Press, 1988); Mary Campbell, *The Witness and the Other World: Exotic Travel Writing, 400–1600*; Tzvetan Todorov, *The Conquest of America*; and *Nous et les autres: La réflexion française sur la diversité humaine* (Paris: Seuil, 1989); Edward Said, *Orientalism;* and Christopher L. Miller, *Blank Darkness: Africanist Discourse in French* (Chicago: University of Chicago Press, 1985).

29. In the case of American literature, at least one critic has explicitly connected the theme of the voyage with the evasion of sexuality: "The figure of Rip Van Winkle presides over the birth of the American imagination . . . the typical male protagonist of our fiction has been a man on the run, harried into the forest and out to sea, down the river or into combat— anywhere to avoid 'civilization,' which is to say, the confrontation of a man and a woman which leads to the fall into sex, marriage, and responsibility" (Leslie Fiedler, *Love and Death in the American Novel* [New York: Criterion Books, 1960], xx–xxi).

30. The best-known French women writers of travel literature are Anne-Louise Germaine Necker, Mme. de Staël (*Corinne, ou l'Italie* [1807] and *De l'Allemagne* [1810]), and Flora Tristan (*Pérégrinations d'une paria* [1833] and *Promenades dans Londres* [1840]). For the Classical period, one should also especially note Marie de l'Incarnation (a nun whose experiences in Quebec are recounted in her *Relations spirituelles* [1653]), Marie-Catherine Jumel de Berneville, Mme. d'Aulnoy (*Relation du Voyage d'Espagne* [1691]), and Marie-Anne Le Page, Mme. Du Boccage (*La Colombiade, ou la foi portée au Nouveau Monde* [1756] and *Lettres sur l'Angleterre, la Hollande et l'Italie* [1762]).

31. Teresa de Lauretis, *Technologies of Gender: Essays on Theory, Film and Fiction* (Bloomington: Indiana University Press, 1987), 38 and passim.

32. Melanie Klein, "Early Analysis," and "The Role of the School in the Libidinal Development of the Child," in *Love, Guilt, and Reparation, and Other Essays, 1921–1945* (London: Hogarth Press, 1975), 59–105, especially 92–100.

33. Cf. Louis Van Delft, *Le moraliste classique* (Geneva: Droz, 1982), 173–91; and Jurgens Hahn, *The Origins of the Baroque Concept of "Peregrinatio"* (Chapel Hill: University of North Carolina Press, 1973).

34. The definitive study of the problem is, of course, Pierre and Huguette Chaunu's monumental eight-volume *Séville et l'Atlantique: 1504–1650* (Paris: Armand Colin, 1955–59).

35. See Lucien Febvre and Henri-Jean Martin, *The Coming of the Book: The Impact of Printing, 1450–1800,* tr. David Gerard (London: New Left Books, 1976), especially 159–66; Henri-Jean Martin, *Livre, pouvoirs et société à Paris au XVII*ᵉ *siècle,* 2 vols. (Geneva: Droz, 1969); John Lough, *Writer and Public in France* (Oxford: Clarendon Press, 1978); Elizabeth Eisenstein, *The Printing Press as an Agent of Change: Communications and Cultural Transformation in Early Modern Europe* (Cambridge: Cambridge University Press, 1979); Robert Darnton, *The Business of Enlightenment: A Publishing History of the* Encyclopédie (Cambridge, Mass.: Belknap Press, 1979), and *The Literary Underground of the Old Regime* (Cambridge, Mass.: Harvard University Press, 1982).

36. The term "death of the author" derives from Roland Barthes's famous article of the same name, in *Image—Music—Text,* tr. Stephen Heath (New York: Hill and Wang, 1977),

142–48. Also see Peggy Kamuf, *Signature Pieces: On the Institution of Authorship* (Ithaca, N.Y.: Cornell University Press, 1988).

37. On the symbolic dimension of absolutist monarchy, the key studies are Ernst H. Kantorowicz, *The King's Two Bodies* (Princeton: Princeton University Press, 1957); Louis Marin, *Le portrait du roi* (Paris: Minuit, 1981), and *Le récit est un piège* (Paris: Minuit, 1978); and Jean-Marie Apostolidès, *Le roi-machine* (Paris: Minuit, 1981). More properly psychoanalytic insights are drawn by Norman O. Brown, *Love's Body* (New York: Random House, 1966), especially 3–31; and by Mitchell Greenberg, *Corneille, Classicism, and the Ruses of Symmetry* (Cambridge: Cambridge University Press, 1986). On the important relations between theatricality and royal power, see Stephen Orgel, *The Illusion of Power: Political Theater in the English Renaissance* (Berkeley: University of California Press, 1975); and Timothy Murray, *Theatrical Legitimation: Allegories of Genius in Seventeenth-Century England and France* (New York: Oxford University Press, 1987).

38. Sarah Kofman, *Le respect des femmes* (Paris: Galilée, 1982), especially 71–83. Since Friedrich Engels, *The Origin of the Family, Private Property and the State* (1894), histories of the family and of the division of labor under preindustrial patriarchy have burgeoned. Among recent work, see especially Joan Kelley, "Family and State," in her *Women, History and Theory* (Chicago: University of Chicago Press, 1984), 110–55; Eli Zaretsky, *Capitalism, the Family, and Personal Life,* rev. ed. (New York: Harper and Row, 1986); Louise Tilly and Joan Scott, *Women, Work and Family* (New York: Holt, Rinehart and Winston, 1978); Philippe Ariès, *L'enfant et la vie familiale sous l'Ancien Régime* (Paris: Seuil, 1973); Jacques Donzelot, *La police des familles* (Paris: Minuit, 1977).

39. In addition to the previously mentioned publications by Duchet, de Certeau, and Campbell, also see the articles collected in *Histoires de l'anthropologie: XVI–XIX siècles,* ed. Britta Rupp-Eisenreich (Paris: Klincksieck, 1984); Margaret Hodgen, *Early Anthropology in the Sixteenth and Seventeenth Centuries* (Philadelphia: University of Pennsylvania Press, 1964); and Claude Lévi-Strauss, "Jean-Jacques Rousseau, fondateur des sciences de l'homme," in *Anthropologie structurale* II (Paris: Plon, 1973), 45–56.

40. De Jaucourt is either citing from memory or intentionally abbreviating and altering the passage from Montaigne, which can be found in "Of the Education of Children," *Les Essais de Michel de Montaigne,* ed. Pierre Villey, 3rd ed. (Paris: PUF, 1978), I, xxvi, 153. As for the last sentence of the quotation, it is not to be found in Montaigne and is either de Jaucourt's invention or taken from a text I have so far been unable to identify.

1. Equestrian Montaigne

1. Michel de Montaigne, *Journal de voyage en Italie par la Suisse et l'Allemagne en 1580 et 1581,* ed. M. Rat (Paris: Garnier, n.d.), 1. Unless otherwise noted, all subsequent page references are to this edition. English translations, with some modifications, are taken from Donald M. Frame, *Montaigne's Travel Journal* (1957; rpt. San Francisco: North Point Press, 1983).

2. Maurice Rat, "Introduction" to *Journal de Voyage en Italie* by Montaigne, ed. M. Rat (Paris: Garnier, n.d.), iii–iv. Cf. also Charles Dédéyan, *Essai sur le Journal de voyage de Montaigne,* (Paris: Boivan, n.d.) 27–32, 98–99; Paul Bonnefon, *Montaigne et ses amis* (Paris: Armand Colin, 1898; rpt. Geneva: Slatkine, 1969), II, 1–46; Louis Lautrey, "Introduction" to *Journal de Voyage* by Montaigne (Paris: Hachette, 1906), 1–51; Donald Frame, *Montaigne's Discovery of Man: The Humanization of a Humanist* (New York: Columbia University Press, 1955), 110–20; and Donald Frame, *Montaigne: A Biography* (New York: Harcourt, Brace and World, 1965), 201–22.

3. So does Montaigne describe his relationship to the *Essays* in "Of Giving the Lie," *Les Essais de Michel de Montaigne,* ed. Pierre Villey, 3d ed. (Paris: PUF, 1978), II, xviii, 665. Unless otherwise noted, all subsequent references to the *Essays* are to this edition and will be indicated by volume, chapter, and page numbers only; English translations, with some modifications, are from *The Complete Essays of Montaigne,* tr. Donald M. Frame (Stanford University Press, 1958). For a critical examination of the secretary's role in the production of the journal, see especially Craig B. Brush, "La composition de la première partie du 'Journal de Voyage' de Montaigne," *Revue d'Histoire Littéraire de la France* 71 (1971), 369–84; and Fausta Garavini's introduction to her edition of the *Journal de voyage* (Paris: Folio, 1983), 7–31. One critic, Pierre d'Espezel, in his edition of the *Journal* (Paris: Cité des Livres, 1931), has even offered the rather bizarre suggestion that this secretary was Montaigne himself. Cf. Imbrie Buffum, *L'influence du voyage de Montaigne sur les Essais,* diss., Princeton, 1942 (Princeton: privately printed, 1946), 149.

4. Gilbert Chinard, *L'exotisme américain dans la littérature française au XVIe siècle* (Paris: Hachette, 1911), 201.

5. The term comes from Claude Lévi-Strauss's distinction between two types of societies: "those which practice anthropophagy—that is, which regard the absorption of certain individuals possessing dangerous powers as the only means of neutralizing those powers and even of turning them to profit—and those which, like our own society, adopt what might be called the practice of *anthropemy* (from the Greek *émein,* to vomit); faced with the same problem, the latter type of society has chosen the opposite solution, which consists in ejecting dangerous individuals from the social body and keeping them temporarily or permanently in isolation, away from all contact with their fellows, in establishments specially intended for this purpose. Most of the societies which we call primitive would regard this custom with profound horror; it would make us, in their eyes, guilty of the same barbarity of which we are inclined to accuse them because of their symmetrically opposite behavior" (*Tristes Tropiques,* tr. John and Doreen Weightman [New York: Atheneum, 1973], 442). For a more philosophical analysis of cannibalism and cultural appropriation in relation to Montaigne's autobiographical project, see Jean Marc Blanchard, "Of Cannibalism and Autobiography," *MLN* 93 (1978), 654–76; as well as his more recent *Trois portraits de Montaigne: Essai sur la representation à la Renaissance* (Paris: Nizet, 1990), especially pp. 107–202. And on cannibalism as a misogynist trope in anthropological discourse, see Dean MacCannell, "Cannibalism Today," in his *The Tourist Papers* (London: Routledge, forthcoming).

6. Such is the thesis initially advanced by Pierre Villey in his monumental *Les sources et l'évolution des Essais de Montaigne* (Paris: Hachette, 1908) and further developed by Donald Frame in *Montaigne's Discovery of Man.* For Imbrie Buffum (*L'influence du voyage de Montaigne sur les Essais*), the trip to Italy explains an entire set of oppositional reversals in Montaigne's opus: from bookish learning to lived experience, from impersonality to personality, from solitude to society, from the critique of customs to their defense, from "diversity" to "unity," etc. For a critique of the "evolutionary" approach to the *Essays,* see Raymond C. La Charité, "Montaigne's Early Personal Essays," *Romanic Review* 62 (1971); and more recently, Jules Brody, *Lectures de Montaigne* (Lexington, Ky.: French Forum, 1982). See also Richard L. Regosin, "Recent Trends in Montaigne Scholarship: A Post-Structuralist Perspective," *Renaissance Quarterly* 37 (1984), 34–54; and Steven Rendell, "Reading Montaigne," *Diacritics* 15 (no. 2: Summer 1985), 44–53.

7. Frame, *Montaigne's Discovery of Man,* 163.

8. See especially Buffum, *L'influence du voyage;* Dédéyan, *Essai sur le Journal,* 124–51; Marcel Tetel, "*Journal de voyage en Italie* et les *Essais:* Étude d'intertextualité," in Floyd Gray and Marcel Tetel, eds., *Textes et intertextes: Études sur le XVIe siècle pour Alfred Glauser* (Paris: Nizet, 1979), 173–91; and *Montaigne* (New York: Twayne, 1974), 114–16; Craig

B. Brush, "The Essayist Is Learned: Montaigne's *Journal de Voyage* and the *Essais,*" *Romanic Review* 62 (1971); Lino Pertile, "Montaigne in Italia: Arte, tecnica e scienza dal *Journal* agli *Essais,*" *Saggi e Ricerche di Letteratura Francese* 12 (1973), 49–92; Claude Blum, "Montaigne, écrivain du voyage. Notes sur l'imaginaire du voyage à la Renaissance," in François Moureau and René Bernouilli, *Autour du Journal de voyage de Montaigne, 1580-1980* (Geneva and Paris: Slatkine, 1982), 3–11.

9. The reference is to Jacques Derrida, *Of Grammatology,* tr. Gayatri Chakravorty Spivak (Baltimore: Johns Hopkins University Press, 1974), 141–64.

10. On prolific commentary as a discursive practice in the Renaissance, see Terence Cave, *The Cornucopian Text: Problems of Writing in the French Renaissance* (Oxford: 1979). Also see Antoine Compagnon, *La seconde main* (Paris: Seuil, 1979); Lawrence Kritzman, *Destruction/Découverte: Le fonctionnement de la rhétorique dans les* Essais *de Montaigne* (Lexington, Ky.: French Forum, 1980); François Rigolot, *Le texte de la Renaissance: Des Rhétoriqueurs à Montaigne* (Geneva: Droz, 1982); and André Tournon, *Montaigne: La glose et l'essai* (Lyon: Presses Universitaires de Lyon, 1983).

11. While, to my knowledge, there exists no complete bibliography of French travels to Italy, help can be found in the bibliography of foreign voyagers to Italy placed at the end of Alessandro D'Ancona's edition of Montaigne's *Journal: L'Italia alla fine del secolo XVI: Giornale del viaggio di Michele de Montaigne in Italia* (Città di Castello: S. Lapi, 1895), as well as in the bibliographies of Ludwig Schudt, *Italienreisen im 17. und 18. Jahrhundert* (Vienna and Munich: Schroll, 1959) and Hermann Harder, *Le Président de Brosses et le voyage en Italie au dix-huitième siècle* (Geneva: Slatkine, 1981). The main problem with these bibliographies, however, is that they are complete only till the beginning of the nineteenth century. Further help can then be found in Gian Carlo Menichelli, *Viaggiatori francesi reali o immaginari nell'Italia dell'ottocento* (Rome: Edizioni di Storia e Letteratura, 1962). See also Emile Picot, *Les Français italianisants au XVIᵉ siècle* (Paris: Champion, 1906).

12. "On échoue toujours à parler de ce qu'on aime," *Tel Quel* 85 (Autumn, 1980), 33.

13. The relevant passage is as follows: "There is in particular one country, beyond the Alps, that deserves the curiosity of all those whose education has been cultivated through letters. Barely is one on the Gallic frontier along the road between Rimini and Cesena than one finds engraved in marble, that famous senatus consultum which consigned to the gods below and declared to be sacriligious and parricidal anyone who crossed the Rubicon, now called the *Pisatello,* with an army, legion, or cohort. It is on the edge of this river or stream that Caesar stopped awhile, and there freedom, which was about to expire under his arms, still cost him a bit of remorse. If I delay crossing the Rubicon, he said to his head officers, I am lost; and if I cross it, how many unhappy people I shall make! Then, after having reflected on this a few moments, he flings himself into the little river and crosses it, shouting (as happens in risky enterprises) the following: 'I think no more of it, the die is cast.' He arrives in Rimini, takes over Umbria, Etruria and Rome, mounts the throne and perishes soon after by a tragic death" (Louis de Jaucourt, "Voyage," *Encyclopédie* XVII, 477).

14. Cited in Villey's edition of the *Essays,* 1208.

15. Dédéyan, *Essai sur le Journal de Voyage,* 30, 98–105. More suggestively, Marcel Tetel ("Montaigne et Le Tasse: Intertexte et Voyage," in Pierre Michel, François Moureau, Robert Granderoute, and Claude Blum, eds., *Montaigne et les Essais, 1580-1980* [Paris: Champion and Geneva: Slatkine, 1983], 306–19) has shown how Montaigne's observations on Italian culture constitute a structured response to Torquato Tasso's *Paragone dell'Italia alla Francia* (1572). The rivalry between the two cultures is thus doubled by Montaigne's rivalry as a writer with his cisalpine contemporary.

16. *Essays* II, ii, 344.

17. Cf. Jules Michelet, who begins the volume on the Renaissance in his *Histoire de France* with Charles VIII's invasion of Italy in 1494 (*Oeuvres complètes,* ed. P. Viallaneix [Paris: Flammarion, 1971–82], VII, 113ff.).

18. As will be seen below, this ambiguous relationship can be shown to be eminently Oedipal in motivation.

19. Pierre Michel ("Le passage de Montaigne dans l'est de la France," in Moureau and Bernouilli, *Autour du Journal de voyage de Montaigne,* 13) suggests that some of Montaigne's descriptions of sites visited may have been less informed by direct observation than by literary reminiscences of contemporary geographical guide books such as Charles Estienne's *Le Guide des chemins de France* (Paris, 1552) or Sebastien Münster's *Cosmographie universelle* (Paris, 1552), a copy of which we know Montaigne owned. Elsewhere, his secretary reports how Montaigne makes up for the loss of a French guide in Rome by reading up himself on the city to the point that "in a few days he could easily have guided his guide" (*Journal,* 103). Likely candidates among the books studied by Montaigne in Rome include Lucio Mauro, *Le antichità della città di Roma* (Venice, 1542), and Flavio Biondo, *Roma ristaurata et Italia illustrata* (Venice, 1542).

20. See, for example, E. M. W. Tillyard, *The Elizabethan World Picture* (New York: Random House, n.d.); Mikhail Bakhtin, *Rabelais and His World,* tr. H. Iswolsky (Cambridge, Mass.: MIT Press, 1968), especially 303–436; Michel Foucault, *Les mots et les choses: Une archéologie des sciences humaines* (Paris: Gallimard, 1966), 32–59; Louis Marin, "Les corps utopiques rabelaisiens," *Littérature* 21 (February 1976), 35–51, rpt. in *La parole mangée* (Paris: Méridians Klincksieck, 1986), 89–120; John C. O'Neill, *Five Bodies: The Human Shape of Modern Society* (Ithaca, N.Y.: Cornell University Press, 1985).

21. This story is retold in *Essays* I, xxi, 99.

22. Cf. Montaigne's final, negative judgment on the medicinal properties of mineral water: "Only fools let themselves be persuaded that this hard, solid body that is baked in our kidneys can be dissolved by liquid concoctions. Therefore, once it is in motion, there is nothing to do but give it passage; for it will take this passage anyway" (III, xiii, 1094). In regards to Montaigne's self-therapy and visits to major European spas, see Alain-Marc Rieu, "Montaigne: Physiologie de la mémoire et du langage dans le 'Journal de voyage,'" in Moureau and Bernouilli, *Autour du Journal de voyage de Montaigne,* 55–66; Jean-Claude Carron, "Lecture du *Journal de Voyage* de Montaigne: L'errance thérapeutique de l'essayiste," in Michel et al., eds., *Montaigne et les* Essais, 271–78; and Irma S. Majer, "Montaigne's Cure: Stones and Roman Ruins," *MLN* 97 (1982), 958–74.

23. Cf. Garavini, Brush, "La composition de la première partie," and Dédéyan, *Essais.*

24. "An idiom that I could neither bend nor turn out of its common course" (III, v, 873). Numerous critics have alluded, gleefully as it were, to Montaigne's poor command of Italian: Dédéyan, *Essai,* 162–64; D'Ancona, *L'Italia,* 419; Frame, *Montaigne: A Biography,* 219. Nevertheless, some attempt has been made to argue the opposite by Aldo Rosellini, "Quelques remarques sur l'italien du 'Journal du voyage' de Michel de Montaigne," *Zeitschrift für romanische Philologie* 83 (1967), 381–408.

25. The essay, "Of Coaches," also offers Montaigne's strongest critique of European colonialism in the New World. Interestingly, the horse figures again within this critique as an unfair advantage for the conquistadors, "mounted on great unknown monsters, opposed to men who have never seen...a horse" (III, vi, 909). The very last line of the essay also describes the fall—both literal and figural—of the last king of Peru at the hands of "a horseman" who "pulled him to the ground" (III, vi, 915). Cf. Tom Conley, "Cataparalysis," *Diacritics* 8 (Fall 1978), 41–59.

26. The title was bought by Montaigne's great-grandfather, Ramon Eyquem, only a little over fifty years before Montaigne's birth. Relevant information on Montaigne's ancestry can

be found in Frame, *Montaigne: A Biography,* 3–28; Théophile Malvezin, *Michel de Montaigne: Son origine, sa famille* (Bordeaux, 1895; rpt. Geneva: Slatkine, 1970); Paul Bonnefon, *Montaigne et ses amis,* I, 21; and Roger Trinquet, *La jeunesse de Montaigne: Ses origines familiales, son enfance et ses études* (Paris: Nizet, 1972).

27. While numerous critics have mentioned the "importance" of this essay, only a very few have given more than passing attention to this text crucial to the genesis of the *Essays* in its specifically *discursive* aspect. The culprit no doubt is the (to my mind) exaggerated emphasis placed by mainstream Montaigne criticism on the psychobiographical origins of the *Essays* as a mourning for the loss of the author's friend, Estienne de La Boétie. Among the few exceptions are Jean Starobinski, *Montaigne en mouvement* (Paris: Gallimard, 1982), 33–36; Richard L. Regosin, *The Matter of My Book: Montaigne's Essais as the Book of the Self* (Berkeley: University of California Press, 1977), 105–6ff; and Glyn P. Norton, *Montaigne and the Introspective Mind* (The Hague: Mouton, 1975), 25–28.

28. If one discounts the *b* and *c* strata written later, only one reference to a horse appears before I, viii. While I do not have the space to comment on this passage, I can remark briefly, looking forward to the rest of my analysis, that it is not without significance that the horse appears in the context of an exemplary death: "[Captain Bayard] having fought as long as he had strength, and feeling himself faint and slipping from his horse, ordered his steward to lay him down at the foot of a tree, but in such a way that he should die with his face turned toward the enemy; as he did" (I, iii, 18).

29. This tradition goes back, of course, to the Classical writers Montaigne knew so well, among whom idleness (*otium*) was both an ideal to be attained and a state whose realization as often as not coincided with a paradoxical exacerbation of the woes it was supposed to put to rest. Some touchstones among Roman writers include Catullus, 50 and 51, Horace, *Odes,* II, 16, and Seneca's *De Tranquillitate Animi* and *De Otio.* Cf. J.-M. André, *Recherches sur l'otium romain, Annales de l'université de Besançon,* 52 (Paris: Belles Lettres, 1962). On Montaigne's relationship to the Latin moralists' notion of *otium,* see Hugo Friedrich, *Montaigne,* tr. R. Rovini (Paris: Gallimard, 1968), 269.

30. The word *rêverie,* as here employed by Montaigne in the sense of foolishness or *sottise* should not be confused with its modern French equivalent, meaning a trance or daydream. On the changing senses of this word, see Arnaud Tripet, *La rêverie littéraire; Essai sur Rousseau* (Geneva: Droz, 1979), 7–33; and Robert J. Morrissey, *La rêverie jusqu'à Rousseau: Recherches sur un topos littéraire* (Lexington, Ky.: French Forum, 1984).

31. Madness as a kind of motion, motion as a kind of madness, is this not what we find crystallized—precisely at the time of the Renaissance—in the Brantian figure of the *Narrenschiff* or ship of fools? Cf. Michel Foucault, *Histoire de la folie à l'age classique,* 2nd ed. (Paris: Gallimard, 1972), 13–55.

32. In all probability, Montaigne found this piece of information in Plutarch's "Precepts of Marriage," available to him in Amyot's French translation. The relevant part of the text is as follows: "No woman has ever produced a child all alone and without the company of man, but there have indeed been women who produce masses lacking the form of a reasonable creature [*des amas sans forme de creature raisonnable*], and resembling a lump of flesh [*piece de chair*]," *Oeuvres morales de Plutarque,* tr. Jacques Amyot, ed. E. Clavier (Paris: Cussac, 1802), XV, 30.

33. Villey, *Les sources et l'évolution des Essais de Montaigne.* On the "therapeutic" underpinnings of Montaigne's thought, see Philip P. Hallie, *The Scar of Montaigne: An Essay in Personal Philosophy* (Middletown, Conn.: Wesleyan University Press, 1966).

34. While the English pun on "pen" and "penis" is unjustifiable on the level of Montaigne's French text, I maintain its use here because of its explanatory power to designate in shorthand, as it were, the phallocratically sanctioned analogy manifestly operative in "Of Idleness"

between writing as phallic activity and misogynist theories of generation enabled by a gendered opposition between form and matter.

35. The pun is warranted by the fact that *montaigne* was a common spelling of *montagne* in the sixteenth century. For some considerations on how Montaigne plays upon the meaning of his name, see Tom Conley, "Cataparalysis," "*De Capsula Totae:* Lecture de Montaigne, 'De trois commerces,' *L'Esprit Créateur* 28 (no. 1: Spring 1988), 18–26; and François Rigolot, "La *Pente* du 'repentir': Un exemple de remotivation du signifiant dans les *Essais* de Montaigne," in Donald Frame and Mary McKinley, eds., *Columbia Montaigne Conference Papers* (Lexington, Ky.: French Forum, 1981), 119–34.

36. Cf. I, xxxix, 241; III, iii, 821. Many critics have commented on Montaigne's use of spatial metaphors. The most ambitious and systematic in this regard are Regosin, *The Matter of My Book,* and Brody, *Lectures de Montaigne,* especially 28–54; as well as Rigolot, "La *Pente* du 'repentir,'" and Conley, "*De Capsula Totae.*"

37. In his study on literary self-portraiture, *Miroirs d'encre: Rhétorique de l'autoportrait,* (Paris, Seuil, 1980), Michel Beaujour argues that such a paradoxical reversal of personality into impersonality is a distinctive trait of the genre in question. The very attempt to represent the self in language consecrates the loss of that self, as that representation can only occur through recourse to a set of coded, impersonal schemata whose foundations Beaujour is able to locate quite convincingly in the topics of ancient rhetoric. Literary self-portraiture then structures itself as an encyclopedic *discursus* of those *topoi* or common *places,* that is, as a running through of rhetorical possibilities. As opposed to autobiography (understood as a narrative structure recounting the writer's life chronologically), self-portraiture would presuppose a "space," or topology, of the subject in language. Furthermore, this topology is oriented by "an economy which is that of the [writer's] body" (334). Self-portraiture thus phrases the text as a topographical body.

38. *Detours of Desire: Studies in the French Baroque* (Columbus: Miami University/Ohio State University Press Joint Imprint Series, 1984), 57–58.

39. Louis Marin has also insisted on the impossible vision of the *skeletos* in his reading of "De l'exercitation" ("Le tombeau de Montaigne," in *La voix excommuniée: Essais de mémoire* [Paris: Galilée, 1981], 133–56). Cf. also Tom Conley, "Un test de style," *Oeuvres et Critiques* VIII (1–2: 1983), 195–209; and Timothy Murray, "Translating Montaigne's Crypts: Melancholic Relations and the Sites of Altarbiography," forthcoming in *Bucknell Review.*

40. *Journal,* 103–5. Montaigne's description, itself inspired by Joachim Du Bellay's *Les Antiquités de Rome* (1558), models a long series of such meditations on the Roman ruins, not the least significant of which is Freud's extended metaphor of the unconscious as the unimaginable simultaneity of all the historical Romes copresented in their architectural completion (Sigmund Freud, *Civilization and Its Discontents, The Standard Edition of the Complete Psychological Works* [hereafter referred to as S.E.], tr. J. Strachey [London: Hogarth, 1955–73)] XXI, 69–70).

41. Nakedness as the privileged metaphor of sincerity is also explicitly linked by Montaigne to his primitivist tendencies right from the opening "To the Reader": "Had I been placed among those nations which are said to live still in the sweet freedom of nature's first laws, I assure you I should very gladly have portrayed myself here entire and wholly naked." On the theme of "native nudity" in Renaissance travel literature, see Geoffroy Atkinson, *Les Nouveaux Horizons de la Renaissance française* (Paris: Droz, 1935), 62–73, 329–31.

42. As Derrida has argued, the category of experience, despite (or rather because of) its claims to attaining a concrete empiricism, does not for that matter escape the metaphysics of presence: "The notion of experience, even where one would like to use it to destroy metaphysics or speculation, continues to be, in one or another point of its functioning, fundamentally inscribed within onto-theology: at least by the value of *presence,* whose implication it can

never reduce by itself. Experience is always the relationship with a plenitude, whether it be sensory simplicity or the infinite presence of God. Even up to Hegel and Husserl, one could show, for this very reason, the complicity of a certain sensationalism and of a certain theology. The onto-theological idea of sensibility or experience, the opposition of passivity and activity, constitute a profound homogeneity, hidden under the diversity of metaphysical systems" (*Of Grammatology,* 283; Derrida's emphasis).

43. Cf. Pietro Pucci, *The Violence of Pity in Euripedes' Medea* (Ithaca, N.Y., and London: Cornell University Press, 1980), 3–32, 84–85.

44. On the distinction between penis and phallus, see Jacques Lacan, "The Signification of the Phallus," in *Ecrits: A Selection,* tr. A. Sheridan (New York: Norton, 1977), 281–91. Useful commentary on the penis/phallus distinction can be found in Fredric Jameson, "Imaginary and Symbolic in Lacan: Marxism, Psychoanalytic Criticism and the Problem of the Subject," *Yale French Studies* 55/56 (1977), 352–53; Jane Gallop, *Reading Lacan* (Ithaca, N.Y.: Cornell University Press, 1985), 133–56; Ellie Ragland-Sullivan, *Jacques Lacan and the Philosophy of Psychoanalysis* (Urbana and Chicago: University of Illinois Press, 1986), 267–308.

45. In an important chapter of his *Lectures de Montaigne* on "Montaigne et la mort," Jules Brody has finally demonstrated the coherence of this essay, traditionally seen in terms of the "contradiction" between the early and the late Montaigne (93–144).

46. Cf. William Shakespeare, "the undiscovered country from whose bourn no traveler returns," *Hamlet* III, i, 79–80.

47. Sigmund Freud, *The Interpretation of Dreams, S.E.,* V, 385.

48. Both Marin ("Le tombeau de Montaigne," 141) and Conley ("Un test de style," 199) similarly comment upon Montaigne's overdetermined use of the word *moyau* in this context.

49. Cf. Alain-Marc Rieu's intriguing hypothesis of Montaigne's travel as a cure for melancholy in his "Montaigne: physiologie de la mémoire."

50. Since I first wrote these lines, both Irma S. Majer ("Montaigne's Cure,") and Antoine Compagnon (*Nous, Michel de Montaigne* [Paris: Seuil, 1980]) have made much of these connections between Pierre, *pierre,* and *père.* For Compagnon, they mark the point at which what he calls Montaigne's "unrestrained nominalism" (143) is checked by a realism which posits a universal in the father's name: "Now, there is one name for which Montaigne manages a singular treatment, a name which is an exception to his theory and which tends to be granted a substance *in re.* This unique name, always the same, which would escape the universal inconsistency of the *flatus vocis,* of the wind and voice, is not in truth the name of just anything nor, moreover, of just anybody: it is the very name of matter itself and furthermore, the name of the father [*le nom du père*], Pierre" (171). Compagnon documents how the word *pierre* is repeatedly used to refer to substance or matter itself while the name *Pierre* is employed, in example after example, as "the canonical forename, the forename of forenames" (171). Thus, at the stony substratum of the *Essays* is found a rock or *pierre* of stability upon which can be built "an ontology of the seed" (184), which makes of fatherhood itself a universal. Thanks to this ontology of the seed, we are allowed to "go beyond the alternative between life and death," to "resolve the fundamental state of discontinuity and to integrate time" (182). Such a continuity is achieved by the conservation of the father—both in his name and in the materiality of his body—in the son, a conservation literalized, as Compagnon points out, in the practice of cannibalism, which Montaigne describes with the utmost fascination. If, in the first moment, nothing seems more horrible to Montaigne than eating one's father, in a second moment, this disgust is reversed into a reverential *dégustation* which makes of the son's body "the most worthy and honorable sepulture, [the sons] lodging within themselves and, as it were, within their marrow the bodies of their fathers and their remains, bringing them in a way back to life and regenerating them by transmutation into their living flesh by

means of digestion and nourishment" (II, xii, 581). This incorporation by the son of the father conserves the latter ("re-generates" him) in both name and body. This incorporation of the father quite clearly recalls Freud's analysis in *Totem and Taboo, S.E.* XIII, a work that surprisingly is never mentioned by Compagnon. It is only a step from this theory of the father's re-incarnation in the son to the positing of a universal law in *Essays* II, xxxvii according to which sons resemble their fathers.

51. Compagnon can thus read Montaigne's inability to maintain his father's property (the chateau and domain of Montaigne) and his more serious inability to produce a male heir as a kind of betrayal of the father. On the other hand, Montaigne assures his own immortality through another kind of procreation, that of writing. Instead of the name of the father, we have the name of the author, Michel de Montaigne, instituted *after the fact* as "a formal reality" at once universal and particular (229–30). Thus the solution offered by this *nom d'auteur* also, according to Compagnon, allows Montaigne to supersede the opposition between realism and nominalism.

52. The continuity postulated by Compagnon's "ontology of the seed" would then require a certain discontinuity that makes it virtually indistinguishable from the "mereological" ontology of Montaigne's radical nominalism.

53. Cf. *Essays* I, xxvi, 173; II, xvii, 639; III, ii, 810; III, ix, 996–97.

54. "Here you have, a bit more decently, some excrements of an aged mind, sometimes hard, sometimes loose, and always undigested" (III, ix, 946).

55. Compagnon, *Nous,* 198.

56. Compagnon, 115 and passim.

57. Compagnon's conclusion, 198.

58. "La vie et l'oeuvre de Montaigne," in *Essays,* xvii. Cf. Malvezin, *Michel de Montaigne,* 11.

59. The aftereffects of this patronymic displacement remain almost hagiographically inscribed in the regional topography. Saint-Michel, the village adjacent to the Eyquem château, is known today by the name of its proudest son: Saint-Michel-de-Montaigne. I find myself in disagreement with Majer's interpretation ("Montaigne's Cure") whereby Montaigne's trip to Rome would "cure" him of an unresolved Oedipal rivalry with the father to the extent that Rome would symbolize the mother. It seems to me, however, that Montaigne's Oedipal make-up is considerably more problematic. References to his mother in the *Essays* are no more present after his travels than before, and while some writers may have imagined Rome as maternal, I see no evidence that Montaigne did. On the contrary, Montaigne's Rome is an eminently masculinized one, peopled by his favorite Roman heroes, the shade of his father, and even as Dorothy Gabe Colemen has shown (*The Gallo-Roman Muse: Aspects of Roman Literary Tradition in Sixteenth-Century France* [Cambridge: Cambridge University Press, 1979], 156–57), the ghost of the long-lost and ever-mourned La Boétie. While Montaigne was in rivalry with his father, there was also an intense desire for him. As for his mother, Antoinette de Louppes, the biographers inform us not only that she outlived her illustrious son but also that upon the death of Pierre Eyquem in 1568, she became the official executor of his will and managed the household affairs of the Montaigne château until about 1587, when she left the domain permanently. The reasons for this departure remain unclear, but strife between her and Michel seems possible. In any case, rather than going to find the mother in Rome, it seems more likely that Montaigne left home precisely to get away from his mother and to refind his father in the eternal city. On Montaigne's mother, see Cecile Insdorf, *Montaigne and Feminism* (Chapel Hill: North Carolina Studies in the Romance Languages and Literatures, 1977), 43–47; Frame, *Montaigne: A Biography,* 16–28; Malvezin, *Michel de Montaigne;* Trinquet, *La jeunesse de Montaigne,* 117–59.

60. Some touchstones in the debate over Montaigne's politics are Frieda S. Brown, *Religious and Political Conservatism in the* Essais *of Montaigne* (Geneva: Droz, 1963); Friedrich, *Montaigne,* 195-210; Francis Jeanson, *Montaigne par lui-même* (Paris: Seuil, n.d.), 62-74; Jeffrey Mehlmann, "La Boétie's Montaigne," *Oxford Literary Review* 4 (no. 1: 1979), 45-61; Timothy Reiss, "Montaigne and the Subject of Polity," in Patricia Parker and David Quint, eds., *Literary Theory/Renaissance Texts* (Baltimore: Johns Hopkins University Press, 1986), 115-49; Manfred Kölsch, *Recht und Macht bei Montaigne: Ein Beitrag zur Erforschung des Grundlagen von Staat und Recht* (Berlin: Duncker and Humblot, 1974); Anna Maria Battista, *Alle origini del pensiero politico libertino: Montaigne e Charron* (Milan: A. Giuffrè, 1966); Max Horkheimer, "Montaigne und die Funktion der Skepsis," in *Kritische Theorie: Eine Dokumentation* (Frankfurt: S. Fischer, 1968), II, 201-59; Starobinski, *Montaigne en mouvement,* 293-367.

61. Cf. Tzvetan Todorov, "L'etre et l'autre," tr. Pierre Saint-Amand, *Yale French Studies* 64 (1983), 113-44; and "The Morality of Conquest," tr. Jeanne Ferguson, *Diogenes* 125 (1984), 89-102. Other critics resituate the reductionism Todorov sees by ironizing or otherwise complicating the way analogy works in Montaigne: Michel de Certeau, *The Writing of History,* tr. Tom Conley (New York: Columbia University Press, 1988), 209-43; and "Montaigne's 'Of Cannibals': The Savage 'I'," in *Heterologies: Discourse on the Other,* tr. Brian Massumi (Minneapolis: University of Minnesota Press, 1986), 67-79; Gérard Defaux, "Un cannibale en haut de chausses: Montaigne, la différence et la logique de l'identité," *MLN* 97 (1982), 919-57; Jean Marc Blanchard, "Of Cannibalism and Autobiography," *MLN* 93 (1978), 654-76; Steven Rendell, "Dialectical Structures and Tactics in Montaigne's *Des Cannibales,*" *Pacific Coast Philology* 12 (1977), 56-63; Marcel Bataillon, "Montaigne et les conquérants de l'or," *Studi Francesi* (1959), 353-67; Frank Lestringant, "Le Cannibalisme des 'Cannibales,'" *Bulletin de la Société des Amis de Montaigne* 9-10 and 11-12 (1982), 27-40, 19-38; Tom Conley, "Montaigne and the New World," *Hispanic Issues* 4 (1989), 225-62. For more general considerations of the *bon sauvage* myth, see Hayden White, "The Noble Savage Theme as Fetich," in Freddi Chiappelli, ed., *First Images of America: The Impact of the New World on the Old* (Berkeley: University of California Press, 1976), I, 121-35; Michèle Duchet, *Anthropologie et histoire au siècle des lumières,* rev. ed. (Paris: Flammarion, 1977).

62. One of the most endearing moments of Michel Butor's *Essais sur les Essais* (Paris: Gallimard, 1968) is no doubt the imaginary dialogue he stages between Montaigne and his wife, who wants to know what it is her husband spends all his time doing in the seclusion of his library. On Montaigne's attitudes toward women, see Insdorf, *Montaigne and Feminism,* and Abraham C. Keller, "Montaigne on Women," in Wolfgang Leiner, ed., *Onze nouvelles études sur l'image de la femme dans la littérature française du dix-septième siècle* (Tübingen: Gunter Narr and Paris: Jean-Michel Place, 1984), 33-37.

63. *Essays,* II, vi, 376.

64. On the relation between siegecraft and ego-construction as elaborated in terms of the textual production of classical France, see Joan DeJean, *Literary Fortifications: Rousseau, Laclos, Sade* (Princeton: Princeton University Press, 1984).

65. Rigolot sees the ensconcement of Montaigne in the height of his name and dominion as the condition for the very writing of the *Essays* and the reason for their self-deprecatory manner: "It is because he is 'perched' up on top of his 'mountain'—literally and figuratively—that he can...embrace 'a life that is low and without luster' and fearlessly proclaim the *mediocrity* of his discourse" ("La *Pente* du repentir," 132).

66. Such an Oedipal ambiguity can, of course, be called upon to explain Montaigne's systematic undercutting of Sebond (and, for that matter, of theological discourse in general) in essay II, xii, which claims to be an "apology" for his father's favorite theologian. On the issue of Montaigne's relation to his father, the vast current of Montaigne criticism has taken

at face value Montaigne's description of him as "the best father there ever was." A few recent critics, however, have begun to analyze the possibilities of Oedipal rivalry: Frederic Rider, *The Dialectic of Selfhood in Montaigne* (Stanford: Stanford University Press, 1973); Antoine Compagnon, *Nous, Michel de Montaigne;* Mitchell Greenberg, "Montaigne at the Crossroads: Textual Conundrums in the *Essais,*" in *Detours of Desire,* 41–59, and "L'écho de Montaigne," *Oeuvres et Critiques* 8 (nos. 1–2: 1983), 115–25; Denis Hollier, "Le siège," *Oeuvres et Critiques* 8 (nos. 1–2: 1983), 45–58; and François Rigolot, "Montaigne's Purloined Letters," *Yale French Studies* 64 (1983), 145–66. While these critics tend to insist, quite rightly, on Montaigne's structured inadequacy vis-à-vis his real father as well as his symbolic or literary fathers (Socrates, Plutarch, the Latin moralists), this is to forget the obvious, the historical triumph of Montaigne over his father(s). In the terminology advanced by Harold Bloom (*The Anxiety of Influence* [Oxford: Oxford University Press,1973]), Montaigne is a "strong" writer, easily able to overcome his various predecessors. After all, nearly all we know of Pierre Eyquem comes from what his son, Michel de Montaigne, says about him.

2. Cartesian Coordinates

1. *Les Nouveaux Horizons de la Renaissance française* (Paris: Droz, 1935), 254–61, 402–5. A particular favorite for ridicule, in this regard, was Augustine's contention that life in the antipodes was impossible: "Among Christians, those who deny that the earth is round, believe it impossible and against nature to be able to walk with one's head below and one's feet above: even Lactantius and Saint Augustine believe this because, among other reasons, they found no mention of it in Scripture.... Nevertheless, even though the word of God does not clarify this for us, it does not follow that the Antipodes do not exist. For, as it is impious to seek the articles of one's faith elsewhere, so it is also a great superstition to believe and to consider true only what is expressed in the Scriptures" (Henri Lancelot Du Voisin de La Popelinière, *Les trois mondes* [Paris, 1582]; cited in Atkinson, 259–60). In a 1588 addition to the *Apology for Raymond Sebond,* Montaigne follows suit: "It would have been Pyrrhonizing, a thousand years ago, to cast in doubt the science of cosmography, and the opinions that were accepted about it by one and all; it was heresy to admit the existence of the Antipodes. Behold in our century an infinite extent of terra firma.... which has just been discovered" [*Essays* II, xii, 571–72]. Should we be surprised, then, if this same critical *topos* resurfaces in Descartes's often haughty responses to objections made against him? "One should believe a single person who says, with no intention of lying, that he has seen or understood something more than one ought to believe a thousand others who deny this only because they have not been able to see or understand it: just as in the discovery of the antipodes we have believed the reports of a few sailors who have circumnavigated the globe rather than thousands of philosophers who refused to believe that the earth was round" (René Descartes, "Lettre à M. Clerselier," January 12, 1646, in *Oeuvres de Descartes,* ed. Charles Adam and Paul Tannery, rev. ed., [Paris: Vrin, 1973–82], IX-1, 210). Cf. "Réponses aux Sixièmes Objections," IX-1, 227, 229; **VII, 424, 426.** All subsequent references to Descartes will be to this edition and will be marked directly in the text only by page number and, where necessary, by the title and the volume number of the work cited. Since I will refer to the Latin only as necessary for the sake of emphasis or to underscore significant departures from the French, references to the Latin text will be indicated with volume and page numbers in boldface. For the same reason, and because the leading English translations inevitably rely on a mix of the French and Latin versions, all English translations of Descartes (whether from French or from Latin) are my own. I have, however, carefully consulted the following translations: *Descartes: Philosophical Writings,* tr. and ed. Elizabeth Anscombe and Peter Thomas Geach, rev. ed. (Indianapolis: Bobbs-Merrill, 1971); *The Philosophical Writings of Descartes,* 2 vols., tr. John

Cottingham, Robert Stoothof, and Dugald Murdoch (Cambridge: Cambridge University Press, 1984).

2. On the libertine movement in French letters, see J. S. Spink, *French Free-Thought From Gassendi to Voltaire* (London: Athlone, 1960); and René Pintard, *Le libertinage érudit dans la première moitié du dix-septième siècle* (Paris: Boivin, 1943). On its literary ramifications, see Joan DeJean, *Libertine Strategies: Freedom and the Novel in Seventeenth-Century France* (Columbus: Ohio State University Press, 1981).

3. Savinien de Cyrano de Bergerac, *L'Autre Monde, ou les estats et empires de la lune* in *Oeuvres complètes,* ed. Jacques Prévot (Paris: Belin, 1977), 359, my emphasis. Cf. Gérard Genette, "L'univers réversible," in *Figures I* (Paris: Seuil, 1966), 18–20. The progressive familiarization of a putatively other world is also strikingly demonstrated by Descartes in his *The World* as well as Part Five of the *Discourse on Method.* There, the accumulating wealth of detail and ever-greater particularity of description inevitably disclose this "fiction" of a purely deductive physics (and physiology, in the ensuing *Treatise on Man*) as a systematic explication of *the* world in which we live. Similarly, the Orients to be found in Voltaire's tales or Montesquieu's *Persian Letters* do not succeed in being anything more than, as Roland Barthes puts it, "some kinds of empty boxes, mobile signs with no content of their own, degree zeros of humanity, which one quickly uses to signify oneself." Concludes Barthes, "this is the paradox of the Voltairian voyage: to manifest an immobility" ("Le dernier des écrivains heureux," in *Essais critiques* [Paris: Seuil, 1964], 98–99).

4. On the notion of neutralization in utopic discourse, see Louis Marin, *Utopiques: Jeux d'espace* (Paris: Minuit, 1973). Also see Fredric Jameson, "Of Islands and Trenches: Neutralization and the Production of Utopian Discourse," *Diacritics* 7 (no. 2: Summer 1977), 2–21. Other important recent work on the question of utopias can be found in Gilles Lapouge, *Utopie et civilisation* (Paris: Flammarion, 1978); Alexandre Cioranescu, *L'avenir du passé: Utopie et littérature* (Paris: Gallimard, 1972); Raymond Trousson, *Voyages au pays de nulle part: Histoire littéraire de la pensée utopique* (Brussels: Publications de la Faculté de Philosophie et Lettres, 1975); Maurice de Gandillac and Catherine Piron, eds., *Le discours utopique* (Paris: U.G.E. 10/18, 1978); Pierre Furter and Gérard Raulet, eds., *Stratégies de l'utopie* (Paris: Galilée, 1979); Wilhelm Vosskamp, ed., *Utopieforschung: Interdisziplinäre Studien zur neuzeitlichen Utopie* (Stuttgart: J. B. Metzler, 1982); Peter Ruppert, *Reader in a Strange Land: The Activity of Reading Literary Utopias* (Athens: University of Georgia Press, 1986).

5. An exemplary reading that brings out the figural underpinnings in a key text of the British tradition, John Locke's *Essay on Human Understanding,* can be found in Paul de Man, "The Epistemology of Metaphor," *Critical Inquiry* 5 (no. 1: Autumn 1978), 13–30. For a wide-ranging discussion of the ways in which a particular metaphor (the ocular) has informed the history of modern philosophy in Great Britain as well as on the Continent, see especially Richard Rorty, *Philosophy and the Mirror of Nature* (Princeton: Princeton University Press, 1979).

6. To be precise, exactly one instance of Montaigne's name occurs in the entire Cartesian corpus: in a letter to Newcastle (November 23, 1646), Descartes mentions Montaigne's name among those of philosophers who attribute thought and understanding to animals, a view often lambasted by Descartes in his infamous theory of animals as mere "automatons." On the discreet but decisive influence of Montaigne on Descartes, see, among others, Léon Brunschvicg, *Descartes et Pascal, lecteurs de Montaigne* (Neuchâtel: La Baconnière,1945); Richard H. Popkin, *The History of Skepticism from Erasmus to Spinoza* (Berkeley: University of California Press, 1979), 172–213; Alan M. Boase, *The Fortunes of Montaigne: A History of the Essays in France, 1580–1669* (London: Methuen,1935), 209–37; Benjamin Woodbridge, "The *Discours de la méthode* and the Spirit of the Renaissance," *Romanic Review* 25 (1933),

136-42; Gilbert Gadoffre, "Le *Discours de la méthode* et l'histoire littéraire," *French Studies* 2 (1948), 301-14 ; Alexandre Koyré, *Entretiens sur Descartes* (New York and Paris: Brentano, 1944); François Paré, "Descartes et Montaigne, autobiographes," *Etudes littéraires* 17 (1984), 381-94; Philippe Desan, *Naissance de la méthode* (Paris: Nizet, 1987), especially 115-59. Finally, much on the relation between Descartes and Montaigne can be found in Etienne Gilson's extensive commentaries in his edition of the *Discours de la méthode* (Paris: Vrin, 1930).

7. Nathan Edelman, "The Mixed Metaphor in Descartes," *Romanic Review* 41 (1950), 167-78; rpt. in *The Eye of the Beholder: Essays in French Literature,* ed. Jules Brody (Baltimore: Johns Hopkins University Press, 1974), 107-20. While Edelman is not the first to have noticed Descartes's metaphorical preferences, he is, at least as far as I can tell, the first to have argued for the decisive influence of such elements in Descartes's style on the development of his thought. Also see, on this same topic, Th. Spoerri, "La puissance métaphorique de Descartes," in M. Gueroult and H. Gouhier, eds., *Descartes* (Paris: Minuit [Cahiers de Royaumont, Philosophie No. 2], 1957), 273-87; G. Nador, "Métaphores de chemins et de labyrinthes chez Descartes," *Revue Philosophique de la France et de l'étranger* 152 (1962), 37-51; and Pierre-Alain Cahné, *Un autre Descartes: Le philosophe et son langage* (Paris: Vrin, 1980), especially 166-71. Other, more recent works stressing the importance of Descartes's use of language that have substantively informed my reading of Descartes include: Jean-Luc Nancy, *Ego sum* (Paris: Flammarion, 1979); Michel Foucault, *Histoire de la folie à l'âge classique,* 2nd ed. (Paris: Gallimard, 1972), 56-58, 583-603; Jacques Derrida, "Cogito and the History of Madness," in *Writing and Difference,* tr. Alan Bass (Chicago: University of Chicago, 1978), 31-63; Jean-François Bordron, "La fonction structurante," in *Structures élémentaires de la signification,* ed. F. Nef (Brussels: Editions Complexe, 1976), 110-42. Along similar lines, also see Sylvie Romanowski, *L'illusion chez Descartes: La structure du discours cartésien* (Paris: Klincksieck, 1974); Timothy J. Reiss, "Cartesian Discourse and Classical Ideology," *Diacritics* 6 (no. 4: Winter 1976), 19-27; and "The 'Concevoir' Motif in Descartes," in J. Van Baelen and D. L. Rubin, eds., *La cohérence intérieur: Études sur la littérature française du XVII^c siècle présentées en hommage à Judd D. Hubert* (Paris: Jean-Michel Place, 1977), 203-22; John Lyons, "The Cartesian Reader and the Methodic Subject," *Esprit Créateur* 21 (no. 2: Summer 1981), 37-47; and "Subjectivity and Imitation in the *Discours de la méthode,*" *Neophilologus* 66 (no. 4: October 1982), 508-24; Jean-Joseph Goux, "Descartes et la perspective," *Esprit Créateur* 25 (no. 1: Spring 1985), 10-20; Dalia Judovitz, *Subjectivity and Representation: The Origins of Modern Thought in Descartes* (Cambridge: Cambridge University Press, 1987).

8. *Meditations on First Philosophy,* IX-1, 18-19. Cf. *La recherche de la vérité* (The Search for Truth), X, 512: "Such general doubts would lead us straight into the ignorance of Socrates or the uncertainty of the Pyrrhonists. These are deep waters, where it seems to me that one may lose one's footing."

9. Cf. *The Search for Truth,* X, 515: "for from this universal doubt, *just as if from a fixed and immovable point* [*veluti è fixo immobilique puncto*], I shall derive the knowledge of God, of you yourself, and of all the things in the world."

10. According to Martial Gueroult, this dilemma points to a systematic opposition throughout Descartes's opus between the persuasive and the convincing: "The first is a deep agreement and close acquiescence, either with sensations or habits, or with the fundamental requirements of our mind; the second is an external constraint in which will, far from being seduced, sees its consent torn from it by the force of reasons. When conviction encounters a persuasion opposed to it, it can be brought to move against itself with difficulty" (*Descartes' Philosophy Interpreted according to the Order of Reasons,* tr. Roger Ariew et al. [Minneapolis: University

of Minnesota Press, 1984] I, 299n). Cf. Henri Gouhier's remarks on the difference between *assensio* and *persuasio* (*La pensée métaphysique de Descartes* [Paris: Vrin, 1967], 91–95ff).

11. Cf. Gueroult, *Descartes' Philosophy:* "The analysis of the piece of wax has appeared as a decisive and brilliant verification of the conclusions imposed by the order of reasons" (I, 127).

12. Cf. Nancy's claim in *Ego sum* that the subject's continued existence is contingent upon his *continued* enunciation of the *cogito*. The argument is based on the following line from the Second Meditation: "This proposition: *I am, I exist,* is necessarily true, every time that I pronounce it, or that I conceive it in my mind" (IX-1, 19). The temporal problem of the *cogito*'s continuity or discontinuity is, of course, one of the traditional areas of debate among readers of Descartes. As his own first reader, Descartes was himself aware of the problem: "It might just happen that if I ceased to think, I would at the same time cease to be or to exist" (IX-1, 418). Early and eloquent reformulations of this dilemma are found in David Hume's *Treatise of Human Nature,* ed. L. A. Selby-Bigge (Oxford: Clarendon, 1888) and Kant's *Critique of Pure Reason,* ed. and tr. N. K. Smith (New York: St. Martin's, 1929), 341–44. In the wake of Jaako Hintikka's immensely influential and fiercely contested article, "*Cogito, Ergo Sum:* Inference or Performance?" (*Philosophical Review* 71 [1962], 3–23), current debates on this issue have tended to question the fundamental Cartesian dictum in terms of performative utterance. In a similar but more rigorously semiotic vein, Bordron ("La fonction structurante") has analyzed the *cogito* in terms of a slippage between *énonciation* and *énoncé.* Even more recently, Jean-François Lyotard has argued the necessity of the subject's proper name to provide a solution of continuity between the not necessarily identical pronouns of *I think* and *I am* (*The Differend: Phrases in Dispute* [Minneapolis: University of Minnesota Press, 1988], 46).

13. Our formulation of an *erro, ergo sum* turns out to be not too far from the *ambulo, ergo sum,* whose validity Descartes denies in his responses to Pierre Gassendi's materialist objections to the *cogito,* namely, that any of one's actions, whether intellectual or corporeal, is sufficient to prove one's existence ("Fifth Objections," **VII,** 259–61). Predictably, Descartes's rebuttal is that a proposition such as *I walk, therefore I am* is only certain insofar as *I think* that I am walking, since I could imagine myself walking even though I may be only dreaming. As a result, all that can be inferred is the existence of the mind that thinks itself to be walking and not that of the body that is in motion (**VII, 352**). Descartes's response thus already calls into action the mind/body split not explicitly developed until the Sixth Meditation to ward off Gassendi's objection as a naïve empiricism. Such a rejoinder could not so easily dispose of the figuratively indecidable *erro, ergo sum* to the extent that the fact of *error* necessarily precedes any distinction between mind and body. The very confusion of the categories could only reinforce the proposition's validity.

14. The pleasures of the famous Cartesian *poêle* were already tested by Montaigne during his trip through southern Germany on his way to Italy. His secretary notes Montaigne's reactions: "Monsieur de Montaigne, who slept in a room with a stove in it [*dans un poile*], praised it highly for feeling all night a pleasant and moderate warmth of air. At least you don't burn your face or your boots, and you are free from the smoke you get in France" (*Journal,* 24). Later, in the *Essays,* Montaigne compares the relative merits of French chimney and German *poêle:* "A German pleased me at Augsburg by attacking the disadvantages of our fireplaces [*noz fouyers*] by the same argument we ordinarily use to condemn their stoves [*poyles*]. For in truth, that stifling heat, and the smell of that material they are made of when it gets hot, gives most of those who are not used to them a headache; not me. But after all, since this heat is even, constant and general, without flame, smoke, or the wind that the opening of our chimneys brings us, it has what it takes in other respects for comparison with ours" (III, xiii, 1080). In line, however, with his predictable Latin affinities, both modes of

heating are considered subservient to a highly overdetermined third: "Why don't we imitate Roman architecture? For they say that in ancient times the fire was made only outside their houses, and at the foot of them; whence the heat was breathed into the entire dwelling by pipes, contrived in the thickness of the walls that surrounded the rooms that were to be warmed. This I have seen clearly indicated, I don't know where, in Seneca" (ibid.). As for the horse, it dramatically reappears in one of Descartes's most notable successors, Giambattista Vico, who resorts to it precisely for the purposes of differentiating himself from Descartes: "We shall not here feign what René Descartes craftily feigned as to the method of his studies simply in order to exalt his own philosophy and mathematics and degrade all the other studies included in divine and human erudition. Rather, with the candor proper to a historian, we shall narrate plainly and step by step the entire series of vicissitudes, in order that the proper and natural causes of his [Vico's] particular development as a man of letters be known. Just as a high-spirited horse, long and well trained in war and long afterwards let out to pasture at will in the fields, if he happens to hear the sound of a trumpet feels again the martial appetite rise in him and is eager to be mounted by the cavalryman and led into battle; so Vico, though he had wandered from the straight course of a well disciplined early youth was soon spurred by his genius to take up again the abandoned path, and set off again on his way" (*The Autobiography of Giambattista Vico*, tr. Max Harold Fisch and Thomas Goddard Bergin [Ithaca, N.Y.: Cornell University Press, 1944], 113–14). Vico's revision of Descartes's autobiographical rhetoric has been critically examined by Juliana Schiesari in an as yet unpublished paper, "His-story: Vico's Autobiography in the Third Person," read at the Modern Language Association convention in December 1988.

15. While it is worth noting that Descartes takes this metaphor from medieval theological allegory where it is rampant (cf. Nador, "Métaphores de chemins," 39–41), it is the peculiarity of his discourse to link the allegorical imagery of morality with the basis of "scientific" inquiry. The intelligent decision would seem to be for Descartes indistinguishable from the morally correct one, a slippage queried by none other than the Jansenist Antoine Arnauld in the "Fourth Objections" (IX–1, 167–68). In Kantian terms, there would be no distinction in Descartes between pure and practical reason. But if the road to God and the road to truth are the same road, and if the destination is to be reached through a moral rationality or a rational morality, then one can already see the possibility as well as the necessity for Descartes's proving God's existence by rational proof alone.

16. The "dark wood of error" is, of course, a longstanding literary *topos*, celebrated examples of which can be found in the opening cantos of Dante's *Inferno* and Spenser's *Faerie Queene*. A modern, parodic version of it can be found in Samuel Beckett's *Molloy*, tr. Patrick Bowles (New York: Grove Press, 1955), in which the hero rejects Descartes's advice of following a straight line and seeks instead to crawl out of the wood within which he is entrapped by moving in an ever-widening spiral (115–24). Despite the efforts of Ruby Cohn (*Samuel Beckett: the Comic Gamut* [New Brunswick, N.J.: Rutgers University Press, 1962], 10–16) and Hugh Kenner (*Samuel Beckett: A Critical Study* [New York: Grove Press, 1961], especially the chapter on "The Cartesian Centaur," 117–32), not much seems to have been done in terms of Beckett as a critical reader of Descartes. Not only is Cartesianism a persistent subtext of his novels and plays, but his first published work, "Whoroscope" (Paris: Hours Press, 1930), was a prize-winning poem about Descartes, and he did extensive research on Descartes for his master's degree while serving as a visiting lecturer at the Ecole Normale Supérieure in Paris.

17. Cf. Nancy, *Ego sum*, 104–15.

18. *Discourse*, VI, 6.

19. The historical veracity of Descartes's account of his own philosophical development has drawn serious reservations from twentieth-century critics. Ferdinand Alquié, in particular,

has insisted on a slow, lifelong process of maturation in Descartes's philosophy. He consequently refuses to read any inklings of the later works in the earlier ones, to the point of claiming that the *cogito* of the *Discourse* is not yet the "true *cogito*," whose proper formulation must await the publication of the *Meditations* (*La découverte métaphysique de l'homme chez Descartes*, rev. ed. [Paris: PUF, 1966], 133ff). Others, such as Georges Poulet ("Le songe de Descartes," in *Etudes sur le temps humain* [Paris: Plon, 1949], I, 63-92); Bertram D. Lewin (*Dreams and the Uses of Regression* [New York: International Universities Press, 1958]); and, to a lesser extent, Gregor Sebba (*The Dream of Descartes* [Carbondale and Edwardsville: Southern Illinois University Press, 1987]), see the entirety of Descartes's philosophical project inscribed in the early references to the dream. Needless to say, between the two extremes, innumerable variations and positions exist. For some overviews of the critical terrain, see Geneviève Rodis-Lewis, *L'oeuvre de Descartes* (Paris: Vrin, 1971), 45-59, 448-54

20. While references to the dream occur in the *Cogitationes Privatae* (**X, 216-18**), whatever text Descartes may have written has disappeared. Scholars are thus obliged to follow the version given by Adrien Baillet in his *Vie de Monsieur Des-Cartes* ([Paris: Horthemels, 1691; rpt. Geneva: Slatkine, 1970], I, 81-86), reproduced by Adam and Tannery, *Oeuvres*, X, 179-88. Baillet's text can be given considerable credence, however, since what could be called his biographical method often consists merely in the verbatim lifting of phrases from Descartes's writings, including now-lost manuscripts to which Baillet had access. In fact, Baillet's biography could be said, in general, to retranscribe the autobiographical passages in Descartes from first to third person. Textual problems notwithstanding, Descartes's dream has drawn considerable interpretive attention. See, in particular, Poulet, "Le songe"; Sebba, *Dream;* Lewin, *Dreams;* Sigmund Freud, "Brief an Maxime Leroy über einem Traum des Cartesius," in *Gesammelte Werke* (London: Imago, 1948), XIV, 558-60; Maxime Le Roy, *Le philosophe au masque* (Paris: Rieder, 1929), I, 79-96; Jacques Maritain, *Le songe de Descartes* (Paris: Corrêa, 1932); Henri Gouhier, *Les Premières Pensées de Descartes* (Paris: Vrin, 1958); Stephen Schönberger, "A Dream of Descartes: Reflections on the Unconscious Determinants of the Sciences," *International Journal of Psychology* 20 (January 1939), 45-57; Iago Galston, "Descartes and Modern Psychiatric Thought," *Isis* 35 (Spring 1944), 118-28; J. O. Wisdom, "Three Dreams of Descartes," *International Journal of Psychoanalysis* 28 (1947), 118-28; L. Feuer, "The Dream of Descartes," *American Imago* 20 (1959), 3-26; Ben-Ami Scharfstein, "Descartes's Dreams," *Philosophical Forum* 1 (1968-69), 293-317; Roberta Recht, "'The Foundations of an Admirable Science': Descartes's Dreams of 10 November 1619," *Humanities in Society* 4 (nos. 2-3, Spring-Summer 1981), 203-19; Jacques Barchilon, "Les songes de Descartes du 10 novembre 1619, et leur interprétation," *Papers on French Seventeenth-Century Literature* 11 (no. 20: 1984), 99-113; Jack Rochford Vrooman, *René Descartes: A Biography* (New York: Putnam, 1970), 45-67; Marie-Louise von Franz, *Der Traum des Descartes,* in *Zeitlose Dokumente des Seele* (Zurich: Rascher, 1952), 49-119; Karl Stern, *The Flight from Woman* (New York: Farrar, Strauss and Giroux, 1965), 75-105.

21. Here, I find myself both in agreement and at variance with Lucien Goldman's understanding of Descartes as he who opens up the infinite spaces that alarm Pascal (*Le Dieu caché: Étude sur la vision tragique dans les Pensées de Pascal et dans le théâtre de Racine* [Paris: Gallimard, 1959], 36-45). While my reading corroborates such a discovery of infinity in Descartes's writing, it also maintains that a denial of this infinity is already or simultaneously underway there. In fact, I would go so far as to argue that the denial of infinity or "error" is a defining gesture of Cartesianism itself. Even in his physics, the implicit postulation of the infinity of the universe is reduced to the merely "indefinite," as Alexandre Koyré has shown, through the "identification of extension and matter" (*From the Closed World to the Infinite Universe* [Baltimore: Johns Hopkins Press, 1957], 101ff). To explain the existence of movement within this voidless world, Descartes is obliged to resort to his infamous theory

of vortices (tourbillons, cf. Le Monde, XI, 18–21; Principles of Philosophy IX–2, 71–84; VIII–1, 49–62), by which the movement of one object necessarily displaces another, which in turn displaces another and another, until we return to the original object set in motion. As such, the hop of a flea would necessarily be felt around the world. This absolute cosmological economy of travel is guaranteed, of course, by God, who is the "first cause" of this motion whose pathways describe perfect circles and whose quantity remains constant throughout the universe (Principes, IX–2, 81–84; VIII–1, 58–62).

22. An object of aesthetic contemplation is "mathematically sublime" if its size is so great that the imagination can no longer "comprehend" it as a whole even while that faculty persists in its attempts to "apprehend" that object through a process of sequential approximations. Immanuel Kant, Critique of Judgment, tr. J. H. Bernard (New York: Hafner Press, 1951), 86–99.

23. As Descartes states elsewhere, "God alone is the author of every movement in the world" (Le Monde, XI, 46).

24. "The idea of infinity as comprehending all of being, comprehends all of what is true in things," A. Clerselier (April 23, 1649), V, 355–56. Cf. Alquié, La decouverte, 218–38; and Rodis-Lewis, L'oeuvre de Descartes, 286ff.

25. A long and implicitly puritanical tradition has placed the sole source of Cartesian error in the faculty of the will: from at least Spinoza (Parts I and II of Descartes's Principles of Philosophy Demonstrated in the Geometric Manner, in Collected Works of Spinoza, ed. Edwin Curley [Princeton: Princeton University Press, 1985], 256–60) through Rodis-Lewis, L'oeuvre de Descartes, 311–13, and Susan Bordo (The Flight to Objectivity: Essays on Cartesianism and Culture [Albany: SUNY Press, 1987], 78–82). Nonetheless, it seems to me that Descartes's analysis merely points, in a geometrically inspired fashion, to a zone of nonintersection between two God-given, hence perfect, faculties: "Since God is not deceitful, the faculty of knowing that He gave us cannot fail, nor even the faculty of the will" (Principles, IX–2, 43; VII–1, 21; my emphasis). As a result, to follow Alquié, La decouverte, "the Fourth Meditation did not completely exculpate God, nor did it fully ground man's responsibility" (286). As for his objections to the Méditations, the ever-recalcitrant Gassendi takes the opposite tack: "The fault seems to lie less with the free will for not judging correctly than with the understanding for not indicating correctly" (VII, 317). Cf. also Gottfried Wilhelm Leibniz, "I do not admit that errors are more dependent upon the will than upon the intellect" (Critical Thoughts on the General Part of the Principles of Descartes [1692], in L. Loemker, ed., Philosophical Papers and Letters [Chicago: Chicago University Press, 1956], II, 637ff).

26. Among those critics who read Descartes's work as more driven by the need—negatively, as it were—to contain error than by the positive desire to ground truth as certitude, see especially Romanowski, L'illusion, 159, 186, and passim; and Alquié, La decouverte, 17–37, and passim. It is also worth noting that the major work of Descartes's most prominent successor in France, Malebranche's La recherche de la vérité, is fundamentally organized as a reflection on ways to overcome the chief obstacle to truth, error.

27. Maurice Blanchot, Le pas au-delà (Paris: Gallimard, 1973). See also Jacques Derrida, "Pas," Gramma 3–4 (1976), 111–215.

28. While the original 1619 poêle experience may have had little to do (at least in the eyes of some critiques, most notably that of Alquié) with Descartes's subsequent meditations carried out in Holland after 1628, the phantasmic space of the stove-heated room recurs as the narrative setting for both the Discourse and the Meditations, as when Descartes has some trouble doubting that he is "here, sitting close to the fire, dressed in a housecoat" (IX–1, 14; VII, 18), or when he demonstrates the melting of the wax piece by putting it near the fire "even while I am speaking [dum loquor]" (IX–1, 23; VII, 30; cf. Charles Adam, Vie et oeuvres de Descartes: Étude historique, in Oeuvres de Descartes, ed. Adam and Tannery, XII, 130). The

coziness of the hearth thus helps construct an illusion of immediacy conducive to the text's persuasive power. Even his move to Holland is justified by that country's prolific use of the *poêle* (cf. the letter to Balzac of May 5, 1631, analyzed below). The private space of the warm room could be said, therefore, to supply the representational parameters for the subject as individualistic consciousness. In this respect, Leibniz's concept of the monad, which has "no windows through which anything could enter or depart," is but a cooled-down version of the Cartesian locus of subjectivity (*The Monadology* [1714], in *Philosophical Papers*, II, 1044–45ff). The proximateness of Being in the Cartesian system is also cogently noted by Hegel: "The demand which rests at the basis of Descartes's reasonings thus is that what is recognized as true should be able to maintain the position of having the thought therein *at home with itself*. . . . The thinking subject as the simple immediacy of *being-at-home-with-me* is the very same thing as what is called Being. . . . Thought, the Notion, the spiritual, the self conscious, is what is *at home with itself*, and its opposite is contained in what is extended, spatial, separated, not at home with itself" (Georg Wilhelm Friedrich Hegel, *Lectures on the History of Philosophy*, tr. E. S. Haldane and Frances H. Simson [New York: Humanities Press, 1955], III, 226, 229, 244; my emphasis).

29. Cf. *Discourse*, Fifth Part, VI, 46–54; *Treatise on Man*, XI, 123–30. As magisterially demonstrated by Etienne Gilson, the thermodynamic theory of the circulation distinguishes Descartes both from scholastic views and from those of his contemporary, William Harvey (*Etudes sur le rôle de la pensée médiévale dans la formation du système cartésien* [Paris: Vrin, 1930], 51–100).

30. Cf. Gueroult, *Descartes' Philosophy*, I, 30, 73, 99–100, and passim. The metaphor of methodical doubt as the emptying of a container is itself further elaborated by Descartes as the overturning of a basketful of apples to separate the good from the rotten ("Seventh Objections with Notes by the Author," **VII, 481, 512**). This procedure is also extensively analyzed by Bordo *Flight to Objectivity* from a feminist perspective in terms of a purification ritual, whose ultimate historical horizon is the "masculinization of thought" enacted by the seventeenth-century discourse of objective science (16–17 and passim).

31. Once again, we find ourselves to be rephrasing the gist of Gassendi's objections, namely that since "all ideas come from without," the faculty that conceives them, "not being outside of itself, cannot transmit its own species into itself, nor consequently can it bring forth any notion of itself" (**VII, 279–80, 292** and passim).

32. In the face of Père Bourdin's objections that Cartesian doubt risks undermining all possible knowledge, Descartes at great length and with considerable humor insists upon the *heuristic* quality of his doubt by elaborating the metaphor of excavating one's way down to the bedrock ("Seventh Objections," **VII**, especially **544–61**). On the other hand, it indeed remains an open question as to whether Descartes's inaugural moments of skepticism do or do not overshadow the touted stability of his subsequent, foundational principles. Cf. Edelman, "Mixed Metaphor," 174–76; Popkin, *History of Skepticism*, 193–213; and Henri Lefebvre, *Descartes* (Paris: Hier et Aujourd'hui, 1947).

33. On this sale, see the letters to his elder brother (April 3, 1622) and to his father (May 22, 1622). Cf. Baillet, *Vie* I, 116–17; Adam, *Vie*, 63.

34. While early biographers, such as Baillet (I, 117–18) and the now-discredited Pierre Borel (*Vitae Renati Cartesi, Summi Philosophi, Compendium* [Paris: 1656]) and even Elizabeth Haldane (*Descartes: His Life and Times* [London; John Murray, 1905], 89–95), blithely send Descartes through all sorts of points on the Italian peninsula and have him experience various adventures in great detail, more scrupulous scholars (such as Adam, *Vie*, 63–67; Vrooman, *René Descartes*, 69; Henri Gouhier, *Premières Pensées*, 104–6; Le Roy, *Le philosophe*, I, 107–18; and Gustave Cohen, *Ecrivains français en Hollande dans la première moitié du XVIIᵉ siècle* [Paris: Champion, 1920], 412–13) are left with precious little to go on, except for the

fact that Descartes did indeed travel to Italy in 1622. Perhaps a travelogue such as Montaigne's exists and has yet to be discovered. In any case, Montaigne's *Journal* was not yet known in Descartes's time and so could have had no influence on him, save through the allusions made in the *Essays.*

35. In 1644, 1647, and 1648. For details of these trips, see Baillet, *Vie* II, 215–48, 323–30, 338–50; Adam, *Vie,* 432–75; and Cohen, *Ecrivains français,* 579–85, 635–47.

36. *Discourse,* VI, 31.

37. Which is not at all to imply that Descartes himself is unaware of the problem: It is not the *Discourse* nor the *Meditations,* nor even the comedy he wrote for Christina of Sweden (see XI, 661–62), nor his fictional dialogue, *The Search for Truth,* but the *Principles of Philosophy,* the most purely philosophical of his works and a work written in the traditional style of the treatise, which in his 1647 preface to the French translation he enjoins his reader to read "in its entirety just as if it were a *novel"* (IX-2, 11; my emphasis). Cf. the remark attributed to Pascal by Antoine Menjot: "The late M. Pascal called Cartesianism 'the Romance of Nature, something like the story of Don Quixote'" (*Pensées,* ed. L. Lafuma, tr. A. J. Krailsheimer [Harmondsworth: Penguin, 1966], 356).

3. Montesquieu's Grand *Tour*

1. Normand Doiron, "L'art de voyager: pour une définition du récit de voyage à l'époque classique," *Poétique* 73 (February 1988), 83–108.

2. Ibid., 85.

3. The text of Montesquieu's travelogue was first published by Baron Albert de Montesquieu as *Voyages de Montesquieu* (Bordeaux: Gounouilhou, 1894–96), well over a century and a half after the trip took place. Unless otherwise noted, all subsequent references to the work of Charles-Louis de Secondat de Montesquieu will be to the *Oeuvres complètes* edited by Roger Caillois (Paris: Gallimard, 1949–51), and will be indicated only as necessary by title, volume, and page number. With some modifications, translations are by Christopher Betts for the *Persian Letters* (Harmondsworth: Penguin, 1973); and by Thomas Nugent for *The Spirit of the Laws* (New York: Hafner, 1949). All other translations of texts by Montesquieu are my own.

4. Cf., for example, Robert Shackleton, *Montesquieu: A Critical Biography* (Oxford: Oxford University Press, 1961), 136, 171–74; Pierre Barrière, *Un grand provincial: Charles-Louis de Secondat, Baron de La Brède et de Montesquieu* (Bordeaux: Delmas, 1946), 153ff; and J. Robert Loy, *Montesquieu* (New York: Twayne, 1968), 24.

5. On reputed changes in Montesquieu's political thinking, see Paul Janet, *Histoire de la science politique dans ses rapports avec la morale* (Paris: Félix Alcan, 1887), II, 468–77; Robert Shackleton, "La genèse de l'*Esprit des lois,"* *Revue d'Histoire littéraire de la France* 52 (1952), 425–38; Henri Barckhausen, "Introduction," *Voyages de Montesquieu,* xii (republished in his *Montesquieu: Ses idées et ses oeuvres d'après les papiers de La Brède* [Paris: Hachette, 1907]); Badreddine Kassem, *Décadence et absolutisme dans l'oeuvre de Montesquieu* (Geneva: Droz, 1960), 157–77; Robert Derathé, "Introduction," *De l'esprit des lois,* by Montesquieu (Paris: Garnier, 1973), iii–vi; and Sante A. Viselli and Alexandre L. Amprimoz, "Voyage et esprit chez Montesquieu," *USF Language Quarterly* 25 (no. 1–2, Fall–Winter, 1986), 47. Also see Georges Benrekassa's critique of such an "evolutionary perspective," in *La politique et sa mémoire: Le politique et l'historique dans la pensée des lumières* (Paris: Payot, 1983), 296–97; and Hermann Harder's insistence upon the differences between the *Voyage* and *The Spirit of the Laws* (*Le Président des Brosses et le voyage en Italie au dix-huitième siècle* [Geneva: Slatkine, 1981], 117–29). On the voyage as a possible cause of Montesquieu's climatological ideas, see Robert Shackleton, "The Evolution of Montesquieu's

Theory of Climate," *Revue internationale de philosophie* fasc. 3–4 (1955), 317–39; and Micheline Fort Harris, "Le séjour de Montesquieu en Italie (août 1728—juillet 1729); chronologie et commentaires," *SVEC* 127 (1974), 190–96.

6. Joseph Dedieu, *Montesquieu: L'homme et l'oeuvre* (Paris: Boivin, 1943), 68.

7. Jean Starobinski, *Montesquieu par lui-même* (Paris: Seuil, 1953), 39.

8. This dialectical approach is exemplified by Starobinski's extended discussion of the contradictions in Montesquieu's concept of liberty (ibid., 60–113).

9. Louis Marin, *Etudes sémiologiques* (Paris: Klincksieck, 1971), 19–23 and passim.

10. Dean McCannell, *The Tourist: A New Theory of the Leisure Class* (New York: Schocken, 1976). See also Jonathan Culler, "The Semiotics of Tourism," *American Journal of Semiotics* 1, (no. 1–2: 1981), 127–40; and my "Sightseers: The Tourist as Theorist," *Diacritics* 10 (Winter 1980), 3–14.

11. On the history of the grand tour, see William Edward Mead, *The Grand Tour in the Eighteenth Century* (Boston and New York: Houghton Mifflin, 1914); Paul F. Kirby, *The Grand Tour in Italy, 1700–1800* (New York: Vanni, 1952); Anthony Burgess and Francis Haskell, *The Age of the Grand Tour* (New York: Crown, 1967); and Robert Shackleton, "The Grand Tour in the Eighteenth Century," *Studies in Eighteenth-Century Culture* 1 (1971), 127–42. The popularity of the grand tour, even as early as the late seventeenth century, was noted by François Deseine in his *Nouveau voyage d'Italie* (Paris, 1699): "The custom of traveling is today so common, especially among northern peoples, that a man who has never left his country is held without esteem. It is so true that voyages form one's judgment and perfect a man that he is said to be like those plants that can only bear good fruit after they have been transplanted."

12. Or, as Montesquieu puts it in another context, "The soul thus remains in a state of uncertainty between what it *sees* and what it *knows*" (*Essai sur le goût,* 11, 1256; emphasis added).

13. The classic problem of perspectivism in the *Persian Letters* has most recently been addressed by Tzvetan Todorov, "Réflexions sur les *Lettres persanes,*" *Romanic Review* 74 (1983), 306–15. See also Kevin Newmark's response to Todorov, "Leaving Home without It," *Stanford French Review* 11 (Spring 1987) 17–32; Suzanne Pucci, "Orientalism and Representations of Exteriority in Montesquieu's *Lettres persanes,*" *The Eighteenth Century: Theory and Interpretation* 26 (1985), 263–79; and "Letters From the Harem: Veiled Figures of Writing in Montesquieu's *Lettres persanes,*" in Elizabeth C. Goldsmith, ed., *Writing the Female Voice: Essays on Epistolary Literature* (Boston: Northeastern University Press, 1989), 114–34. The classic essay on the imbrication of sexuality and power in the letters is Aram Vartanian, "Eroticism and Politics in the *Lettres persanes,*" *Romanic Review* 60 (1969), 23–33. On the question of perspective as it pertains more generally to eighteenth-century travel narrative, see Percy Adams, "Perception and the Eighteenth-Century Traveler," *The Eighteenth Century: Theory and Interpretation* 26 (1985), 139–57; and Barbara Marie Stafford, *Voyage Into Substance: Art, Science, Nature, and the Illustrated Travel Account, 1760–1840* (Cambridge, Mass.: MIT Press, 1984).

14. In an as yet unpublished paper delivered at the Modern Language Association convention in December 1987, Sylvie Romanovsky also discusses this scene and the relation between mobility and knowledge as part of a wider gender imbalance in the *Persian Letters.* See also Suzanne Pucci, "Letters from the Harem."

15. Cf. Harris, *Le séjour,* 103.

16. Cf. the October 5, 1728, report of the French *chargé d'affaires* in Milan, Leblond, to the Ministère d'Affaires Étrangères: "As this tour does not seem to me to be very much in accord with a man who travels simply out of curiosity, I have my suspicions that there may be some other reasons for this trip, which make me believe that it is my honorable duty to

give you an account of it" (cited in Françoise Weil, "Promenades dans Rome en 1729 avec Montesquieu," *Technique, art, science: Revue de l'enseignement technique* 121 (October 1958), 2. On Montesquieu's diplomatic ambitions, see his letter to the Abbé d'Olivet of May 10, 1728: "A few days ago, I wrote to Monsieur the Cardinal [Fleury] and to Monsieur de Chauvelin [Keeper of the Seals] that I would be more than happy to be employed by them at foreign courts, and that I had worked hard to make myself capable of such missions" (*Oeuvres complètes de Montesquieu,* ed. André Masson et al. [Paris: Nagel, 1950–55], III, 892: all ensuing references to this edition will be signaled by the name "Masson" followed by the volume and page number). Cf. *Mes Pensées* I, 987; and Louis Desgraves, *Montesquieu* (Paris: Mazarine, 1986), 173, 180–81.

17. Cf. Frances Yates, *The Art of Memory* (Chicago: University of Chicago Press, 1966); and Michel Beaujour, *Miroirs d'encre* (Paris: Seuil, 1980), 79–168.

18. A more nuanced view of China does appear much later (book XIX, 562–71), but, as we shall see, it is no doubt because by that point, the static cartography of governmental natures has had to confront the temporal problem of history. Cf. Elie Carcassonne, "La Chine dans l'*Esprit des lois,*" *Revue d'histoire littéraire de la France* 31 (1924), 193–205. On the *topos* of the "sage Chinois," see Paul Hazard, *La crise de la conscience européenne, 1680–1715* (Paris: Boivin, 1935) 19–22; Virgile Pinot, *La Chine et la formation de l'esprit philosophique en France (1640–1740)* (Paris: Guethner, 1932); and René Etiemble, *L'Orient philosophique au XVIIIe siècle* (Paris: Centre de documentation universitaire, 1957–58). For an accessible and readable compilation of the Jesuit Relations from China, see Isabelle and Jean-Louis Vissière, eds., *Lettres édifiantes et curieuses de Chine par des missionnaires jésuites, 1702–1776* (Paris: Garnier-Flammarion, 1979). For more of Montesquieu's reactions to these letters, as well as his friendship with the Chinese scholar Arcadio Hoange, see the notes grouped under the title *Geographica* in Masson II, 956–63.

19. Often erroneously considered the inventor of such climatological schemas, Montesquieu follows a tradition going back to antiquity, renovated by Louis Le Roy's *De la vicissitude ou variété des choses en l'univers* (Paris, 1575); Jean Bodin's *Methodus ad facilem historiarum cognitionem* (Paris, 1572) and *Les six livres de la République* (Lyon, 1576); and John Arbuthnot's *Essay Concerning the Effects of Air on Human Bodies* (London, 1733). On the innovativeness of Montesquieu's climatological thinking as set against the background of the materialist critique of climate theories, see Benrekassa, *La Politique,* 179–256. Also Etienne Fournol, *Bodin précurseur de Montesquieu* (Paris: A. Rousseau, 1896); Robert Shackleton, "The Evolution of Montesquieu's Theory of Climate"; Jean Ehrard, *L'idée de nature en France dans la première moitié du XVIIIe siècle* (Paris: PUF, 1956), 691–736; and André Merquiol, "Montesquieu et la géographie politique," *Revue internationale d'histoire politique et constitutionnelle* 7 (1957), 127–46.

20. Does not Montesquieu describe himself when he describes the pleasures of the northerner as "hunting, traveling, war, and wine" (*The Spirit of the Laws,* 477)? On Montesquieu's ethnocentrism, see in particular Carminella Biondi, "Montesquieu razzista?" *Studi francesi* 27 (no. 81: 3, 1983), 474–77; and Benrekassa, who argues not only that the system is conceived "to come back ultimately to Europe" but also, given Montesquieu's positioning of Asians among "peoples who are closer to the south" (*Essai sur les causes qui peuvent affecter les esprits et les caractères,* I, 61), that the north-south opposition is itself reducible to one between Europe and Asia (*La politique,* 217).

21. By combining the characteristics Montesquieu assigns to despotism, we can conclude that the despotic land is a land without difference, whether temporal (no history), spatial (no topography), or social (no classes). Cf. Louis Althusser, *Montesquieu: La politique et l'histoire* (Paris: PUF, 1959), 82–97; and Alain Grosrichard, *Structure du sérail: La fiction du despotisme asiatique dans l'Occident classique* (Paris: Seuil, 1979), 100–101.

22. Given Montesquieu's altitudinal penchant, a critic such as Voltaire, in his commentaries on *The Spirit of the Laws,* has no trouble finding counterexamples of lowland republics and mountainous despotisms as well as pointing out various mistakes in Montesquieu's geography (*Essais sur les moeurs,* in *Oeuvres complètes,* ed. Louis Moland [Paris: Garnier Frères, 1877–85], XIII, 179; cf. *Dictionnaire philosophique,* article "Esprit des lois," XX, 6–7; *Commentaire sur quelques principales maximes* de l'Esprit des lois, XXX, 442–45), and the more sober and incisive Destutt de Tracy is easily able to argue against the reductionism of a system that thinks only in terms of "degrees of latitude and degrees of heat" (*Commentaire sur* l'Esprit des lois *de Montesquieu* [Paris: Mme. Lévi, 1828], 268–69).

23. In his *Dictionnaire philosophique,* Voltaire criticizes the then-modish expression and claims its origin to be Gascon (article "Franc ou Franq; France, François, Français," *Oeuvres complètes* XIX, 190). Interestingly enough, Montesquieu's home province is Gascony.

24. Readers of the travelogue have often been taken aback by the text's dryness as well as by the apparent impassivity of Montesquieu's reactions to what he sees. Cf. Jean Ehrard, *Montesquieu, critique d'art* (Paris: PUF, 1965), 69, 136; Desgraves, *Montesquieu,* 207; and Harris, *Le séjour,* 81, 130, 140, 150, 163, 174.

25. In a line struck from his letter to Mme. de Lambert of November 9, 1728, Montesquieu offers a social concomitant for his view from the tower: "Here is how I travel: I arrive in a city; within three days, I know everybody there" (Masson III, 922, n. b).

26. "Since I have been in Italy, I have opened my eyes upon the arts, about which I previously had no idea; it is an entirely new country for me," writes Montesquieu to Mme. de Lambert on December 26, 1728 (Masson III, 927). On the progressive development of Montesquieu's sensitivity to art during his trip to Italy, see Ehrard, *Montesquieu, critique d'art;* and Barrière, "L'expérience italienne de Montesquieu," *Rivista di letterature moderne* (January–March 1952), 15–28.

27. Pierre Barrière, "Montesquieu voyageur," in *Actes du Congrès Montesquieu,* ed. Louis Desgraves (Bordeaux: Delmas, 1956), 62. Cf. "L'expérience italienne," 25.

28. Letter to Mme. de Lambert, December 26, 1728 (Masson III, 928).

29. Cf. 825–26 and Caillois's note, 1615. The most thorough examination of the chronology of Montesquieu's travel is the one undertaken by Harris (*Le séjour*), who is driven to conclude that in counterdistinction to the meticulous order of Edward Gibbon's travelogue, "it must be said that Montesquieu treats dates with more abandon than when he set up Rica and Usbek's itinerary" (71, 74).

30. See Harris, 73–74, 121, 189–90.

31. On the impersonality of Montesquieu's voice in the travelogue, see Harris, 72, 119, 174, 185. On the question of Montesquieu's Cartesianism (mediated by Malebranche as well as by Fontenelle), see Barrière, *Un grand provincial,* 312–13; E. Buss, "Montesquieu und Cartesius," *Philosophische Monatshefte* 4 (Wintersemester 1869–70), 1–38; Gustave Lanson, "L'influence de la philosophie cartésienne sur la littérature française," *Revue de métaphysique et de morale* 4 (1896), 517–50, especially 540–46; and "Le déterminisme historique et l'idéalisme social dans l'*Esprit des lois,*" *Revue de métaphysique et de morale* 23 (1916), 177–202; Charles-Jacques Beyer, "Montesquieu et l'esprit cartésien," in *Actes du Congrès Montesquieu,* 159–73. On the other side, Georges Benrekassa asserts that "no one dares any more to see in Montesquieu, as Lanson once did, a Cartesian disposition," *Montesquieu* (Paris: PUF, 1968), 22. But perhaps it is Montesquieu's own reflection on Descartes that is the most suggestive: "Descartes taught those who came after him to discover even his errors [*ses erreurs mêmes*]" (*Mes Pensées,* II, 1548).

32. Among the panoply of proposed sites are Santa Trinità-dei-Monti, the Pincian hill, the Capitoline hill, the Janiculum, and the cupola of Saint Peter's Basilica (see Ehrard, *Montesquieu, critique d'art,* 70; Desgraves, *Montesquieu,* 207; and Jean Rousset, "Se promener

dans Rome au XVIII^c siècle," in Raymond Trousson, ed., *Thèmes et figures du siècle des Lumières: Mélanges offerts à Roland Mortier* [Geneva: Droz, 1980], 243).

33. François-Maximilien Misson, *Nouveau voyage d'Italie fait en l'année 1688* (De Hague, 1691); François Deseine, *Nouveau voyage d'Italie* (Paris, 1699); Bernard de Montfaucon, *Diarium italicum. Sive monumentum veterum, bibliothecarum, musaeorum, &c. Notitiae singulares in itinerario italico collectae* (Paris, 1702); Etienne de Silhouette, *Voyage de France, d'Espagne, de Portugal et d'Italie, du 22 avril 1729 au 6 février 1730* (Paris, 1730); Le Père Jean-Baptiste Labat, *Voyages en Espagne et en Italie* (Paris, 1730); Charles de Brosses, *Lettres familières d'Italie en 1739 et en 1740* (Paris, 1799); Joseph Jérome de Lalande, *Voyage d'un Français en Italie* (Paris, 1769); Gilbert Burnet, *Some Letters containing an account of what seemed most remarkable in Switzerland, Italy, France and Germany* (Amsterdam, 1687); Joseph Addison, *Remarks on Several Parts of Italy, &c, in the years 1701, 1702, 1703* (London, 1705); Tobias Smollett, *Travels through France and Italy* (London, 1766). Edward Gibbon's travelogue of 1764 was only recently published as *Gibbon's Journey from Geneva to Rome,* ed. G. Bonnard (London: Nelson, 1961). Johann Wolfgang von Goethe's *Italienische Reise* of 1786-88 appeared in various bits and pieces until its first integral publication at Stuttgart in 1862. As they became available, the earlier of these travelogues served as guidebooks for later travelers, who often carried them in their baggage. See Pierre Laubriet, "Les guides de voyages au début du XVIII^c siècle," *SVEC* 32 (1965), 269-325; Ludwig Schudt, *Italienreisen im 17. und 18. Jahrhundert* (Vienna and Munich: Schroll, 1959); Hermann Harder, *Le Président de Brosses;* and Rousset, "Se promener dans Rome," 239-50. Nevertheless, as Shackleton points out, "if one excludes the specialized *Diarium Italicum* of Montfaucon, [Montesquieu's] is the first travel account since the *Journal de voyage* of Montaigne to be written by a Frenchman *of literary eminence*" (*A Critical Biography*, 91; emphasis added).

34. Among the most developed examples of this *topos* is the one undertaken by Freud in *Civilization and Its Discontents, S.E.* XXI, 69-70. The attempt to view all of Rome's past in its "simultaneity" and not just as accumulated ruins gives Freud one of his most suggestive analogies for the structure of the unconscious in its unrepresentability. Montesquieu's Rome would have been an especially jumbled one, since systematic archeological excavation of the ancient city did not begin for another century (see Harris, *Le séjour,* 152).

35. The text of the document is reproduced at the end of "Of Vanity," *Essays* III, ix, 999-1000; and the story of its difficult procurement is recounted in the *Travel Journal,* 129-30. Near the end of his life, Montesquieu wrote to an unidentified addressee that his stay in Rome some twenty-five years earlier remained "the happiest time of my life and the time during which I learned the most," February 21, 1754 (Masson III, 1496).

36. Cf. the letters of November 14, 1748 (1144); November 19, 1748 (1145); December 2, 1748 (1148, 1150); December 28, 1748 (1150, 1151); January 9, 1749 (1162-63); January 10, 1749 (1163); January 31, 1749 (1175); March 4, 1749 (1196-97); April 2, 1749 (1215); April 23, 1749 (1227-28); May 20, 1749 (1231-32); June 7, 1749 (1239-40) (all page numbers refer to Masson III).

37. A very similar description of Saint Peter's is used by Kant to explain the notion of the sublime. *Critique of Judgement,* tr. J. H. Bernard (New York: Hafner Press, 1951), 90-91.

38. Cf. Althusser: "that man who set off alone and truly discovered the new lands of history" (*Montesquieu,* 122); or Ernst Cassirer, who refers to Montesquieu as "the first thinker to grasp and to express clearly the concept of 'ideal types' in history" (*The Philosophy of the Enlightenment,* tr. F. Koelln and J. Pettegrove [Princeton: Princeton University Press, 1951], 210). Also see René Hubert, "La notion du devenir historique dans la philosophie de Montesquieu," *Revue de métaphysique et de morale* 46 (1939), 587-610.

39. In what is indubitably the most rigorous inquiry into the problem of Montesquieu's historicism, Suzanne Gearhart demonstrates that although "the principle seems to represent the relationship of each government to time—it is what permits a government to reproduce itself, to exist in time, to have a history" (*The Open Boundary of History and Fiction* [Princeton: Princeton University Press, 1984], 138), both despotic and republican forms of goverment are shown to fall outside history: the former as a collapse into the mere "circumstantiality" of events (147-49); the latter as irrecoverably situated in "the distant past" (150-52). As for Montesquieu's preferred form of government, the monarchy, its determined historicity also situates it as an intermediary form, a degenerate version of republicanism which in turn degenerates into despotism: "In this way, a concept of history thus tends ultimately in Montesquieu to dominate historicity, to limit or to subordinate the differences and the contradictions within nature or the origin" (157).

40. As Gearhart rightly observes, "The origin is the moment that makes history intelligible; all history must be continuous with an origin if it is to be history and not some unintelligible process of random change. But though it makes history intelligible, the origin also makes it redundant—the mere illustration of what was already implicitly present at the beginning" (*Open Boundary*, 158-59).

41. On this problem, see Grosrichard's excellent discussion, *Structure du sérail*, 39-76.

42. For Georges Benrekassa, the historical contingency of the Roman changes in government, as Montesquieu describes them, carries out a deconstruction of the "Roman myth" in political thinking: "Henceforth there is no longer any paradigmatic and simplifying origin, but only multiple fractures of history out of which are born difficult questions. . . . Rome, the object of a 'work of mourning,' also exists as a matter in history; *The Spirit of the Laws,* Rome's tomb" (*La politique,* 320-21ff.). As for the celebrated importance of the British constitutional model within the framework of *The Spirit of the Laws,* Benrekassa also convincingly demonstrates Montesquieu's comprehension of the English situation with a larger Latin paradigm, where it figures as the "New Rome in the West" (ibid., 291-96 and 308-20).

43. See Merle Perkins, "Montesquieu on National Power and International Rivalry," *SVEC* 238 (1985), 1-96, who also persistently aligns Montesquieu's internationalism with the plurality of "angles of vision" Montesquieu deploys in approaching his topic (7, 18, 46, 70, 83, 85, 88, 91, 92).

44. The complicity between the science of geography and militarism is probably ageless. Maurice Bouguereau presented the first national atlas of France, *Le théâtre françoys* (Tours, 1594) to Henri IV as an aid to the king's tax collecting and military campaigning (I thank Tom Conley for this reference). Richelieu's ideal of "natural frontiers" and Louis XIV's subsequent combination of warfare and legal manipulation to secure the best possible borders for France testify to the relation between national unity and cartographic representation (Cf. Bruno-Henri Vayssière, "'La' carte de France," and Mireille Pastoureau, "Feuilles d'atlas," both in *Cartes et figures de la terre,* ed. Roger Agache et al. [Paris: Centre Georges Pompidou, 1980], 252-65, 442-54). One of the principal causes of war in early modern Europe was the desire to unify the often disparate feudal holdings of a royal family into the geographically coherent whole of a nation-state.

45. On the preponderance of liquid imagery in Montesquieu, see Corrado Rosso, *Montesquieu moralista: dalle leggi al "bonheur"* (Pisa: Goliardica, 1965), 101-10; and Jane McLelland, "Metaphor in Montesquieu's Theoretical Writings," *SVEC* 199 (1981), 205-24. McLelland is especially cogent in arguing Montesquieu's systematic reprise of his early scientific work on the "hydraulics" of plant life in the later political analogies built around the idea of "channels of power" (208-16). It should be added that the economic principle of Montesquieu's fluid mechanics, whereby every displacement is compensated by another, recalls the

similar economy of displacement in Descartes's physics, as typified most manifestly in his theory of vortices (see chapter 2, n. 21).

46. On Montesquieu's use of travel relations in his work, see Muriel Dodds, *Les récits de voyages sources de* l'Esprit des lois *de Montesquieu* (Paris: Honoré Champion, 1929).

47. "One effect of Montesquieu's history of the French monarchy is that it tends to undermine the very specificity of the principles he defends so vigorously elsewhere," Gearhart, *Open Boundary,* 153. Also Benrekassa, who concludes his lengthy study by noting that Montesquieu's "ambition" in the preface to *The Spirit of the Laws* to see history "bent" to being but "the consequences" of his principles (II, 229) ends by "being ineluctably reversed," meaning that his principles have been bent to the sequence of history (*La Politique,* 355).

48. Viselli and Amprimoz oddly misinterpret the quotation from the *Aeneid* as signaling the beginning of the Virgilian voyage (47). Perhaps David Hume was right to chide Montesquieu for the obscurity of this quotation put in place of a conclusion: "I find a number of people as perplexed as I am in trying to guess the meaning of the last paragraph in your work: *Italiam, Italiam . . .* no doubt for lack of knowing what it is you are alluding to" (Lettre à Montesquieu, April 10, 1749 [Masson III, 1222]).

49. One cannot help but be struck by the abruptness with which Montesquieu ends the treatise, dropping his narrative in the middle of the Middle Ages, an abruptness of ending reminiscent of Stendhal (who, incidentally, was a great reader and admirer of Montesquieu: "It's not exactly love that I have for Montesquieu, it is veneration" [*Voyage dans le midi: Mémoires d'un touriste* III [Paris: Maspero, 1981], 69). But in the case of Montesquieu, the abrupt ending betrays less an aesthetic experimentation than his desire to get out of the text, to be done with it. This exasperation at being caught up in a seemingly endless text, whose expanse is such as to render hopeless any attempt to domesticate it or recuperate it, is precisely what is evoked by this as well as other travel metaphors in *The Spirit of the Laws.* On the *topos* of the nautical voyage as a metaphor of the narrator's progress through the text, see Ernst Curtius, *European Literature and the Latin Middle Ages,* tr. W. Trask (Princeton: Princeton University Press, 1953), 128–30. On the extensiveness of Montesquieu's erudition in pursuit of his magnum opus, see Iris Cox, *Montesquieu and French Laws, SVEC* 218 (1983).

50. Letter to Godefroy de Secondat, December 28, 1744 (Masson III, 1052–53).

51. "Testament de Montesquieu," (Masson III, 1573; emphasis added). On the arranging of Denise's marriage, see Stendhal, *Voyage dans le midi,* 76, 78; Shackleton, *Montesquieu,* 198–200; Barrière, *Grand provincial,* 97ff; Desgraves, *Montesquieu,* 253–57; Jeannette Geffriaud Rosso, *Montesquieu et la féminité* (Pisa: Goliardica, 1977), 42–44. Stendhal's version of the story adds, however, that after this marriage of utter convenience to preserve the name of Montesquieu, Montesquieu's wife did bear him a son, to whom Montesquieu then refused the patronym, "out of respect for the sacrifice he had asked from his daughter" (78). Montesquieu would have succeeded in preserving the name *and* in preventing the rise of a threatening male progeny by designating the latter by the other family name, Secondat, whose etymological sense implicitly relegates its bearer to the status of a mere "follower." Stendhal, that great admirer of the father, had a concomitant disdain for the son, M. de Secondat, whom he calls "that good old fellow [*ce brave homme*]" and accuses of kleptomania (76–78). Unfortunately, Stendhal was not only wrong about the son (who was, in fact, Montesquieu's first-born), but in what is the most thoroughgoing research into the notarial archives to date, Jean Dalat also finds no hard proof for Stendhal's claim of a forced (as opposed to merely an arranged) marriage, even though he does uncover ample evidence of Montesquieu's often petty and occasionally vicious manipulation of his patriarchal rights in order to assure the perpetuation of both his name and his land (*Montesquieu chef de famille en lutte avec ses beaux-parents, sa femme, ses enfants* [Paris: Archives des Lettres Modernes, 1983]). In

any case, Montesquieu's fear that his line would come to an end seems to have been motivated in 1744 by his son's lack of a male heir after four and a half years of marriage. In 1749, however, a son was finally born of this union, the future Général de Montesquieu of American and French Revolutionary War fame. A year earlier, a son had been born to Montesquieu's daughter, Denise, from whom indeed descend the current barons of Montesquieu.

52. *Mes Pensées,* I, 1292.

53. Shackleton, *Montesquieu: A Critical Biography,* 1. Desgraves adds that "from the existing village of Montesquieu, you can still today perceive the ruins of a château that crowns a forlorn and desolate hill" and that already in Montesquieu's time the castle was in ruins (*Montesquieu,* 9, 87).

54. Cf. Voltaire: "I respect Montesquieu even when he falls [*dans ses chutes*], because he picks himself back up [*se relève*] and mounts to the sky [*pour monter au ciel*]" (*Commentaire sur l'Esprit des lois,* XXX, 441).

55. Of the innumerable assessments of Montesquieu's impact on revolutionary thinking and legislation, see especially Bernard Groethuysen, *Philosophie de la Révolution française, précédé de Montesquieu* (Paris: Gallimard, 1956); Renato Galliani, "La fortune de Montesquieu en 1789: Un sondage," *Archives des lettres modernes* 197 (1981), 31–61; Norman Hampson, *Will and Circumstance: Montesquieu, Rousseau and the French Revolution* (Norman: University of Oklahoma Press, 1983); Judith N. Shklar, *Montesquieu* (Oxford: Oxford University Press, 1987), 111–26; and Paul M. Spurlin, "L'influence de Montesquieu sur la constitution américaine," in *Actes du Congrès Montesquieu,* 265–72. On the revolutionary "return to the ancients," see Louis Hautecoeur, *Rome et la renaissance de l'antiquité à la fin du XVIIIᵉ siècle* (Paris: Fontemoing, 1912). I thank Marie-Claire Vallois for this reference.

4. Pedestrian Rousseau

1. See Charles L. Batten, *Pleasurable Instruction: Form and Convention in Eighteenth-Century Travel Literature* (Berkeley: University of California Press, 1978).

2. As Jean Starobinski has eloquently indicated, Rousseau's search for both moral and physical fixity, his desire to "fix down his life [*fixer sa vie*]" and to "fix down his opinions once and for all," is not without relevance to his having spent at least thirty-eight of his sixty-six years in one kind of transient mode or another (*Jean-Jacques Rousseau: La transparence et l'obstacle,* 2nd ed. [Paris: Gallimard, 1971], 63–65, 71–72, and passim).

3. *Emile, ou de l'éducation,* in *Oeuvres complètes de Jean-Jacques Rousseau,* ed. Bernard Gagnebin and Marcel Raymond (Paris: Gallimard, 1959–69), IV, 245. All subsequent references to Rousseau are to this edition and will be indicated only as needed by title, volume, and page number. With some modifications, English translations are taken from the following: *A Discourse on Inequality,* tr. Maurice Cranston (Harmondsworth: Penguin, 1984); *Emile,* tr. Barbara Foxley (1911; rpt. London: Dent, 1974); *The Confessions,* tr. J. M. Cohen (Harmondsworth: Penguin, 1953); *The Reveries of a Solitary,* tr. John Gould Fletcher (1927; rpt. New York: Burt Franklin, 1971). Unless noted, all other English translations of Rousseau are my own.

4. Immanuel Kant, *Critique of Judgement,* tr. J. H. Bernard (New York: Hafner Press, 1951), 73 and passim. Cf. Derrida, "Le Parergon," in *La vérité en peinture* (Paris: Flammarion, 1978), 19–168.

5. Cf. De Jaucourt's article, "Voyageur," in the *Encyclopédie,* XVII, 478. The article states that one must suspect *all* travelers of being liars even if—and in fact precisely because—some of them are not. On duplicitous travel narratives in the eighteenth century, see Percy Adams's classic *Travelers and Travel Liars: 1660–1800* (Berkeley: University of California Press, 1962).

6. On the semiotic import of names as rigorously designative but indeterminate with regard to sense, see Jean-François Lyotard, *The Differend: Phrases in Dispute* (Minneapolis: University of Minnesota, 1988), 32–58.

7. On the general question of authenticity as the value by which a voyage is judged, I refer the reader once more to Dean MacCannell, *The Tourist: A New Theory of the Leisure Class* (New York: Schocken, 1976).

8. This is not the only place Rousseau advances so sweeping a condemnation of travel. Compare the following passage from the preface to *Narcisse:* "The Crusades, commerce, the discovery of the Indies, navigation, long voyages, and still other causes I don't want to go into, have maintained and augmented the disorder. Everything that facilitates communication between one nation and another spreads not their virtues but their crimes, and in every nation it alters the customs which are proper to their climates and to the constitution of their governments" (*Narcisse, ou l'amant de lui-même,* II, 964n). As for Rousseau's defense of national identity, the most questionable statement is no doubt found in his *Considérations sur le gouvernement de la Pologne,* especially I, 959–66, where he sees the solution to Poland's political woes in the delineation of a distinctive "national physiognomy" (960). See, on the question of Rousseau's nationalism, the useful if somewhat misguided work of Alexandre Choulguine, *Les origines de l'esprit national moderne et Jean-Jacques Rousseau, Annales Jean-Jacques Rousseau* 26 (1937), 7–283. And on Rousseau's extensive but selective use of ethnographical information from contemporary travel narratives, see Chinard, *L'Amérique et le rêve exotique dans la littérature française au XVIIe et la XVIIIe siécle* (Paris: Droz, 1934), 341–65; and more recently, Tzvetan Todorov, "La connaissance des autres: Théories et pratiques," *L'Esprit Créateur* 25 (no. 3: Fall 1985), 8–17.

9. This reversal is not unique to Rousseau; it can be found as early as Fontenelle's 1708 "Eloge de Tournefort" ("Philosophers rarely run about in the world, and ordinarily those who do are hardly philosophers; and hence a philosopher's journey is extremely precious," *Oeuvres* [Paris: Jean-François Bastien, 1790], VI, 240–41), and is responsible for the Enlightenment's innovative sponsoring of ambitious expeditions overseas led by scientists and philosophers with specific research agendas. Typical of such journeys were those of Maupertuis (to Lapland in 1736–37) and La Condamine (to Amazonia from 1735 to 1745) to measure the "flattening" of the globe, as well as Bougainville's monumental circumnavigation. Cf. Numa Broc, *Le géographie des philosophes: Géographes et voyageurs français au XVIIIe siècle* (Paris: Ophrys, n.d.), especially 187–92; René Pomeau, "Voyage et lumières dans la littérature française du XVIIIe siècle," *SVEC* 57 (1967), 1269–89; and for a slightly later period, Sergio Moravia, "Philosophie et géographie à la fin du XVIIIe siècle," *SVEC* 57 (1967), 937–1011. On the general question of the relation between travel narratives and the often parallel development of science and aesthetics, see Barbara Maria Stafford, *Voyage into Substance: Art, Science, Nature, and the Illustrated Travel Account, 1760–1840* (Cambridge, Mass.: MIT Press, 1984). As for Rousseau, the philosopher's journey would thus seem to pose somewhat of a double bind. On the one hand, one can only be a "real" philosopher as opposed to a "philosophe de ruelle [salon-dwelling philosopher]" if one travels; on the other hand, one should already be a philosopher in order to travel.

10. Second *Discourse,* III, 214.

11. Ibid.

12. Far from being the aristocratic designation of an entitled property, the surname of Rousseau merely suggests a feature of some ancestral physiognomy: red hair.

13. "Go back to your country, return to the religion of your fathers, follow it in the sincerity of your heart and do not leave it again. . . . When you want to listen to your conscience, a thousand empty obstacles will disappear at the sound of your voice. You will feel that it

is an inexcusable presumption, given the uncertainty in which we are, to profess a religion other than the one in which you are born, and a falsehood not to practice sincerely the one you profess. If you deviate, you deprive yourself of a great excuse before the tribunal of the sovereign judge. Will He not rather pardon the error into which you were born than the one you dared to choose for yourself?" (*Emile,* IV, 631). In the sixth of his *Lettres écrites de la montagne,* Rousseau defends the political theses of *The Social Contract* by claiming that they are patterned after the constitution of his native Geneva: "Everything else being equal, I gave preference to the government *of my country*" (III, 811; emphasis added).

14. As Henri Coulet eloquently states, "the idea of return is affirmed more than the idea of getting installed in a country visited in the course of a journey. . . . After some hesitating and taking of different tacks, the principal goal seems to be that of a political education which Emile could put to use in his own country; his travels will have taught him that settling elsewhere goes against both his duty and his interests" ("L'éducation politique d'Emile," in *Hommage à François Meyer* [Aix-en-Provence: Publications de l'Université de Provence, 1983], 87).

15. Among recent analyses of this pedagogical paradox, see especially Harari, *Scenarios of the Imaginary: Theorizing the French Enlightenment* (Ithaca, N.Y.: Cornell University Press, 1987), 102-32; Suzanne Gearhart, *The Open Boundary of History and Fiction* (Princeton: Princeton University Press, 1984), 277-79; and Joan DeJean, *Literary Fortifications: Rousseau, Laclos, Sade* (Princeton: Princeton University Press, 1984), 120-61; but also Thomas M. Kavanagh, *Writing the Truth: Authority and Desire in Rousseau* (Berkeley: University of California Press, 1987), 78-101, who sees a more ambiguous dialectic between freedom and constraint.

16. Cf. Jacques Derrida, *Of Grammatology,* tr. Gayatri Chakavorty Spivak (Baltimore: Johns Hopkins University Press, 1974), 141-57; Georges May, *Rousseau par lui-même* (Paris: Seuil, n.d.), 129-51; Jean Starobinski, "Jean-Jacques Rousseau et le péril de la réflexion," in *L'oeil vivant* (Paris: Gallimard, 1961), 119ff; Pierre-Paul Clément, *Jean-Jacques Rousseau: De l'éros coupable à l'éros glorieux* (Neuchâtel: La Baconnière, 1976); Victor G. Wexler, "'Made for Man's Delight': Rousseau as Antifeminist," *American Historical Review* 81 (1976), 266-91; Sarah Kofman, *Le respect des femmes* (Paris: Galilée, 1981), 57-150; Peggy Kamuf, *Fictions of Feminine Desire: Disclosures of Heloise* (Lincoln: University of Nebraska Press, 1982), 97-122; Danielle Montet-Clavié, "La femme comme nature morte dans l'oeuvre de Jean-Jacques Rousseau," in Groupe de Recherches Interdisciplinaire d'Etude des Femmes, *La femme et la mort* (Toulouse: Publications de l'Université de Toulouse-Le Mirail, 1984), 59-76; Georges Benrekassa, *Le concentrique et l'excentrique: Marges des Lumières* (Paris: Payot, 1980), 285-303; and Kavanagh, *Writing the Truth.* For a more "sympathetic" view situated on the level of political content, see Joel Schwartz, *The Sexual Politics of Jean-Jacques Rousseau* (Chicago: University of Chicago Press, 1984). On Rousseau's radicalizing influence on progressive women in the late eighteenth century, sexism notwithstanding, see Gita May, "Rousseau's 'Antifeminism' Reconsidered," in Samia I. Spencer, ed., *French Women and the Age of Enlightenment* (Bloomington: Indiana University Press, 1984), 309-17.

17. The canonical analysis is that of Pierre Burgelin, "L'éducation de Sophie," *Annales de la société Jean-Jacques Rousseau* 35 (1959-62), 113-30. More recently, see Nancy J. Senior, "Sophie and the State of Nature," *French Forum* 2 (no. 2: May 1977), 134-46; Nannerl O. Keohane, "'But for Her Sex . . .': The Domestication of Sophie," in J. MacAdam, M. Neumann, and G. Lafrance, eds., *Trent Rousseau Papers* (Ottawa: University of Ottowa Press, 1980), 135-45; and Helen Evans Misenheimer, *Rousseau on the Education of Women* (Washington: University Press of America, 1981).

18. Derrida, *Of Grammatology,* 141-64 and 313-16.

19. The situation is complicated, of course, by the fact that the teacher is *not* Emile's father, although, to the extent that he is a substitute father and is essentially treated as one, the teacher is also himself a simulacrum of the father.

20. He is, in fact, at the very heart of the *oikos,* if we remember the introduction to Rousseau's article for the *Encyclopédie* on political economy: "The word Economy, or Oeconomy, is derived from *oikos,* a house, and *nomos,* law and meant originally only the wise and legitimate government of the house for the common good of the whole family. The meaning of the term was then extended to the government of that great family, the State. To distinguish these two senses of the word, the latter is called *general* or *political* economy, and the former domestic or particular economy. The first only is discussed in the present article. On domestic economy, see *Family Father*" (III, 241; translation modified from *A Discourse on Political Economy,* in *The Social Contract and Discourses,* tr. G. D. H. Cole [New York: Dutton, 1950], 285). Despite the disclaimer, a great deal of the ensuing article is devoted to establishing the differences and similarities between the father of a family and the ruler of a country. I submit that it would not be stretching matters at all to say that in Rousseau it is the father who defines the home, a situation reinforced by the description in book I in the *Confessions,* of Rousseau's motherless childhood home (*Confessions,* I, 7–12).

21. As Minerva-Mentor tells Télémaque, "you have gained well in suffering, since you have acquired wisdom," François de Salignac de La Mothe de Fénelon, *Les Aventures de Télémaque,* ed. Albert Cahen (Paris: Hachette, 1927), I, 365.

22. "The child, doomed to repeat the tutor's imaginary, can do no more than imagine secondhand" (Harari, *Scenarios,* 112).

23. This "incorporation" of the father is one of the key concepts of psychoanalysis. My analysis of the problem has accordingly been informed by a reading of Freud, especially *Totem and Taboo, The Standard Edition of the Complete Psychological Works* (hereafter referred to as *S.E.*), tr. J. Strachey (London: Hogarth, 1955–73), XIII, especially 140–61; "Postscript" to *Psychoanalytic Notes on an Autobiographical Account of a Case of Paranoia, S.E.* XII, 80–82; "The Dissolution of the Oedipus Complex," *S.E.* XIX, 173–79.

24. This proposed conclusion to *Emile et Sophie* was, in point of fact, never written by Rousseau, although we know of it from the likes of Jacques Bernardin de Saint-Pierre and Pierre Prévost, to whom Rousseau would have told the ending of the story. Prévost's account of the "conclusion of the *Solitaires*" can be found in IV, clxiii–clxiv. Bernardin de Saint-Pierre's slightly more detailed rendition can be found in his *La vie et les ouvrages de Jean-Jacques Rousseau,* ed. Maurice Souriau (Paris: Edouard Cornély, 1907), 169–74. Also see Kavanagh's useful note in *Writing the Truth,* 199. Kavanagh, moreover, convincingly argues against those critics who would ignore or dismiss the importance of this lesser-known of Rousseau's works and stresses instead that it is the "essential postscript" to *Emile,* one whose "subject matter [is] already inscribed in *Emile*'s given" (101, 85). Indeed, only a very few other Rousseau critics have paid serious attention to this text: Charles Wirz, "Notes sur 'Emile et Sophie ou les solitaires,'" *Annales Jean-Jacques Rousseau* 36 (1963–65), 291–303; Guy Turbet-Delof, "A propos d' 'Emile et Sophie,'" *Revue d'Histoire littéraire de la France* 64 (1964), 44–59; Nancy J. Senior, "'Les Solitaires' as a Test for Emile and Sophie," *French Review* 49 (no. 4: March 1976), 528–35; and James F. Hamilton, "'Emile et Sophie': A Parody of the Philosopher-King," *Studi francesi* 65–66 (1978), 392–95.

25. *La transparence et l'obstacle,* 153–65. A more nuanced version of Starobinski's thesis, one which allows a more tortured and unpredictable indeterminacy between such opposites as departure/return, illness/cure, and obstacle/transparency, can be found in his recent *Le remède dans le mal: Critique et légitimation de l'artifice à l'âge des Lumières* (Paris: Gallimard, 1989), 165–232. On the dialectic of movement and repose as it figures in the Enlightenment

"mentality" of happiness, see Robert Mauzi, *L'idée du bonheur dans la littérature et la pensée française au XVIIIᵉ siècle* (Paris: Armand Colin, 1985), 125-35, 330-513.

26. The home cannot defend itself against some unspecified enemy from without or within. The *Lettre à d'Alembert sur les spectacles* (1758) could be studied in this context, since it invokes a defense of Rousseau's own fatherland against a plot hatched from without but intended to destroy from within (the establishment of a theater in Geneva). The threat is that of the destruction of the very boundary separating without from within, with the encroachment of a foreign power (France) in Geneva and the latter's subsequent subservience to that power. And in the subsequent *Lettres écrites de la montagne,* Rousseau finds himself in the even stranger position of having to defend his loyalty to the state and religion of Geneva after having been condemned by both. Responding to this perverse attack by the home against one of its own constitutes what Rousseau calls "my final duty to my country" (III, 897). On the Swiss identity of Rousseau, see François Jost, *Jean-Jacques Rousseau Suisse: Étude sur sa personnalité et sa pensée* (Fribourg: Editions Universitaires, 1961), and *Rousseau et la Suisse* (Neuchâtel: Griffon, 1962). For a more nuanced discussion, see Starobinski, "L'écart romanesque," in *La transparence et l'obstacle,* 393-414; and Martina Rudes, "Une patria difficile: Ginevra nella corrispondenza di Jean-Jacques Rousseau (1754-1758)," *Il Lettore di provincia* 15 (no. 57/58: August-September 1984), 57-63.

27. One might note, in regards to this critique of dependency, the high incidence of metaphors of binding in *Emile.* Binding (like the dependency for which it is so often a metaphor) seems to be continually understood by Rousseau as something negative, if not as negativity itself. Witness his famous attack against the use of swaddling clothes because they restrict the child's liberty of movement (IV, 253-56). While there is no space here to pursue a detailed reading of the binding metaphors in *Emile,* it can be surmised that much more is at stake in them than a simple question of child care.

28. The relevant passages can be found in *Confessions,* I, 646; *Reveries,* I, 1041 and 1048; and the first "Lettre à Malesherbes," January 4, 1762, I, 1132. Cf. Starobinski, *La transparence et l'obstacle,* 283-300; and Kavanagh, whose careful study of the "freedom in servitude" theme of *Emile and Sophie* (*Writing the Truth,* 78-101) leads him to an important and original rereading of Rousseau's political writings as less "totalitarian" in inspiration than motivated by an "abiding identification with the voice of the victim" (101ff). On the literary *topos* of freedom in captivity, see Victor Brombert, *La prison romantique: Essai sur l'imaginaire* (Paris: José Corti, 1975), 11-50.

29. This rephrasing of the ontological question of selfhood as a topographical one grounds Alain Grosrichard's psychoanalytic reading of Rousseau's imaginary as caught in an endless series of identifications, a psychologically vertiginous and fatal crack in the Lacanian "mirror stage" that scripts the history of Rousseau's ego development as a harrowing traversal of "a hall of mirrors" in search of an impossible "fixed point" ("'Où suis-je?', 'Que suis-je?' [Réflexions sur la question de la *place* dans l'oeuvre de Jean-Jacques Rousseau, à partir d'un texte des *Rêveries*]," in *Rousseau et Voltaire en 1978: Actes du colloque international de Nice [juin 1978]* [Geneva and Paris: Slatkine, 1981], 338-65).

30. This positing of a (fictional) interlocutor as the enabling condition for the constitution of the subject in discourse is a structure laid bare in the familiar trope of apostrophe. See Jonathan Culler, "Apostrophe," *Diacritics* 7 (Winter 1977), 59-69. Specific studies of the role of the reader in Rousseau can be found in Robert J. Ellrich, *Rousseau and His Reader: The Rhetorical Situation of the Major Works* (Chapel Hill: University of North Carolina Press, 1969); and Huntington Williams, *Rousseau and Romantic Autobiography* (Oxford: Oxford University Press, 1983), 180-217.

31. Consider Rousseau's famous statements near the beginning of the *Discourse on Inequality:* "Let us begin by setting aside all the facts, because they do not affect the question"

(III, 132); "For it is no light enterprise to . . . attain a solid knowledge of a state which no longer exists, which perhaps never existed, and which will probably never exist, yet of which it is necessary to have sound ideas if we are to judge our present state satisfactorily" (III, 123). On the consequences of this positing of truth as a necessary fiction, the canonical studies remain those of Derrida, *Of Grammatology;* and Paul de Man, *Blindness and Insight* (Oxford: Oxford University Press, 1971), 101-41, and *Allegories of Reading: Figural Language in Rousseau, Nietzsche, Rilke, and Proust* (New Haven: Yale University Press, 1979), 135-301. Also see Gearhart's important and brilliant critique of their work in *The Open Boundary,* 234-84. For a historical and ideological situating of Rousseau's concept of nature as critical fiction, see Bronislaw Baczko, *Rousseau: Solitude et communauté,* tr. Claire Brendhel-Lamhout (Paris and De Hague: Mouton, 1974), 59-154.

32. On the congruencies between Rousseau's anthropological history of the different "ages of man" as presented in the two Discourses and the *chronological* organization of the first book of the *Confessions,* see Philippe Lejeune, *Le pacte autobiographique* (Paris: Seuil, 1975), 87-163. For some considerations on Rousseau as the possible originator of autobiography, at least in its modern form, a claim already modeled by Rousseau himself in the opening line of the *Confessions* ["I form an enterprise which has no precedent," 5], see Lejeune, *L'autobiographie en France* (Paris: Armand Colin, 1971) and *Le pacte autobiographique,* 311-41; also Michael Sprinker, "The End of Autobiography," in James Olney, ed., *Autobiography: Essays Theoretical and Critical* (Princeton: Princeton University Press, 1980), 323-26. Other essays included in this same volume that are pertinent to the question are James Olney, "Autobiography and the Cultural Moment: A Theoretical, Historical, and Bibliographical Introduction," especially 5-6; Georges Gusdorf, "Conditions and Limits of Autobiography," tr. James Olney, 28-48; and Jean Starobinski, "The Style of Autobiography," tr. Seymour Chatman, 73-83. Also see Lionel Gossman's seminal articles, "Time and History in Rousseau," *SVEC* 30 (1964), 311-49; and "The Innocent Art of Confession and Reverie," *Daedalus* 107 (no. 3: Summer 1978), 59-77. By far the most sophisticated and ambitious examinations of Rousseau as autobiographer are Huntington Williams, *Rousseau and Romantic Autobiography,* and Ellen Burt's forthcoming *Rousseau's Autobiographics.*

33. Among the most overt statements in this regard are the following: "There is a certain *succession* of affects and ideas which modify those that follow them, and which it is necessary to know in order to pass judgment upon them. I am trying throughout to explain the first causes well so as to give a feeling for the sequential chain of effects" (*Confessions,* 175, emphasis added); "I have only one faithful guide on which I can count; namely, the chain of feelings which have marked the *succession* of my being, and through the succession of events which have acted as a cause or effect of my being" (ibid, I, 278, emphasis added); "But from these first acts of goodness, poured out with effusion of heart, were born chains of *successive* engagements that I had not foreseen, and of which I could no longer shake off the yoke" (*Reveries,* I, 1051, emphasis added). On this "genetic" dimension of Rousseau's autobiographical writing, see Starobinski, *La transparence et l'obstacle,* 230-32ff.

34. This correlation between moral and topographical height is underscored in the famous twenty-third letter of *La Nouvelle Héloïse:* "It seems that by rising above [*en s'élevant au dessus*] the domain of men, one leaves all low and earthly feelings behind, and that as one nears the ethereal regions, the soul contracts some of their inalterable purity" (78). For a detailed reading of the relation between the moral and the physical in this passage, as well as of Rousseau's literary predecessors in this *topos,* see Christie McDonald-Vance, *The Extravagant Shepherd: A Study of the Pastoral Vision in Rousseau's* Nouvelle Héloïse, *SVEC* 105 (1973), especially 58-70. While for Daniel Mornet, the modern taste for mountain scenery would have originated, almost singlehandedly, with Rousseau (*Le sentiment de la nature en France de Jean-Jacques Rousseau à Bernardin de Saint-Pierre: Essai sur les rapports de la*

littérature et des moeurs [Paris: Hachette, 1907], 259–60ff.), Barbara Stafford more judiciously situates *La Nouvelle Héloïse* within the context of the Enlightenment's emerging interest in mountains, an interest whose decisive publication would have been that of Johann Jacob Scheuchzer's *Itinera Helvetica* in 1708 (*Voyage into Substance,* 88–89ff., and 362).

35. While Rousseau was in Turin at the time of Montesquieu's visit there in 1728, there is no account of their meeting each other, which is unsurprising, as their difference in social rank and prestige would have made such an encounter unlikely, if not meaningless had it occurred. See Luigi Firpo, "Rousseau e Montesquieu a Torino," *Nouvelles de la République des Lettres* 2 (1981), 67–89; and Robert Shackleton, "Montesquieu, Dupin, and the Early Writings of Rousseau," in Simon Harvey, Marian Hobson, David Kelley, Samuel S. B. Taylor, eds., *Reappraisals of Rousseau: Studies in Honour of R. A. Leigh* (Manchester: Manchester University Press, 1980), 234. For Montesquieu's reactions to Turin, see *Voyage,* I, 604–17.

36. Zulietta's indignant response is too good to pass up: "Zanetto lascia le Donne, e studia la mathematica [Johnny, give up women and study mathematics]" (*Confessions,* 322). On Rousseau's adventure in Venice, see Clément, *Jean-Jaques Rousseau,* 203–21; Madeleine B. Ellis, *Rousseau's Venetian Story: An Essay upon Art and Truth in* Les Confessions (Baltimore: Johns Hopkins Press, 1966); Giuseppe Scaraffia, "Venezia, Rousseau e Casanova," in Centre d'Etudes Franco-Italiennes, Universités de Turin et de Savoie, *Mélanges à la mémoire de Franco Simone: France et Italie dans la culture européenne* (Geneva: Slatkine, 1981), II, 561–71; and Lester Crocker, *Jean-Jacques Rousseau* (New York: Macmillan, 1968–73), I, 156–59.

37. May, *Rousseau par lui-même,* 129–51.

38. On Rousseau's trip to England, see Louis J. Courtois, *Le séjour de Jean-Jacques Rousseau en Angleterre (1766–1767)* (Geneva: Jullien, 1911); Margaret H. Peoples, *La querelle Rousseau-Hume, Annales Jean-Jacques Rousseau* 18 (1927–28), 1–331; Henri Roddier, *Jean-Jacques Rousseau en Angleterre au XVIIIe siècle* (Paris: Boivin, 1950), especially 259–306; Jacques Voisine, *Jean-Jacques Rousseau en Angleterre à l'époque romantique: Les écrits autobiographiques et la légende* (Paris: Didier, 1956), 13–55; Edward Duffy, *Rousseau in England* (Berkeley: University of California Press, 1979), 9–31; and Crocker, *Jean-Jacques Rousseau* II, 265–302.

39. The patriarchal arrangement of Clarens is the implicit discovery of Etienne Gilson's classic "La méthode de M. de Wolmar" (in *Les Idées et les lettres* [Paris: Vrin, 1932], 275–98), and the explicit object of more recent studies, including Tony Tanner, "Julie et 'la Maison paternelle': Another Look at Rousseau's *La Nouvelle Héloïse,*" *Daedalus* 105 (no. 1: Winter 1976), 23–45; Kamuf, *Fictions of Feminine Desire,* 97–122; DeJean, *Literary Fortifications,* 161–90; and Kavanagh, *Writing the Truth,* 1–21.

40. In a stylistic reading of this passage from the *Confessions* (quoted by me here and throughout the following pages), Huntington Williams argues that Rousseau's syntax so successfully mimes the "repetitive physical movement of walking" that, through a "rhetorical tour de force," it actually "elevate[s] Rousseau to the same exalted state described in the narrative" (*Rousseau and Romantic Autobiography,* 10–13). Despite the manifest ingenuity of the analysis, one is still left wondering why Rousseau should persist in lamenting those ecstatic moments of rambling reverie as irretrievably lost in the past, if as Williams claims, "the present act of writing creates this past anew" (13).

41. Cf. "Mon portrait," I, 1128. On the vexed question of Rousseau's "malady," see especially Starobinski's "Sur la maladie de Rousseau," in *La transparence et l'obstacle,* 430–44; Clément, *Jean-Jacques Rousseau,* 273–93; and Kofman, who astutely associates Rousseau's Armenian attire and urinary disorder to a desire to "be" the mother and to give birth to a child as if one were "passing a stone" through the urethra (*Le respect des femmes,* 148–50). Of course, such a fantasy of castration and feminization can also be shown to condition his

erotic investments in various kinds of phallic women from Mlle. Lambercier, who spanks him, to Mme. d'Houdetot, whose surprise visit dressed in nothing less than an *equestrian* outfit triggers Rousseau's sense of being truly in love for "the first and only" time: "On this trip, she was on horseback and dressed as a man [*à cheval et en homme*]. Although I am not very fond of such masquerades, the air of romance about this one charmed me, and this time it was love.... the first and only love in all my life, one whose consequences make it forever memorable" (*Confessions*, I, 439).

42. "Not for long did my imagination leave this lovely land deserted. I populated it with beings after my own heart, and casting out opinions, prejudices and all fake passions, I transported into nature's refuges men worthy of inhabiting them. Out of these men, I formed a charming society to which I did not feel unworthy of belonging. I fabricated a golden age to suit my fancy, and filling those lovely days with all the scenes my heart could still desire, I became emotional to the point of tears in considering the true pleasures of humanity, pleasures that are so delicious and so pure, and that are henceforth so distant from men" (I, 1140). If we accept what Rousseau says in book IX of the *Confessions* (I, 430ff.), his novel *La Nouvelle Héloïse* would have been conceived and elaborated out of exactly such a fantasy. And in a letter to Jacob Vernet, dated November 29, 1760, he similarly projects the writing of *Emile* as the outcome of his reveries while walking: "A kind of treatise on education, full of my customary reveries and the final fruit of my rustic promenades [*dernier fruit de mes promenades champêtres*], remains to be published by me" (*Correspondance complète de Jean-Jacques Rousseau*, ed. R. A. Leigh [Geneva: Institut et Musée Voltaire; and Oxford: Voltaire Foundation, 1965–89], VII, 332).

43. *Confessions*, I, 162.

44. Ibid.

45. On the predicament of happiness as a problem of consciousness, see Georges Poulet, *Etudes sur le temps humain I* (Paris: Plon, 1949), 220–35.

46. Compare the following passage from "Mon portrait": "I never do anything except during my strolls, the countryside is my study; the mere aspect of a table, paper and books is tedious to me, the accoutrements of work discourage me, if I sit down to write I find nothing and the need to be witty takes it away" (I, 1128).

47. Cf. the description of the "Illumination" at Vincennes in the second "Lettre à Malesherbes": "If I could ever have written a quarter of what I saw and felt under this tree, with what clarity I would have made evident the contradictions of the social system.... All that I could retain of these swarms of great truths that enlightened me for a quarter of an hour under this tree has been feebly scattered into my three major writings" (I, 1135–36).

48. Perhaps nowhere is this contradiction between travel and writing so ironically presented as in Rousseau's persuading Diderot and Grimm to accompany him on a long-desired tour of Italy on foot only to see the project transmuted into a mere exercise in writing: "For a long while, I searched Paris for two comrades sharing my taste, each willing to contribute fifty *louis* from his purse and a year of his time for a joint tour of Italy on foot.... I remember talking with such passion of the project to Diderot and Grimm that I finally gave them the same urge. I thought I had it all settled: but soon it all reduced itself to a mere journey on paper [*un voyage par écrit*], in which Grimm found nothing more pleasant than getting Diderot to commit various impieties and handing me over to the Inquisition in his stead" (*Confessions*, I, 59).

49. *Reveries*, I, 999.

50. According to the etymology set forth by Wartburg, the words *rêver* and *rêverie* would be derived from a hypothetical Latin word, *reexvagus*, meaning "to roam about, to wander for one's pleasure, to take a pleasant walk [*vagabonder, errer pour son plaisir, faire une promenade joyeuse*]" (*Französisches Etymologisches Wörterbuch* [Basel: Zbinden, 1960], X,

184). Adds Marcel Raymond, "it is a question of leaving oneself, of leaving one's natural character, of deviating from the beaten path, of going astray, of going out of bounds [*extravaguer*]" (*Jean-Jacques Rousseau: La quête de soi et la rêverie* [Paris: José Corti, 1962], 159ff.). The *rêverie* thus already implies a *promenade* and vice versa. Cf. Arnaud Tripet, *La rêverie littéraire: Essai sur Rousseau* (Geneva: Droz, 1979); Robert J. Morrissey, *La rêverie jusqu'à Rousseau: Recherches sur un topos littéraire* (Lexington, Ky.: French Forum, 1984); and Huntington Williams, *Rousseau and Romantic Autobiography,* 9-22.

51. Cf. *Rousseau juge de Jean-Jacques* (*Dialogues*), 1, 845-47.

52. Morrissey correctly sees in this reverie of prior reveries an "embedded phenomenon" that is the culmination of Rousseau's attempts to turn the reverie into a "state of autarky": "To fall into a reverie over former reveries [*rêver à ses rêveries d'autrefois*] appears as a means of enriching them, of making them live more fully" (154ff.). Such a second-degree reverie thus also ironically reconfirms Tripet's original insight into the reverie as a melancholy means to recover "a lost place and a shattered unity": "[The reverie] does not exist without some alienation from which it attempts in turn to depart, so as to live . . . in an anteriority which the reverie helps us recapture" (*La rêverie littéraire,* 26). Cf. Starobinski's discussion of what he calls "secondary reverie" ("Rêverie et transmutation," in *La transparence et l'obstacle,* 415-29).

53. Among the many studies of the analogies between writing and botanizing in the *Rêveries,* see especially Kavanagh, *Writing the Truth,* 165-80; Starobinski, *La transparence et l'obstacle,* 278-82; McDonald-Vance, *Extravagant Shepherd,* 70-73; Gossman, "The Innocent Art," 72-74; David Scott, "Rousseau and Flowers: The Poetry of Botany," *SVEC* 182 (1979), 73-86; Pierre Saint-Amand, "Rousseau contre la science: L'exemple de la botanique dans les textes autobiographiques," *SVEC* 219 (1983), 159-67; Jenny H. Batlay, "L'herbier, journal de rêveries, comme substitut d'une écriture autobiographique chez Rousseau," in *Rousseau et Voltaire en 1978,* 8-18; and in a more phenomenological register, John C. O'Neal, *Seeing and Observing: Rousseau's Rhetoric of Perception* (Saratoga, Cal.: Anma Libri, 1985), 122-38. On the relation between the "affective memory" of the herbarium and the temporal problem of consciousness, see Poulet, *Etudes,* 226-35.

54. J.-B. Pontalis, *Entre le rêve et la douleur* (Paris: Gallimard, 1977), 156.

55. It was Robert Osmont who first analyzed the resemblances between Montaigne's and Rousseau's accidents in his "Contribution à l'étude psychologique des *Rêveries du promeneur solitaire,*" *Annales Jean-Jacques Rousseau* 23 (1934), 54-55. Also see Henri Roddier's "Introduction" to *Les Rêveries* (Paris: Garnier, 1960), lxvi-lxvii; and Huntington Williams, *Rousseau and Romantic Autobiography,* 4-5.

56. Honoré de Balzac, *Le Père Goriot,* in *La comédie humaine* (Paris: Gallimard, 1976-81), III, 290. The Père Lachaise cemetery was opened in 1804, the culmination of a reform movement in burial practices that replaced the old charnel house with the landscaped garden (see Richard A. Etlin, *The Architecture of Death: The Transformation of the Cemetery in Eighteenth-Century Paris* [Cambridge, Mass.: MIT Press, 1984]). As Etlin also shows, Rousseau's own "natural" tomb, as landscaped by the Marquis de Girardin on the Ile des Peupliers near Ermenonville, represented an important turn in the fortunes of this movement (204-9). An editorial note to the Pléiade edition of *Le Père Goriot* (1330) signals the publication of guidebooks for the modish strollers and "tourists" who began frequenting the cemetery early on, defining it as *the* place in Paris to take a walk: *Le conducteur au cimetière de l'Est ou du Père-Lachaise* (Paris: Plass, 1820); and *Promenade sérieuse au cimetière du Père-Lachaise ou du Mont Louis près de Paris* (Paris: Lachevardière, 1826).

57. Notice that Rousseau's view of the city, here as well as in the *Profession of Faith of a Savoyard Vicar,* is not only from on high (as Montesquieu would have prescribed) but also

from outside the city, thus preserving its gazer from the risk of immersion in a corrupt urbanity.

58. On Rousseau's postaccident plenitude in indifferentiation, see also Poulet, *Etudes,* 215. Lionel Gossman has also perceptively noted the dissolution of even the most basic opposition in the *Rêveries:* "what is often called life—immediacy, presence, plenitude, enjoyment—is closely akin to death" ("The Innocent Art," 71).

59. More Rousseauist than Rousseau himself in recounting the accident, Bernardin de Saint-Pierre also applies the word *écorché* in describing the philosopher's wounds: "One of those Great Danes that the vanity of rich people allows to run ahead of their coaches, to the misfortune of folks on foot, knocked [Jean-Jacques Rousseau] so roughly onto the pavement that he lost all consciousness. Some charitable passersby picked him up: his upper lip was split, the thumb of his right hand was all skinned [*ecorché*]. He came back to himself [*il revint à lui*]. They wanted to hire him a carriage, but he didn't want one for fear of catching a chill. He came back home on foot [*Il revint chés lui à pied*]; a doctor came running: [Rousseau] thanked him for his friendship but refused his help. Instead, he was content to wash his wounds, which after a few days healed perfectly. 'It's nature who cures,' he said, 'not men'" (*La vie et les ouvrages,* 49).

60. Cf. *Aeneid* II, 293–97 and passim. My critique of the theological reference point finds an eloquent fellow traveler in Sartre's relativist reproach to François Mauriac for assuming the position of God in relation to the characters in his novels: "As do the rest of our authors, he wanted to ignore that the theory of relativity applies integrally to the novelistic universe, that in a true novel there is, no more than in the world of Einstein, no place for a privileged observer, and that in a novelistic system, there exists, no more than in a physical system, no experiment that can reveal whether that system is in motion or at rest" (*Situations* I [Paris: Gallimard, 1947], 56–57).

61. On the status of the signature (or its absence) in Rousseau, see Ellen Burt, "Rousseau the Scribe," *Studies in Romanticism* 18 (Winter 1979), 629–67; and Peggy Kamuf, *Signature Pieces: On the Institution of Authorship,* especially 21–120.

62. Since Rousseau's time, Saint-Pierre has been renamed the Ile Rousseau, and the rue Plâtrière similarly redubbed the rue Jean-Jacques Rousseau. While such a naming of a place after a person is not unusual, it does afford us an interesting contrast with the cases of Montaigne and Montesquieu, whose names are derived from a previously existing place, the ownership of which gives its possessor leave to apply the name to himself. True to the ethics of *Emile,* and despite his flaunted nostalgia for his birthplace of Geneva, Rousseau's home turns out to correspond to any number of those places where he happened to stay, write, and walk.

63. Developed most elaborately with respect to the case of the Wolfman (*From the History of an Infantile Neurosis,* in *S.E.* XVII, 7–122), the important psychoanalytic concept of *Nachträglichkeit* has been defined by Jean Laplanche and Jean-Baptiste Pontalis: "Experiences, impressions, and memory-traces may be revised at a later date to fit in with fresh experiences or with the attainment of a new stage of development. They may in that event be endowed not only with a new meaning but also with psychical effectiveness" ("Deferred Action," in *The Language of Psycho-Analysis,* tr. Donald Nicholson-Smith [New York: Norton, 1973], 111).

Index

Georges Van Den Abbeele is professor of French at the University of California—Davis. He is the translator of Jean-François Lyotard's *The Differend: Phrases in Dispute* and has published numerous essays on early modern literature and contemporary theories in *Diacritics, Esprit Créateur, Romantic Review, French Studies,* and *Stanford French Review.* He is also a member of The Miami Theory Collective and the coeditor of *Community at Loose Ends* (Minnesota, 1991).